Mayan Journeys

CCIS Anthologies, 4
CENTER FOR COMPARATIVE IMMIGRATION STUDIES, UCSD

Contributors

Yesenia Acosta
Alex Barreno
Guadalupe Castillo
María de Jesús Cen Montuy
Wayne A. Cornelius
Rebecca Dames
David Fitzgerald
Angela García
Daisy García
Paola Guzmán
Zoila Jiménez-Pacheco
Ann Kimball
Pedro Lewin Fischer
Blair Lyman
Alejandra Maciel
Luis Manzanero Rodríguez
Alpha Martell
Vanessa Molina
Amérika Niño
Patricia Pasillas
Maribel Pineda
Sonia Prelat
Oscar Ramos
Andrea Rodríguez
Juan Rodríguez de la Gala
Ileana Beatriz Ruiz Alonso
Milton Jovanni Sarria
Arturo Severo Vázquez
Travis Silva
Mirian Solís Lizama
Luis Tapia
Edith Tejeda Sandoval
Jennifer Wittlinger

MAYAN JOURNEYS

U.S.-BOUND MIGRATION FROM A

NEW SENDING COMMUNITY

edited by

Wayne A. Cornelius

David Fitzgerald

Pedro Lewin Fischer

LA JOLLA, CALIFORNIA

CENTER FOR COMPARATIVE IMMIGRATION STUDIES, UCSD

Printed in the United States of America

Cover design by Debra B. Topping.
Cover photograph by David Fitzgerald.
Interior photographs by Wayne Cornelius, David Fitzgerald,
Pedro Lewin Fischer, Vanessa Molina, and Sara Zapata.

ISBN–13: 978-0-9702838-8-7 (cloth)
ISBN–13: 978-0-9702838-9-4 (paper)

Library of Congress Cataloging-in-Publication Data

Mayan journeys : U.S.-bound migration from a new sending community /
edited by Wayne A. Cornelius, David Fitzgerald, and Pedro Lewin Fischer.
    p. cm. -- (CCIS anthologies ; 4)
  Includes bibliographical references.
  ISBN 978-0-9702838-8-7 (cloth cover) -- ISBN 978-0-9702838-9-4 (pbk.) 1.
United States--Emigration and immigration--Social aspects. 2. Mayas--
Migrations. 3. Mexicans--United States. I. Cornelius, Wayne A., 1945- II.
Fitzgerald, David, 1972-. III. Lewin F., Pedro. IV. University of California,
San Diego. Center for Comparative Immigration Studies. IV. Title. V. Series.

JV6475.M39 2007
304.8'73001749742--dc22

                                                               2007033246

CONTENTS

PREFACE

This book is the second in a series of volumes reporting the results of fieldwork conducted by the Mexican Migration Field Research and Training Program (MMFRP) at the University of California, San Diego.[1] The MMFRP seeks to document and explain changes in migration and settlement behavior by restudying, in great depth, the same set of three migrant-sending communities in rural Mexico and their U.S. urban satellite communities at three-year intervals. The substantive focuses vary from year to year, but one constant is the impact of changes in U.S. immigration law and policy on migration behavior.

The MMFRP's research sites were purposively selected to enable us to test hypotheses in diverse socioeconomic and cultural contexts. The towns differ markedly in terms of levels of economic development (they are classified by Mexico's National Population Council as high-, medium-, and low-marginality *municipios*); ethnic composition (one is mestizo, two are indigenous [Maya and Mixteco]); and density of U.S. migration experience (ranging from 38 to 70 percent of residents having migrated internationally). All three sites are small towns, with 2005 populations numbering between 1,264 and 2,645 inhabitants.

Tunkás, Yucatán, our research community for 2006, was chosen because we believe it to be typical of the localities in southern Mexico that have become increasingly important sources of migration to the United States in recent years. Historically, the state of Yucatán has experienced very little U.S.-bound migration, partly because of the great distances involved and because there was minimal direct U.S. labor recruitment

---

[1] The first volume is *Impacts of Border Enforcement on Mexican Migration: The View from Sending Communities*, edited by Wayne A. Cornelius and Jessa M. Lewis (La Jolla: Center for Comparative Immigration Studies, UCSD, 2007). The third volume is *Four Generations of Norteños: New Research from the Cradle of Mexican Migration*, edited by Wayne A. Cornelius, David Fitzgerald, and Scott Borger (La Jolla: Center for Comparative Immigration Studies, UCSD, in press).

in the area. The spectacular growth of the tourism industry along the "Mayan Riviera" of Cancún and its coastal neighbors beginning in the 1970s provided a trampoline for migration to the United States. Many internal migrants from towns like Tunkás for the first time entered a monetarized economy, where they acquired a taste for dollars and developed skills useful in the restaurant and hotel industries. Since the 1980s, migrations to Cancún and the United States have risen together. Indeed, we found that having prior migratory experience within Mexico increases the probability of U.S. migration among Tunkaseños by 28 percent.

Newly emerging sending communities like Tunkás—the town is still in its first generation of migration to the United States—are living laboratories for the study of Mexican migration because they can shed light on processes of transborder network formation, the establishment of satellite communities in the United States, and the learning of border-crossing strategies. In theory, international migration control should be more effective in stemming unauthorized migration from a new sending community, which has less-developed social networks for eluding the Border Patrol than do established sending communities. However, Tunkaseños were just as likely as migrants from the historical Mexican sending regions to be able to circumvent recent U.S. border enforcement measures. Tunkaseños were also equally well informed about the risks and costs of illegally crossing the border, yet they generally remain undeterred.

Beyond its relative youth as a migrant-sending community, Tunkás has several other attributes that open new avenues for migration research. In contrast to the more prosperous traditional labor-exporting communities in Mexico's west-central plateau region, Tunkás has extensive low-end poverty and poverty-related health problems. The local economy does not produce enough well-paying jobs to keep its residents from migrating to the United States or to regional growth centers like the Mayan Riviera or the state capital of Mérida. As in other parts of Mexico, family remittances are primarily used for daily consumption and housing. Collective remittances have been directed to improving sports facilities rather than to basic infrastructure or job-creating investments. The most promising local alternative to migration is beekeeping, which has attractive export options and would be even more profitable if value could be added locally by processing honey and other bee products in Tunkás.

Migration from the Yucatán Peninsula and other parts of south/ southeastern Mexico is increasing the ethnic complexity of the Mexican immigrant population in the United States. Two-thirds of Tunkaseño migrants speak Maya as well as Spanish. Given their exposure to other Mexicans and to Latin Americans of diverse backgrounds in the United States, the longer a Tunkaseño migrant has lived in the United States, the more likely he or she is to identify with a broader identity such as Mexican or Latin American—while at the same time symbolically taking pride in Mayan accomplishments and traditions.

In the central-western Mexican states that have historically dominated migration to the United States, one of the most common complaints about the migrants' impacts on sending communities is their introduction of Evangelicalism and other religious affiliations identified with the United States, in sharp contradistinction to an overwhelmingly Catholic Mexico. In Tunkás, a quarter of the population is Evangelical, yet Evangelicals and Catholics have very similar migration histories. Evangelicalism is not associated with migration in this case because Evangelical churches in Tunkás began in the early twentieth century and thus predate U.S. migration flows.

The Mexican Migration Field Research and Training Program is, first and foremost, a vehicle for training the next generation of international migration scholars and practitioners in the United States and Mexico. With the exception of the co-editors, all of the contributors to this volume were students—mostly undergraduates—at the time of their participation in the project. Our binational field research team consisted of thirty-one students trained by us (their faculty mentors) to conduct survey research, semi-structured interviews, and ethnographic observation in the research site. In Tunkás, data collection was completed within a two-week period coinciding with the annual fiesta honoring the town's patron saint (January–February 2006). Interviewing of U.S.-based Tunkaseño migrants was conducted during February 2006 in their principal destination communities in the Los Angeles–Orange County metropolitan area.

The universe for the survey interviews in Tunkás was every adult aged 15 to 65 with U.S. migration experience and all household heads in the same age bracket. Working from satellite images and an existing map, we first created a map of all inhabited houses in the town. We made up to four attempts at different times of day to contact the household head, or an adult acting as the household head, in all of the inhabited dwellings. Each adult with U.S. migration experience was surveyed. Where migrants were absent throughout our fieldwork period, we asked their closest family member for information about the migrant's experiences and demographic attributes. The oldest child aged 15 or above in each inhabited dwelling was interviewed as well to create a sample of potential migrants. Information was also gathered from neighbors on the former occupants of all uninhabited houses in the town to document cases of whole-family migration to the United States.

In Tunkás, 201 migrants were interviewed directly, and detailed information about 172 absent migrants was collected from family members. In addition, 296 nonmigrants were interviewed. The rejection rate was 4 percent. At the end of each survey interview, the respondent was asked to provide contact information for family members living in the United States. These contacts were the basis of a snowball sample with multiple points of entry of 55 Tunkaseños living in Los Angeles and Orange counties who were not present in their hometown at the time of the fieldwork. A total of 724 survey interviews yielded data on 4,120 individuals. The team also conducted 60 in-depth, semi-structured interviews with key informants and migrants, and these were digitally recorded and transcribed for analysis. The chapters that follow exhibit a rich blend of survey and qualitative data that enhances the explanation of results and suggests new research possibilities.

This book and the field research on which it is based were made possible by grants from the Ford Foundation, the Tinker Foundation, and the Metropolis Project/Foundation for Population, Migration, and Environment. Supplemental support was provided by the Provost of Eleanor Roosevelt College, the Senior Vice Chancellor, the Dean of Humanities, and the Center for the Study of Race and Ethnicity at the University of California, San Diego. We are grateful to our institutional partner in Yucatán, El Centro INAH Yucatán, for administrative and logistical support. Graduate student research assistants Scott Borger, Angela García, Edith Tejeda, and Leah Muse-Orlinoff made invaluable contributions to the project. As always, we are indebted to Sandra del Castillo for her expert editing and design work.

Particular thanks are due to Tunkás's former Municipal President, Jorge Elías Kuh, and his staff for their unstinting cooperation and interest in our research. David Carrillo, a leader of the town's apiculture industry, was very helpful in gathering information on this key sector of the economy. In the state capital of Mérida, Lic. Rita Candelaria Chuil Gómez, head of the Department of Agrarian Development in the Procuraduría Agraria, kindly gave us access to the agrarian reform records pertaining to Tunkás.

In our research communities in Yucatán and Southern California, hundreds of Tunkaseños welcomed us into their homes and gave generously of their time to share with us their experiences, struggles, and aspirations. We hope that this volume is a faithful representation of their lives as migrants and potential migrants and of their hopes for their community. We look forward to returning often.

Wayne A. Cornelius
David Fitzgerald
Pedro Lewin Fischer
La Jolla, California
August 1, 2007

Los Angeles–based Tunkás residents participate in a demonstration protesting the U.S. House of Representatives' restrictive immigration bill, May 2006.

1 Yucatán as an Emerging Migrant-Sending Region

PEDRO LEWIN FISCHER

ETHNOGRAPHIC GLIMPSES OF TRANSNATIONAL SPACES

Migrants exist simultaneously in different geographic locations, and herein lies one of their greatest strengths:

> *Our Yucatecan countrymen in Denver remember that they are not alone. Cenotillo is behind them.*—Migrants' supporters in Cenotillo, Yucatán.

> *Mr. Bush, Remember that the United States was built by migrants. Up with the labor force; "no" to oppression. Bring down this wall of shame.*—Supporters in Santa Elena, Yucatán.

> *Stop criminalizing our people of Maní who are in the United States.*—Supporters in Maní, Yucatán.

> *The United States is rich thanks to our migrants. If this law goes forward, those of us here, the migrants' families, will suffer. Why? Because we depend on the workers who are over there, far away. So I, as part of the migrant committee of this* municipio, *am happy to be participating in this event in support of our family members and friends who are in the United States. And it's not just here, my friends, that we are holding these events, but also in Peto and all across Yucatán.*—Supporters in Oxkutzcab, Yucatán.

Translation by Sandra del Castillo.

We invite everyone to join us in sending a message to those who live, struggle, labor, and strive in the United States. This is a movement to reach out to the migrant, to tell him he is not alone. That we are concerned for his welfare. That we are not insensitive to his problems. And that we are calling for a peaceful mobilization in support of better living conditions both for the migrants and for ourselves and that, thanks to these migrants, we have been better off for these many years.—Supporters in Peto, Yucatán.

Anyone unfamiliar with international migration from Yucatán may surmise from the preceding statements that this is a migration with a long history and with strong political linkages uniting the migrants' communities of origin in Mexico with their communities of destination in the United States. This is not the case.

The preceding statements appeared on posters that family and friends of Mayan migrants created to raise awareness in their hometowns and to express solidarity with their compatriots who live and work in the United States, unaware that their messages would be picked up by the national media.[1] Migrants in the United States had asked their families and communities in Mexico to mobilize against H.R. 4437. This bill, proposed by F. James Sensenbrenner, Jr. (R-Wisconsin), chairman of the Committee on the Judiciary in the U.S. House of Representatives, was passed by the House in December 2005. It sought to upgrade border security and enhance workplace enforcement to identify and repatriate undocumented migrants. The bill was strongly opposed by many migrant organizations in the United States and, as we observed in Yucatán, by the communities from which migrants come.[2]

South of the border, in a speech opening the annual fiesta in Cenotillo, in eastern Yucatán, the municipal president noted the arrival of several hundred migrants returning from San Bernardino, California. Disregarding differences between migrants and nonmigrants, he spoke

---

[1] Some of the posters were reproduced in *Por Esto* (Mérida) on May 2, 2006.

[2] The U.S. Senate declined to approve HR 4437. However, a more narrowly drawn substitute bill, the Secure Fence Act of 2006, was enacted by both houses of Congress and signed by President George W. Bush.

of "community morality," exhorting both migrants and nonmigrants to participate in a ritual of communality. Moments later, dozens of video cameras appeared as the migrants sought to record—for themselves and for those unable to return—a portrait of their town, even as it was being altered by the very same returned migrants who were there, seeking to experience the town's "authenticity." During video recordings and conversations, at dances, and across generations, one hears English, Spanish, and Maya spoken, sometimes in that order. A young woman of Cenotillo, garbed in an impeccable indigenous costume, speaks English, understands Maya, but speaks no Spanish. The young men next to her wear T-shirts with images of Chicago and Los Angeles. When the moment arrives for the migrants to return to the United States, another two hundred, mostly young people join those who, with their digital memories in hand, head north once again.

On any given day in Oxkutzcab, which is the region's leading sender of international migrants, the streets are filled with pedicabs whose umbrellas advertise Western Union, Dinero en Minutos, and other companies that provide money transfer services. Alongside a traditional Mayan home, a two-story house is under construction. Its balcony will provide sunset views and a place to remember the Golden Gate Bridge and the experiences of living clandestinely in San Francisco's "Maya Town." The building's architecture clearly reflects new ways of visualizing domestic space, even if these are not yet fully integrated into daily activities.

Another day, more than three hundred people from Oxkutzcab gather at the offices of the municipal president because the governor is about to announce a new program for migrants. As the authorities present an 87-page booklet entitled "Guide for the Yucatecan Migrant," they acknowledge the debt owed to residents who have been forced to leave their community and are now in the United States. The officials' words evoke curiosity, uncertainty, suspicion, hope, and expectation among the audience, whose members hope for a future in which migrants can leave the clandestine life of an illegal behind and begin to enjoy social acceptance and the rights of U.S. citizenship.

On yet another day, the annual town fiesta in Peto brings together town residents from both sides of the border. Some are seated in the plaza; others are present virtually, seen and heard on a giant screen erected in the town square. A greeting from family members in San Rafael, California, recalls ties of kinship, friendship, and solidarity. Any ethnographer who remembers the Yucatán Peninsula as it existed some twenty years ago or more would be very puzzled by this new ethnographic reality and by the dynamic relations that Yucatán and its contexts, both national and international, have woven over the course of the last three decades.

SENDING REGIONS AND INDIGENOUS MIGRATION

Efforts to differentiate the various phases and zones of out-migration from Mexico have identified four key regions: (1) the historical or traditional region, comprising the states of Aguascalientes, Colima, Durango, Guanajuato, Jalisco, Michoacán, Nayarit, San Luis Potosí, and Zacatecas; (2) the Center, including the Federal District, Guerrero, Hidalgo, México State, Morelos, Oaxaca, Puebla, Querétaro, and Tlaxcala; (3) the border region or North, made up of Baja California, Baja California Sur, Coahuila, Chihuahua, Nuevo León, Sinaloa, Sonora, and Tamaulipas; and (4) the South/Southeast, composed of Campeche, Chiapas, Quintana Roo, Tabasco, Veracruz, and Yucatán (Corona 2000; Durand 1998; Durand and Massey 2003). If we accept the classification developed by Mexico's National Population Council (CONAPO), region 4 would also include Oaxaca and Guerrero, states that, according to Durand and Massey, are part of the Center (see figure 1.1). CONAPO bases its regional classification on historical tradition, the intensity of migration flows, and geographic proximity (CONAPO 2005a). Basing their regionalization on geographic and migratory criteria, Durand and Massey assert that Guerrero has never been part of Mexico's southern region and that, along with Oaxaca, it has a much older migratory tradition than the states that compose Mexico's South/Southeast region.

Both sources agree, however, that any regionalization scheme results from the application of specific research objectives. The scheme followed in this chapter underscores an important sociocultural phenomenon—the rapid growth of the indigenous component of Mexico-to-U.S. migration flows over the last twenty-five years, especially from the 1990s onward. Recent flows of undocumented migrants out of Mex-

ico have originated primarily in the southern states, where 54.7 percent of
Mexico's indigenous population is concentrated (see figure 1.2, table 1.1).

Figure 1.1 Mexico's Migration Regions

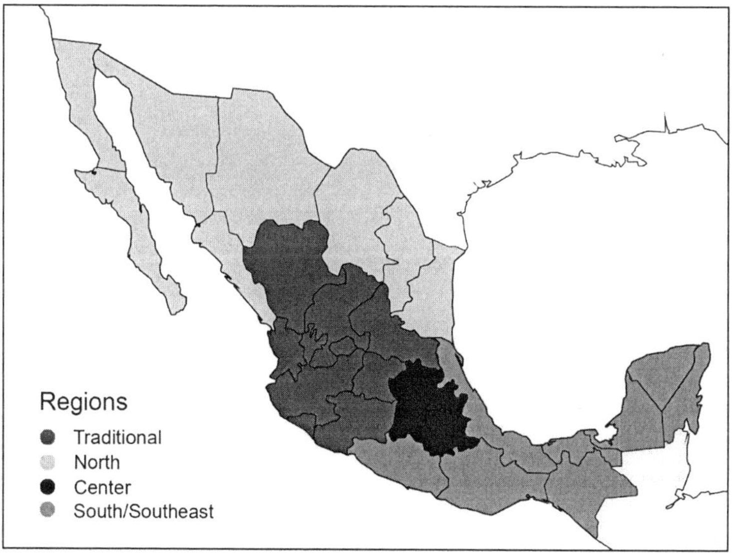

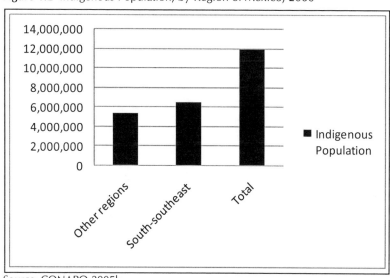

Figure 1.2 Indigenous Population, by Region of Mexico, 2000

Source: CONAPO 2005b.

Table 1.1 Indigenous Populations of South/Southeastern States, 2000

State[a]	Population		Share of Indigenous Population within:	
	Total	Indigenous	State (%)	Nation (%)
Oaxaca	3,429,409	1,911,338	55.7	16.1
Chiapas	3,785,292	1,170,132	30.9	9.8
Veracruz	6,877,295	1,163,363	16.9	9.8
Yucatán	1,650,438	1,080,733	65.5	9.1
Guerrero	3,054,917	569,639	18.6	4.8
Quintana Roo	863,651	393,562	45.6	3.3
Campeche	687,157	212,245	30.9	1.8
Other	75,405,237	5,395,998		45.3
Total	95,753,396	11,897,010		100.00

Source: CONAPO 2005b.

[a] Tabasco is included in the "Other" category because of the small size of its indigenous population.

From a chronological perspective, the "historical/traditional" region was the first in Mexico to experience international out-migration, which began in the nineteenth century. In the twentieth century, this region provided large numbers of laborers to the United States during World War II and throughout the Bracero Program (1942–1964). The states of the South/Southeast are the most recent contributors to U.S.-bound migration, making this Mexico's "youngest" migration region and the one with the largest indigenous component in its migrating population (Durand and Massey 2003; Fox and Rivera-Salgado 2004). Yucatecan migrants, especially Mayan Yucatecos, are illustrative of the emerging indigenous migration to the United States.

Of Mexico's four migration regions, the historical region and the North continue to send the largest absolute numbers of migrants. However, various macroeconomic factors have made the Center and the South/Southeast the largest sources of migrants relative to these areas' populations. These are the only regions to have increases in their migrating population as a share of total population during the last fifteen years (see figure 1.3).

Figure 1.3 Share of Population Living in U.S. by Birth Region in Mexico

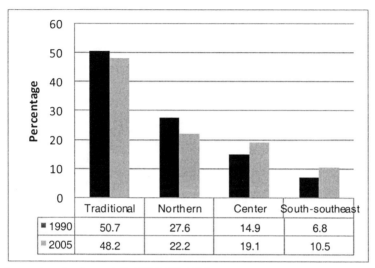

	Traditional	Northern	Center	South-southeast
▪ 1990	50.7	27.6	14.9	6.8
▪ 2005	48.2	22.2	19.1	10.5

Source (also for figure 1.4): CONAPO 2005a.

If we examine the estimated numbers of undocumented migrants returning to Mexico in different periods, the upsurge in migration from the South/Southeast is even more noteworthy. The growth of its share of migrants returned from the United States between 1993 and 2004 outpaces all other regions (see figure 1.4).

Figure 1.4 Undocumented Returning Migrants, by Region of Origin

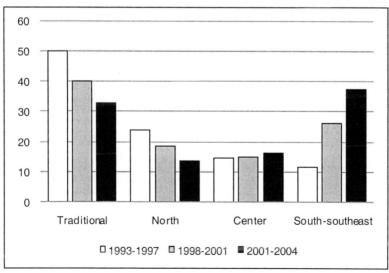

THE YUCATÁN PENINSULA: A REGIONAL MIGRATION SYSTEM

There is no doubt that migration has become a vital ingredient in the restructuring of relationships between Mexico and the United States. Migrant remittances have acquired a level of economic importance on par with Mexico's petroleum and tourism sectors, and migration is persistently the most sensitive issue in U.S.-Mexican relations. This is the context surrounding the current out-migration from the states of the Yucatán Peninsula: Campeche, Quintana Roo, and Yucatán. The peninsula's growing importance as a source of migrants to the United States is linked to three basic elements in the regional political economy: urban growth, the decline of agriculture, and the intense development of the tourism corridor, principally in Quintana Roo.

Population growth rates remained fairly uniform across the three states until the 1960s, with Campeche's population growing at 4.5 percent during that decade, Quintana Roo's by 7.1 percent, and Yucatán's by 2.2 percent. During the 1970s, however, the development of Cancún as a tourism center and the associated inflow of workers from across the region sparked a growth spurt in Quintana Roo, with the state's population growing by 15.1 percent (see figure 1.5).

Figure 1.5 Average Annual Population Growth in the Yucatán Peninsula, 1960–2005

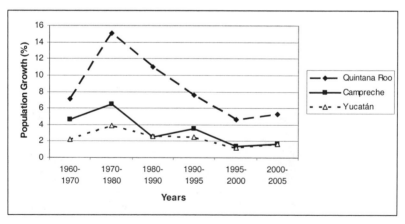

Sources: INEGI, *Censos de Población y Vivienda,* 1960–2000; *Conteos de Población y Vivienda,* 1995 and 2005.

Beginning with the re-creation of Cancún as a tourist destination and the later construction of the "Mayan Riviera," Quintana Roo experienced a significant inflow of migrants from other parts of Mexico. Only 42 percent of the state's residents in 2000 were born in the state (INEGI 2000). The largest contingent of internal migrants came from Yucatán State, especially after 1990 (see figure 1.6).

Figure 1.6 Migrants to Quintana Roo, 1970–2000, by State of Origin

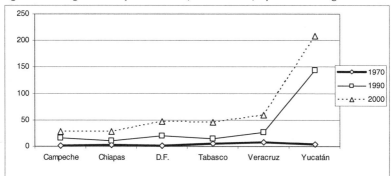

Sources: INEGI, *Censos de Población y Vivienda*, 1970–2000.

It is very common for Yucatecan families to have at least one relative in Quintana Roo or the Mayan Riviera, paralleling the nationwide trend among Mexican families to have relatives in the United States. There are many municipios that have lost the majority of their population to Cancún or Cozumel. For example, in Dzemul, the municipal president claims that the town has lost 4,000 of its previous inhabitants to migration to the region's tourism centers, and these out-migrants typically have been gone for a minimum of five years. In Dzemul, at least two generations of townspeople have now established themselves in Cancún (author interview with Leticia Murúa and Juan Torres Bosco, November 2006).

In terms of monthly income, Campeche and Yucatán fall below the national average, but Quintana Roo exceeds the average income level for Mexicans overall. In nearly all economic sectors, wages in Quintana Roo were nearly double those found in Yucatán, a difference which, when combined with the dynamism of Quintana Roo's tourism-driven economy, is a virtually endless incentive for migration to Mexico's Caribbean coast (Lewin and Guzmán 2005a).

In sum, the Yucatán Peninsula presents a regional migration system in which Yucatán stands out as the primary migrant-sending state, while Quintana Roo is the primary pole of attraction. The principal catalyst has been the development of the tourism corridor along the peninsula's Caribbean coast. This migration follows circuits that link the region's three states with one another. Urban growth, especially in the state capitals, is directly tied to tourism development.

The cultural dimension of the "Mayan world" has also exerted significant influence on the area's economic development. This is true not only because the majority of the workforce has been drawn from the rural Mayan communities of Yucatán, but also because the national and international image of this region as a world-class tourist destination has been woven around a symbolic construction in which "cultural authenticity" and "natural beauty" are employed to heighten the allure of tourism activities. The city of Playa del Carmen, which had a mere 500 residents in 1980, now is a major tourist attraction that draws visitors from around the world. The town's rate of growth has been phenomenal. Ranging between 18 and 30 percent between 2000 and 2004, its growth rate even outpaced that of nearby Cancún, which grew between 7 and 11 percent annually (*La Jornada*, March 17, 2006). The displacement of population toward state capitals and tourism centers has completely changed the sociodemographic profile of the area's indigenous population, with major consequences for current and future migration patterns.

REGIONAL DEVELOPMENT, ECONOMIC CRISIS, AND MIGRATION IN YUCATÁN

Despite Yucatán's relatively small size and homogeneous topography, at different moments in its history the state has been divided into several regions differentiated by economic activities. The first instance of such specialization began in 1890, when the state consisted of three economic regions devoted to the production of henequen, corn, and cattle/sugarcane. Booms in timber extraction and agriculture followed in the early 1960s, and by 1972 coastal fishing had become another important sector.

More than half of Yucatán's municipios lie in the henequen zone, in the north/northeastern portion of the state, which covers a fourth of the state's area and contains more than half of its labor force (Fraga 1992). The crisis in henequen production began in the 1970s, when the federal government began to privilege industrial development over agriculture (Villanueva 1990: 79–84). The establishment of the Banco de Yucatán in 1962 and of the cordage company Cordemex in 1964 significantly changed the production process in the henequen industry. Prior to 1967, most henequen had been processed by individual small landowners, but in 1967 Cordemex installed fiber-removing machines, and by 1981, 42 percent of henequen was processed by the Banco de Yucatán and 43 percent by Cordemex. Only 15 percent was processed by small private producers (Villanueva 1990: 81).

During the second half of the 1970s, Yucatán's henequen sector suffered further assaults with a drop in international prices, the emergence of new competitors such as Brazil and Tanzania, and the development of synthetic fibers and new technologies. These changes are clearly reflected in production and employment figures from the period. From 1965 to 1980, the percentage of the state's workers employed in the cordage industry fell from 54 to 14 percent (Macosay and Vallado 1988, cited in Baños Ramírez 1996: 82; Villanueva 1990: 87–88).

The henequen crisis continued throughout the 1980s until the sector virtually disappeared in 1992. Thousands of newly unemployed workers flowed to the cities in search of work that could complement the incomes of their rural households. Many went to Quintana Roo or Mérida. Indeed, Mérida became Mexico's indigenous migration capital. Today there are some 230,000 indigenous people—mostly Mayas—living in Mérida, constituting nearly 30 percent of the city's population (see figure 1.7).

Yucatán's citrus-producing area, encompassing fifteen municipios, adopted its current economic orientation following the implementation of Plan Chac in the 1960s, a program that set out to make this region the key citrus-producing area for the entire state. A substantial number of people were able to purchase irrigated parcels for growing citrus with money they had earned as migrants in the United States (Hervik 2003: 12). Terán Contreras (1987: 186) also notes that in the 1980s more than half of the wealthy campesinos of Oxkutzcab or their children had migrated to the United States, and this had enabled them to acquire land and invest in infrastructure (cited in Fortuny Loret de Mola 2004: 229). The intensification of citrus production initially yielded good results, but these were later undermined as profits went mainly to intermediaries to cover transport and marketing costs (Baños Ramírez 2003: 93; Hervik 2003: 11–13). Today the region's citrus sales are in decline, along with wages and jobs (Fortuny Loret de Mola 2004: 228). This has led to an outflow of population to northern Yucatán, especially the coastal areas (Fraga 1992).

Figure 1.7 Population Growth in Merida, 1950–2000

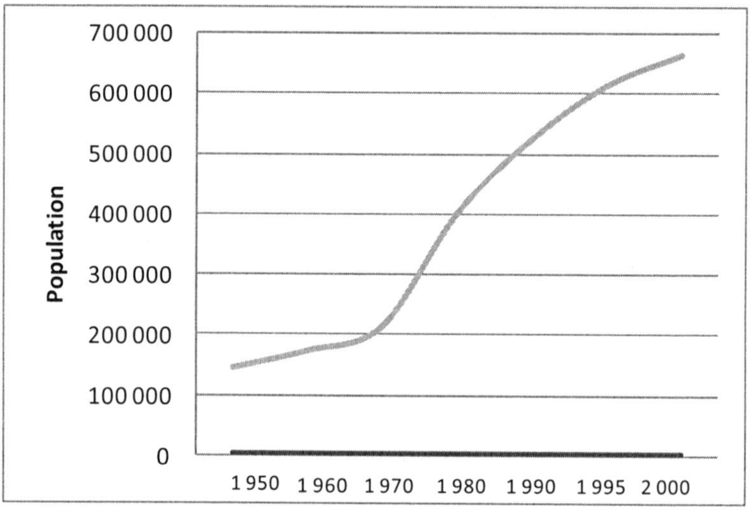

Sources: INEGI, *Censos de Población y Vivienda*, 1950–2000.

The rise of henequen had replaced the previous economy of traditional indigenous communities, which was based on corn production for household consumption. When the milpa gave way to henequen cultivation, this substitution brought many fundamental social changes which, according to Baños Ramírez, culminated in a new type of "rurality" in Yucatán. This new rurality was characterized by the "monopolization of productive assets by a small class of landowners (who decided what, when, and how much to produce); the cultivation of a single product for external markets; the lack of a dynamic internal labor market, leading to the use of a kind of forced labor; the absence of an internal market for consumers; and the development of a sharply asymmetric class structure that permitted a highly unequal income distribution" (Baños Ramírez 1996: 158).

Tunkás is not considered part of the henequen region; rather, it falls within the corn-producing zone even though it lies on its extreme western edge. It abuts the cattle-raising area of northeastern Yucatán as well as the henequen region in the western portion of the state. Nevertheless, so strong was the dynamism of the henequen economy that this sector affected the economic life of many municipios in other regions. Henequen's boom years correlated with high employment, and the sector drew workers not only from the henequen region but also from other areas of the state. Tunkás was among the municipios linked to the henequen industry through labor migration. When henequen disappeared as the driving force in the state economy and the federal government stepped away from direct state-level economic involvement, institutions also lost their capacity to sustain rural production (Solís Lizama 2005: 49).

The region of corn cultivation, which includes twenty-five of the state's most traditional municipios, has experienced phases of economic expansion and contraction beginning with the formation of the corn and cattle haciendas and sugar plantations in the nineteenth century and continuing up to the recovery of some land in the Caste War (Villanueva 1990: 97). Unlike henequen production in the west and citrus production to the south, corn cultivation has been combined with other activities, including beekeeping, small-scale livestock-raising, and, increasingly, wage work. As early as 1982, Villanueva found that 87 percent of regional producers were involved in wage labor. Most of these workers left their communities to work in Mérida or Quintana Roo (Villanueva 1990: 98–99). By the early 1980s corn cultivation accounted for only 36.4 percent of the region's output; honey accounted for 40 percent, and cattle for nearly 30 percent (Villanueva 1990: 128–

29). Falling corn production in Yucatán during the 1980s was particularly notable in the last two years of the decade. This was the worst period for corn at any point between 1980 and 2000 (Baños Ramírez 2003: 90).

Honey production and cattle-raising have also declined over time and become concentrated in the hands of the few large families that have the economic resources to sustain them. In the corn-growing region, the structure of production and land use favored cattle-raising to the detriment of agriculture. This is the case, in part, because land ownership patterns favor cattle-raising. And according to Villanueva, "if the structure of landownership favors private landholders over *ejidatarios*, the dominance of cattle-raising in the structure of production supports the hypothesis that it is the disadvantaged position of the milpa vis-à-vis private property and cattle-raising that explains the decline in corn's productivity and production, and not the characteristics of the production system itself" (Villanueva 1990: 148).

Yucatán has experienced much over the last century. A period of strong economic growth that lasted until the 1970s was followed by the crisis in henequen monoculture and the beginning of the development of tourism centers, especially Cancún, on Mexico's Caribbean coast. The boom years of henequen exports greatly benefited a small number of landholders, but they also created social conditions that undermined the initiative, autonomy, and social mobility of thousands of Yucatecan campesinos (Baños Ramírez 1996: 159). The restructuring of the Yucatecan economy also led to a precipitous fall in the economically active population in agriculture and an equally notable rise in the EAP in the services sector, especially between 1970 and 2000 (see figure 1.8).

The relative importance of rural and urban areas was also reversed in the 1970s, with Yucatán becoming a primarily urban society—giving rise to what Baños Ramírez (2003: 77) calls the establishment of a "post-traditional" order in rural Yucatán. The general context of economic and social crisis in rural Yucatán, demographic growth, urbanization, and differentials between wages within and outside the state paved the path to an intensification of migration, first to the state capital and Quintana Roo, and later to the United States.

Figure 1.8 Economically Active Population in Yucatán, by Sector, 1970–2000

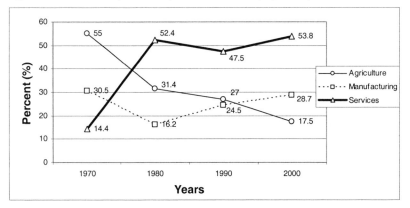

Sources: INEGI, *Censos de Población y Vivienda,* 1970–2000.

MIGRATION AND REMITTANCES

The international migration of Yucatecans to the United States began with the Bracero Program, as people migrated out of central Yucatán as well as Mérida and other of the state's large cities. Yucatecans' incorporation came late in the Bracero Program, principally in the 1950s and early 1960s, shortly before the program's demise. Individuals from more than half of the state's municipalities went to the United States as braceros (Archivo General del Estado, cited in Solís Lizama 2005: 54). However, in contrast to bracero migration from states in western and central Mexico, the flow from Yucatán was relatively small. And unlike the self-perpetuating flows from other sending regions, where the Bracero Program spurred the formation of transnational social networks that encouraged further international migration (Cornelius and Lewis 2007; Durand and Massey 2003), international out-migration from Yucatán came to a virtual halt in the early 1970s, with the development of Cancún as a major tourism destination.

Ironically, this "retention" of Yucatecan migrants in their home state laid the foundation for the later surge in international out-migration from the state. Yucatecans' internal migration to Cancún's tourism sector prepared these workers for international migration, which increased notably beginning in the 1990s (Adler 2004; Fortuny Loret de Mola 2004; Lewin and Guzmán 2005b). Cancún and, later, the

Mayan Riviera became international migration "schools," enabling migrants to develop human capital that they could later apply when migrating internationally. Here they acquired new job skills, expanded their general knowledge base, and learned English (see chapter 4, this volume). Owners of construction companies and hotels in Cancún and Playa del Carmen have confirmed the transition role that Quintana Roo has played for Yucatecan migrants. Some hotel owners expressed frustration with the fact that no sooner are new workers processed through the country's social security system than they abandon their new jobs to head for the United States.

Yucatecan migrants work in hotel construction and restaurants in Playa del Carmen, Akumal, Tulum, Cozumel, and Isla Mujeres, some of the most developed areas in Mexico. An expanding and improved highway infrastructure linking Yucatán and Quintana Roo puts the Mayan Riviera just a few hours away from all of Yucatán's rural population. This First World enclave is just around the corner, so to speak, so Yucatecans, unlike would-be migrants from Oaxaca or Chiapas, need not cross an international frontier to reach the First World. We might even say that Quintana Roo's elaborate tourism development has shifted international frontiers, creating a small "north" within Mexico's "south." It is unlikely that any other area within Mexico today has the same capacity to attract labor.

In the early days of migration from Yucatán, the flow consisted overwhelming of mestizos (Quintal et al. n.d.), but beginning in the early 1980s Mayans from Yucatán joined international migration flows, and their numbers rose steadily through the 1990s. Key factors that have driven contemporary out-migration from Yucatán are socioeconomic in nature: falling demand for henequen and a resulting decline in agricultural activity, increasing job competition between Yucatecan workers and in-migrants from elsewhere in Mexico, the intervention of commercial intermediaries, and natural disasters like hurricanes Gilberto and Isidoro. And eclipsing all of these factors in importance is the pull of U.S. wages, which are up to ten times higher than wages in Yucatán.

Although migrant flows from Yucatán to the United States began to swell in the 1980s, they were not particularly visible until the 1990s, when Yucatecans began to migrate at a more accelerated pace and began to use more solidly established transnational social networks. Today, migrants from Yucatán can be found throughout the United States, though they are concentrated in the Southwest, especially in California. In recent years many Yucatecan migrants have adopted new U.S. destinations. Thus, for example, migrants from Oxkutzcab, who first went to the San Francisco Bay area, began to migrate to Portland, Oregon, where they have encountered *paisanos* from the towns of Maní and Chapab, among others. As their social networks in Oregon consolidated, the new generation of migrants from Oxkutzcab began to travel directly to Portland, without first passing through the Bay area. A similar pattern emerges among migrants from Muna, who first went to Thousand Oaks, California, but after nearly two decades changed their destination to Las Vegas, where there are now over a thousand people from this Yucatecan village. Migrants from Cenotillo, who traditionally concentrated in San Bernardino, California, now head for Denver and the surrounding area. Increasing job competition from other migrants, an eagerness to explore new labor markets, and anti-immigrant sentiments are among the factors that have spurred Yucatecan migrants to move to new migration destinations (Lewin and Guzmán 2005a).

The growth of international migration from Yucatán has been paralleled by an increase in remittances. Although Yucatán does not rank high nationally in terms of total remittances received (see table 1.2), the increase in remittances to the state in recent years is impressive (see figure 1.9). According to Banco de México figures, Yucatán received US$44.5 million in remittances in 2001. By 2006, the remittance flow had reached nearly $114 million.

A comparison of Mexico's migrant-sending areas reveals substantial regional differences in remittance-sending behavior (see table 1.3). Interestingly, migrants from the South/Southeast working in the United States appear to remit funds to their home communities in proportionately higher amounts. For example, in 2005, while the South/Southeast accounted for only one-fifth as many migrants in the United States as the traditional sending region, it nevertheless received fully half as much in remittances as did the states in the traditional sending area. By 2006, the percentage of remittances received by the South/Southeast

Table 1.2 Remittances, by State and Region in Mexico, 2006 (US$ millions)

South/Southeast		Traditional		Center		North	
Campeche	63.3	Aguascalientes	378.2	Federal District	1,551.3	Baja Calif. Sur	24.7
Chiapas	807.6	Colima	166.8	Hidalgo	853.5	Baja California	232.0
Guerrero	1,157.4	Durango	370.9	México	1,926.3	Chihuahua	368.5
Oaxaca	1,198.1	Guanajuato	2,054.8	Morelos	527.8	Coahuila	216.1
Quintana Roo	78.7	Jalisco	1,992.8	Puebla	1,386.0	Nuevo León	285.8
Tabasco	150.1	Michoacán	2,471.5	Querétaro	467.0	Sinaloa	420.1
Veracruz	1,415.2	Nayarit	327.8	Tlaxcala	257.6	Sonora	216.4
Yucatán	113.5	San Luis Potosí	607.4			Tamaulipas	356.3
		Zacatecas	610.5				
Total	4,983.9		8,980.7		6,969.5		2,119.9

Source: Banco de México 2007.

had risen to 55 percent. Comparing the first trimesters of 2006 and 2007, the growth of remittances to Yucatán (27.5 percent) outpaced every other state (the traditional migrant-sending state of Guanajuato ranked second, with remittance growth of 10.1 percent).

Figure 1.9 Remittances to Yucatán, 2003–2006 (US$ millions)

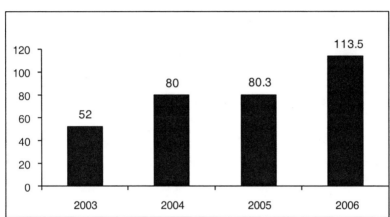

Source: Banco de México 2007.

Table 1.3 Remittances from the United States to Mexico, by Receiving Region (US$ millions)

Region	Population in the United States, 2005	Remittances	
		2005	2006
South/Southeast	1,113,000	4,097	4,983.9
Traditional	5,109,200	8,059	8,980.7
Center	2,024,600	6,097	6,969.5
North	2,353,200	1,780	2,119.9

Sources: CONAPO 2005a: 25–26; Banco de México 2006, 2007.

International out-migration from Yucatán has generated undeniable economic benefits which are being directly capitalized by migrants' families. Many households in migrant-sending communities depend almost entirely on income from remittances. Yet the migration of young people has also caused a rise in violence and the breakdown of family and social relationships within sending communities. Moreover, international migration has been associated with a rise in mental health problems among both migrants and their family members who remain in the home community (see chapter 11, this volume). These social consequences of migration are exacerbated by the fact that most Yucatecan migrants are undocumented. Although these phenomena have appeared only recently, they have already affected many communities in Yucatán, and there is an urgent need for research to help us understand them more fully.

RESEARCH ON YUCATECAN MIGRATION

There have been very few studies of migration from Yucatán. Those that have been conducted are quite recent, reflecting the relative newness of this phenomenon as well as the dominant focus of researchers on internal migration to Mérida and the tourist cities of Quintana Roo. Thus, studies of Yucatecan migration have concentrated primarily on urbanization processes, attempting to understand patterns of economic incorporation and the ways in which migrants remain connected with their communities of origin. These studies were carried out after the 1970s, following the precipitous growth of the state's capital city (Acuña Gallareta 1992; Damián Centeno 1986; Ortega Rojas 1992; Kú Benítez 1998; Reyes Ramírez 1993; Vargas González 1987) and coastal area (Fraga 1992).

Some researchers have provided a historical overview of the changes in migration within the state (see, for example, López Tejero 1987). Some have relied on church records to reveal regional migration flows (Robinson 1980). Also from a historical perspective, Ryder (1977) has studied internal migration beginning in the colonial period, placing it among the population's survival strategies. Others examine the social changes that migration produced, especially the consequences of rural-to-urban migration for processes of production, circulation, and cultural consumption (Hoy Manzanilla 1991; Fernández Repetto 1984). Several scholars have explored the relationship between migration and the henequen crisis and rural transformation in Yucatán more generally (Mena Solís 1985; Baños Ramírez 1996, 2003). Still others have examined the impact of internal migration on cultural or dietary patterns (Balam Pereira 1981; Ryder 1977), both to underscore specific social factors (Ayllón Trujillo 1999) and to uncover the survival strategies associated with rural-to-urban migration (Pacheco Castro 1991). The volume of such studies increased on par with the further development of the tourism sectors in Cancún and the Mayan Riviera (Sierra Sosa 2003; Castellanos 2003).

There were no studies of international migration from the Yucatecan region until the late 1990s. Among the first to study this phenomenon was Ojeda Cerón (1998), whose research focused on migration from Peto in southern Yucatán. The U.S.-bound migration flow from this town began during the second half of the 1970s when a Maryknoll missionary who had been in the region since 1941 helped a group of community members find their way to jobs in California. Ojeda Cerón's work seeks to illuminate migration's impacts on the migrants themselves and their community of origin. He looked at the kinds of work Peteños found in the United States, the difficulties they encountered in that strange and sometimes hostile context, and the weakening of their religiosity. He notes that the transborder networks established by these pioneer migrants, along with the marked salary differentials between Mexico and the United States, opened a path that future waves of international migrants from Peto would follow.

In 2002, Garance Burke published an article in the *San Francisco Chronicle* alerting readers to the presence of a new immigrant community—Yucatecan Mayas—in the San Francisco Bay area (see also Burke 2004). In 2004, Patricia Fortuny Loret de Mola published the results of her ethnographic study of international migrants from Oxkutzcab who had become established in San Francisco. Fortuny's work focuses on the role that religious associations play in constructing and maintaining social networks. Her study of migration behavior among members of an extended family confirmed the embeddedness of the migratory phenomenon in Oxcutzcab. Fortuny Loret de Mola employs the concept of *hetzmek* to demonstrate the capacity of Mayan migrants from this town to travel to distant destinations while maintaining close ties to their community of origin. She found that in Oxkutzcab, when children reach three years of age they are carried piggy-back by their mothers in a practice intended to familiarize children with the notion of traveling over long distances while remaining close to the family. Speaking metaphorically, migrants from Oxkutzcab have transnationalized this local practice, which allows them to inhabit two distinct spaces simultaneously.

Rachel Adler (2004) has examined the characteristics of international migrants from Kaal (a pseudonym) in northern Yucatán whose primary destination is Dallas, Texas. Adopting a human agency perspective, Adler uses the term "migrant agendas" to highlight human agency in migration processes and to explain the social changes catalyzed by migrants' actions. According to Adler, Kaal and its migrant community in Dallas maintain such strong linkages that transnational migration networks affect migrants and nonmigrants alike. For migrants, Dallas has come to represent an extension of Kaal, with the circulation of people, goods, and information serving to lessen the distances between the sending and receiving communities. Migrant agendas are expressed in terms of the ideas and values that migrants ascribe to their reasons for leaving the home community. The objectives of these agendas, according to Adler, are to maintain the extended family, to retain cultural ties to the home community, and to acquire economic standing and prestige in Kaal. These agendas sustain and shape a transnational space that is occupied not only by the migrants but also by the goods and information they circulate.

Although transnational behaviors have served thus far to sustain the linkages between Kaal and its expatriate community in Texas, Adler raises questions about the conditions that may be needed to ensure that this transnational space is preserved. The migrants' undocumented status and the facility they have shown for border crossing are factors that favor the survival of this transnational space. Yet it is essential to consider the effects of other factors, including the collective intent of the migrants themselves and their reasons for separating themselves from the home community.

Solís Lizama (2005) carried out an ethnographic study in Cenotillo, a community near Tunkás that has a relatively long history of migration to the United States. This study confirms the strength of the town's transnational social networks, forged over four decades, and also records significant changes in the migrant population, including the growing participation of young women. Solís Lizama notes that migration has become a kind of rite of passage for the community's youth and an element in the community's cultural repertoire. By identifying various generations of migrants from Cenotillo and their periods of migration, she seeks to understand migration as a factor that helps shape collective identities among both migrants and nonmigrants.

A sense of belonging and a connection to the land are integral elements in the process of recasting identity in Cenotillo. Migrants and nonmigrants share a sense of belonging to the community; their participation in the annual town fiesta and use of the Maya language are important ways of constructing and valuing this sense of belonging. But for those who must leave the community temporarily, their identity as members of the Cenotillo community is filtered through their concurrent identity as international migrants. Inversely, nonmigrants also reconfigure their own sense of community identity, redefined now to include the absent migrants.

Finally, in 2003 a state-level diagnostic study of migration from Yucatán was carried out by Lewin and Guzmán (2005a). It provides a broad overview of Yucatecan migrants' communities of origin, their destinations, the kinds of jobs they fill, the length of their stays, and their approximate numbers in Yucatán, Quintana Roo, and the United States. The study identifies nearly thirty Yucatecan migrant clubs or associations that have been established in various parts of the United States, principally in California, Oregon, and Colorado. The same authors also produced the *Guía del Migrante Yucateco* (Guzmán and Lewin 2004), which summarizes migrants' rights and obligations and is geared to international migrants.

More generally, the diagnostic study demonstrates the need for further, interdisciplinary research to support the design of public policies in a state that is undergoing rapid transformation as a result of international migration. Such policies must address the needs of migrant communities in both Yucatán and the United States. The present volume is another contribution toward this end.

References

Acuña Gallareta, Alma Rosa. 1992. "Condiciones naturales para la reproducción social de los trabajadores migrantes en la ciudad de Mérida." Undergraduate thesis, Universidad Autónoma de Yucatán.

Adler H., Rachel. 2004. *Yucatecans in Dallas, Texas: Breaching the Border, Bridging the Distance.* Boston: Pearson.

Ayllón Trujillo, Ma. Teresa. 1999. *Factores de los procesos migratorios de Yucatán.* Madrid: M. TAT.

Balam Pereira, Gilberto. 1981. *La migración en el área de los centros coordinadores del INI de Yucatán: el bracerismo regional y sus repercusiones sociales.* Valladolid, Yucatán: Centro Coordinador Indigenista.

Banco de México. 2003–2007. *Ingreso por remesas familiares, distribución por entidad federativa.*

Baños Ramírez, Othón. 1996. *Neoliberalismo, reorganización y subsistencia rural: el caso de la zona henequenera de Yucatán 1980–1992.* Mérida: Universidad Autónoma de Yucatán.

———. 2003. *Modernidad, imaginario e identidad rurales: el caso de Yucatán.* México, DF: El Colegio de México.

Burke, Garance. 2004. "Yucatecos and Chiapanecos in San Francisco: Mayan Immigrants Form New Communities." In *Indigenous Mexican Migrants in the United States,* ed. Jonathan Fox and Gaspar Rivera-Salgado. La Jolla, CA: Center for U.S.-Mexican Studies and Center for Comparative Immigration Studies, University of California, San Diego.

Castellanos, María Bianet. 2003. "Gustos and Gender: Yucatec Maya Migration to the Mexican Riviera." PhD dissertation, University of Michigan.

CONAPO (Consejo Nacional de Población). 2005a. *Migración México–Estados Unidos: panorama regional y estatal.* Mexico: CONAPO.

———. 2005b. *Proyecciones de indígenas de México y de las entidades federativas 2000–2010.* Colección Prospectiva. Mexico: CONAPO.

Cornelius, Wayne A., and Jessa M. Lewis, eds. 2007. *Impacts of Border Enforcement on Mexican Migration to the United States: The View from Sending Communities.* La Jolla, CA: Center for Comparative Immigration Studies, University of California, San Diego.

Corona, Rodolfo. 2000. "Mediciones de la migración de mexicanos a Estados Unidos en la década 1990–2000," *Foro Población y Sociedad en el México del Siglo XXI,* October 13–14.

Damián Centeno, D. 1986. "Los migrantes pobres en la ciudad de Mérida: el caso de la colonia Hidalgo." Undergraduate thesis, Universidad Autónoma de Yucatán.

Durand, Jorge. 1998. "Nuevas regiones migratorias." In *Población, Desarrollo y Globalización. V reunión de investigación sociodemográfica en México*, vol. 2, ed. René M. Zenteno. México, DF and Tijuana: Sociedad Mexicana de Demografía/El Colegio de la Frontera Norte.

Durand, Jorge, and Douglas Massey. 2003. *Clandestinos: migración mexicana en los albores del siglo XXI.* Mexico: Miguel Ángel Porrúa.

Fernández Repetto, Francisco Javier. 1984. "Cultura y migración en Yucatán: Xocén y Cuzamá." Undergraduate thesis, Universidad Autónoma de Yucatán.

Fortuny Loret de Mola, Patricia. 2004. "Transnational Hetzmek: entre Oxkutzcab y San Panco." In *Estrategias identitarias: educación y antropología histórica en Yucatán*, ed. Juan A. Castillo Cocóm and Quetzil Castañeda. Mérida: Universidad Pedagógica Nacional.

Fox, Jonathan, and Gaspar Rivera-Salgado, eds. 2004. *Indigenous Mexican Migrants in the United States.* La Jolla, CA: Center for U.S.-Mexican Studies and Center for Comparative Immigration Studies, University of California, San Diego.

Fraga, Julia Elena, ed. 1992. *El proceso de emigración hacia la costa de Yucatán: estudio de cuatro puertos del litoral yucateco.* Mérida: Centro de Investigación y Estudios Avanzados del I.P.N., Unidad Mérida.

Guzmán, Estela, and Pedro Lewin. 2004. *Guía del Migrante Yucateco.* Mérida: Indemaya/Instituto Nacional de Antropología e Historia.

Hervik, Peter. 2003. *Mayan People within and beyond Boundaries: Social Categories and Lived Identity in Yucatán.* New York: Routledge.

Hoy Manzanilla, José Antonio. 1991. "Tixcacal Guardia: migración y cambio social (estudio de caso)." Undergraduate thesis, Universidad Autónoma de Yucatán.

INEGI (Instituto Nacional de Estadística, Geografía e Informática). 1950–2000. *Censo de Población y Vivienda.* Mexico: INEGI.

INEGI. 1995–2005. *Conteo de Población y Vivienda.* Mexico: INEGI.

Kú Benitez, Genny Lucly. 1998. "Migración femenina por días, una alternativa al problema económico del grupo doméstico: el caso de Tekantó." Undergraduate thesis, Universidad Autónoma de Yucatán.

Lewin, Pedro, and Estela Guzmán. 2005a. *Indicadores diagnósticos de la migración en Yucatán.* Mérida: Indemaya/Instituto Nacional de Antropología e Historia.

———. 2005b. "Los migrantes del Mayab," *Revista Camino Blanco* [Instituto de Cultura de Yucatán] 8.

López Tejero, Álvaro Eduardo. 1987. "Flujos migratorios en Yucatán (1950–1980)." Undergraduate thesis, Universidad Autónoma de Yucatán.

Mena Solís, Silvia Concepción. 1985. "La migración en un ejido henequenero: el caso de Ekmul." Undergraduate thesis, Universidad Autónoma de Yucatán.

Ojeda Cerón, Carols Rubén. 1998. "Migración internacional y cambio social: el caso de Peto, Yucatán." Undergraduate thesis, Universidad Autónoma de Yucatán.

Ortega Rojas, Flora Elena. 1992. "Estrategias de supervivencia de las unidades domésticas campesinas: un estudio de caso en la comunidad de Sacnicté, Municipio de Mérida, Yucatán." Undergraduate thesis, Universidad Autónoma de Yucatán.

Pacheco Castro, Jorge Atocha. 1991. "Estrategias económicas y sociales de supervivencia en Cacalchén, Yucatán." Master's thesis, Universidad Nacional Autónoma de México/Escuela Nacional de Antropología e Historia.

Quintal, E. Fanny, et al. n.d. "La migración indígena en la península de Yucatán." In *La migración indígena: causas y efectos en la cultura, en la economía y en la población*, ed. Margarita Nolasco and Miguel A. Rubio. Mexico: Instituto Nacional de Antropología e Historia. Forthcoming 2007.

Reyes Ramírez, Rubén. 1993. "Migración y condiciones socioeconómicas de la población inmigrante: la franja periférica sur de la ciudad de Mérida." Undergraduate thesis, Universidad Autónoma de Yucatán.

Robinson, David, J. 1980. "Migración entre pueblos indígenas en Yucatán colonial." Presented at the Segunda Semana de la Historia, Mérida, Yucatán, February.

Ryder, James W. 1977. *International Migration in Yucatán: Interpretation of Historical Demography and Current Patterns*. Austin: University of Texas Press.

Sierra Sosa, Ligia Aurora. 2003. "Población indígena, migración y mercado de trabajo en Cancún, Quintana Roo, México." PhD dissertation, Universitat Rovira I Virgili, Terragona, Spain.

Solís Lizama, Mirian. 2005. "La migración internacional y su papel en la reconfiguración de la identidad en Cenotillo, Yucatán." Undergraduate thesis, Universidad Autónoma de Yucatán.

Vargas González, T. A. 1987. "Estructura ocupacional y migrantes residentes: el área urbana de Mérida." Undergraduate thesis, Universidad Autónoma de Yucatán.

Villanueva Mukul, Eric. 1990. *La formación de las regiones en la agricultura (el caso de Yucatán)*. Mérida: Maldonado /INI/FCA-UADY/CEDRAC.

Central square and *parroquía* in Tunkás.

2 Tunkás: A New Community of Emigration

TRAVIS SILVA, AMÉRIKA NIÑO, AND MIRIAN SOLÍS LIZAMA

In the late afternoon, one can hear the shouts of the ice cream vendor as he pushes his cart down the streets of Tunkás, a town of just under 3,000 inhabitants settled amid the tropical vegetation covering the Yucatán Peninsula. Streams of men are returning from farmland on the outskirts of town, carrying sacks of corn to sell to the women making tortillas. Doors open as residents emerge to the dusty streets emptied earlier by the oppressive midday heat. In the central square, the ocher walls of the Franciscan church face the *palacio municipal* (town hall) across a plaza shaded by cypress and laurel. Old men gather on benches to remember the Tunkás of their youth. They begin their stories in Mayan and switch to Spanish only upon the arrival of a younger resident who cannot understand the indigenous language. A man in a white cowboy hat calls out to his grandson, who wears an oversized Los Angeles Lakers jersey and a Pittsburgh Pirates baseball cap, while the boy's mother enters the local credit union to collect money wired by her husband in the United States. Yet as Tunkás slowly reawakens, many doors remain shuttered. Husbands, father, and sons are missing. Hundreds of *hijos ausentes* (absent sons) have left Tunkás in search of wage-paying jobs that can sustain their families. Although it is historically and culturally distinct from the traditional cradle of U.S.-bound migration in central-west Mexico, Tunkás is an emerging community of migration.

Tunkás, which means "ugly rocks" in Mayan, is a rural *municipio* (a political division similar to a U.S. county) in the state of Yucatán. Located roughly in the middle of the state (figure 2.1), it is a two-hour drive from Mérida, the state capital, and 40 minutes from Izamál, a city of 40,000. Although Tunkaseños did not start leaving the town in large numbers until the 1970s, migration's impacts on the town are unmistakable. Internal migrants live and work in the beach resort areas in the neighboring state of Quintana Roo. Many men and women exit the bus that arrives from Cancún every Friday night. They have come home to visit family before catching a Sunday afternoon bus back to the resort towns that provide wage employment. Signs of migration to the United States also abound: a few minivans and pickup trucks with California license plates, larger homes being constructed with money sent from the United States, and sporadic English heard alongside Maya and Spanish in the conversations taking place in the plaza. Although its residents did not start leaving until late in the history of U.S.-Mexico migration, today migration to *el norte* is the defining characteristic of the town's social and economic life.

Figure 2.1 Map of the State of Yucatán

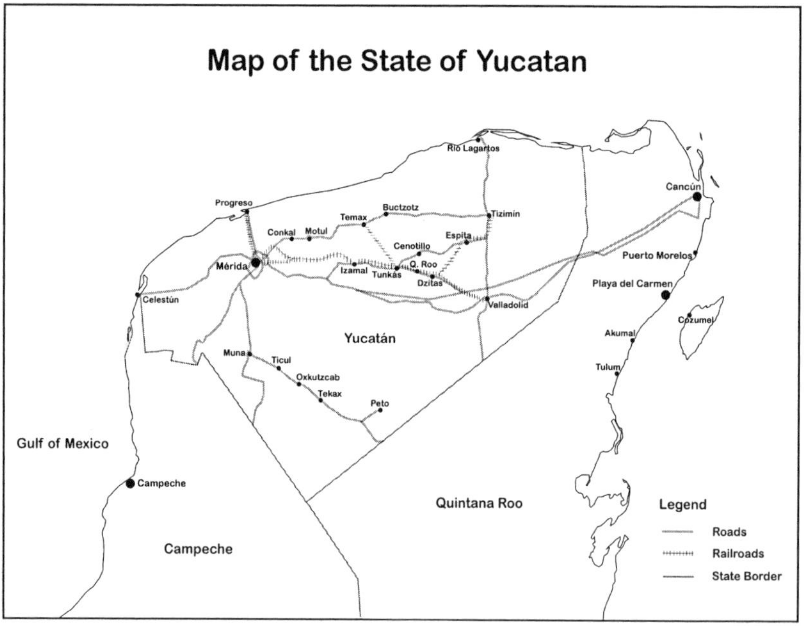

Map of the State of Yucatan

AN ECONOMIC HISTORY OF TUNKÁS

Tunkás emerged from Yucatán's Caste Wars in the early twentieth century as an isolated community. The municipio was dominated by several haciendas producing henequen, the traditional export of the Yucatán Peninsula, and the town's residents were primarily a labor source for the surrounding agricultural area. The state's oligarchic hacienda system, which was rooted in colonial economic practices, was at least partially dismantled by the land reforms of the Mexican Revolution.[1] Wishing to benefit from these land reforms, Tunkás submitted an application in 1918 for an *ejido* to be formed from the lands of eight neighboring haciendas.[2] The owners of these haciendas protested the expropriation of their lands and were able to delay action on Tunkás's application for a decade. Ultimately unsuccessful in their attempts to prevent the formation of an ejido in Tunkás, these landowners lost a portion of their holdings in 1929, when the National Agrarian Commission found that 335 of the 1,349 inhabitants of Tunkás were eligible to be *ejidatarios,* or those with rights to work ejido land. The commission proposed the establishment of a 6,700-hectare ejido in Tunkás (20 hectares per ejidatario). President Emilio Portes Gil approved the proposal on November 7, 1929, and the ejido was established in May of the following year.

By the late 1930s, the population had outgrown the original ejido, and the town submitted an application for its expansion. An additional 7,192 hectares were added by 1945, increasing the size of an individual plot from 20 to 24 hectares and providing for 101 additional ejidatarios. Of this expansion, 3,428 hectares were set aside for public use and were incorporated into the ejido as more men became ejidatarios. The town proposed the next expansion in 1973 and, after legal maneuverings by private landowners who stood to lose property, it was approved seven years later—360 additional hectares, a portion of which was formally set aside for the economic interest of the town's women. Because Tunkás was awarded ejido lands in three distinct phases, the ejido today is fragmented and sits contiguous to privately held farmland (see

---

[1] For a comprehensive discussion of the development of landholding practices in Yucatán, see Joseph 1986: 53–127.

[2] An *ejido* is a form of land tenure begun under the Mexican government's agrarian reform program in 1918. Land was expropriated and redistributed to local farmers who hold usufruct to the land in common but have the right to work an individual plot.

figure 2.2). This fragmentation, along with an increase in the number of ejidatarios, has led to a restriction on the size of individual plots. The average ejido plot in Tunkás is now under 10 hectares—less than half the size of the 1945 plot. Land fragmentation has also compelled some Tunkaseños to cross privately owned land to reach their plots, sometimes creating tension with local landowners. Despite the difficulties associated with Tunkás's ejido, it remains the center of the town's economic life.

Figure 2.2 Map of the Tunkás Ejido

Ejido of Tunkás

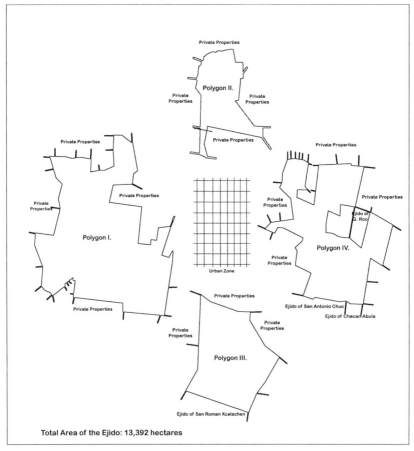

Total Area of the Ejido: 13,392 hectares

During the early days of the ejido, the timber industry was the dominant economic activity. Tunkás and its neighboring municipios supplied wood to furniture makers in various cities in Yucatán. A railroad link between Mérida and Valladolid, established at the turn of the century, ran through Tunkás, providing freight service to carry the wood of the Tunkaseño countryside to urban factories. The era of the furniture wood industry was a period of relative prosperity in Tunkás. According to Vicente Adrián Ake, a local historian, the abundance of jobs in the timber industry minimized emigration from the town during the Bracero Program, which operated from 1942 to 1964:

> Very few migrated from here. When a lot of people went, it was about ten or twelve. This is because there were many jobs here. You could earn money. They paid in real silver coins. You would even see gold coins.

At the industry's peak, each week timber filled two freight trains to Mérida. Wages were relatively high, and jobs in timber cutting or preparation were readily available. No trees were planted, however, and the supply of wood ultimately was exhausted. Commercial cutting declined in the 1950s and ended around 1960.

Apiculture has been a more durable segment of the Tunkaseño economy. Although only a small portion of Tunkás's population engages in beekeeping today, this activity has been a feature of the Yucatán Peninsula since pre-Columbian times.[3] In contemporary Tunkás, commercial beekeeping began around the time that the furniture wood industry collapsed. Initially undertaken as a small-scale enterprise by one family in the 1960s, there is now an association that promotes the interests of Tunkás's thirty-two professional beekeepers. Association

---

[3] Bees provided the ancient Maya with honey and wax (Mann 1973: 217). Honey and bee wax were so highly prized in Mayan society that the Maya paid part of their tribute to Spanish *conquistadores* with these products (Padilla et al. 1992: 565). Keeping bees was also more than an economic activity for the ancient Maya. Their glyphic writing system contained characters influenced by the anatomy of the bee and the value of its products (Crksson 1892: 102).

members export their honey to Europe and Japan through a Mérida-based exporter (see chapter 8, this volume).

Tunkás today relies primarily on the ejido for food. The ejido is divided roughly equally between campesinos, who grow crops, and livestock raisers. The ejido is self-governing through an assembly of ejidatarios, which in turn elects a *comisario ejidal* to act as leader. The comisario directs the day-to-day operations of the ejido and allocates plots to individual farmers. To regulate the number of ejidatarios with access to ejido land, the status of ejidatario is passed from father to son.

The importance of Tunkás's ejido cannot be overstated. Men stream out in the early morning on the kilometer-and-a-half trek to the ejido lands. Today, two-thirds of economically active Tunkaseños work in agriculture (INFDM 2002), and the majority of these men (649 registered ejidatarios) work in the ejido.[4] Beyond its economic significance, the ejido also plays an important role in the social life of the town. One of the town's largest gathering halls is the Casa Ejidal, two blocks off the central plaza, and the ejidatarios have their own *gremio* (guild)[5]— one of Tunkás's few civic associations.

Beginning in 1992, after decades of debate, a national land reform initiative known as PROCEDE was implemented. The goal of this program was to privatize ejido land, as part of an effort to modernize the Mexican economy. The constitutional reform that launched PROCEDE stipulated that ejido privatization must be a collective, local decision. As of this writing, the ejidatarios of Tunkás have declined to privatize their communal holdings through PROCEDE. The opinion of the ejidatarios, however, is not monolithic on this point. Many are proud that their land is still held in common trust, while others believe that privatization is necessary for economic growth. Manuel Tech Uicab, a local official, describes the contentious atmosphere regarding land reform proposals in the town:

---

[4] Interview with Comisario Ejidal Mario Pinzón Canche, February 2006.

[5] Gremios are responsible for the religious aspects of the fiestas held to honor their town's patron saint. Unlike specifically religious organizations, their membership reflects the broad social composition of their community. Thus there are women's and men's gremios, gremios of farmers, migrants to the United States, and so on (Fernández 1995).

> When people speak of what they have tried to do, there is
> a bit of confusion. There have been problems at the time
> of elections when someone mentions that they have the
> idea to privatize here.... The last time this happened, it
> was at the time of elections, and it caused a great commo-
> tion that was published in the newspaper.

Prior to its implementation, PROCEDE's proponents hypothesized that land reform would invigorate Mexico's agrarian economy and thereby relieve the pressures pushing migrants from their hometowns. Opponents, by contrast, believed that upheaval in land use and tenure would create a stream of people heading for the United States. However, Cornelius (1998: 230) found in his study of Tlacuitapa, a longtime migrant-sending community in Los Altos de Jalisco, that ejido privatization had not affected migration patterns, because changes in land tenure did not mitigate the root economic and social problems that push people out of the town. More generally, as the privatization process has unfolded, critics have become increasingly skeptical that it will make ejido agriculture more productive or profitable. Nancy Johnson argues that PROCEDE has been unsuccessful in initiating the recapitalization of the agrarian sector that is needed for further development (Johnson 2001: 305). The general failure of Mexico's land reform program to stem emigration is reflected in the experience of Tunkás. We found that families with ejido rights have the same incidence of migration as families without ejido certificates. Holding ejido land does not seem to influence decisions about internal migration or migration to the United States.

THE HISTORY OF TUNKASEÑO MIGRATION

Though Mexican workers have been crossing to the United States in search of work since the late nineteenth century,[6] several states in the central-west plateau of the country are identified as historic migrant-sending areas: Jalisco, Michoacán, Guanajuato, Zacatecas, Durango, and San Luis Potosí (Durand and Massey 2003: 72). Until recently, these traditional migrant-sending states supplied the bulk of migrants to the

---

[6] For a detailed description of early Mexican migration to the United States, see Cardoso 1980.

United States. By contrast, southern Mexico (including the Yucatán Peninsula) has only recently begun sending migrants to the United States. Durand and Massey (2003: 89) hypothesize that Yucatán and its neighboring states were slow to send migrants north of the border for two reasons: internal migration opportunities relieved the pressure to migrate to the United States, and low regional participation in the Bracero Program meant that these areas did not establish a toehold in the United States that would serve as a springboard for larger-scale migration. While these factors may explain the generalized emergence of Yucatecan migration in the 1980s and 1990s, we found that the bracero experience of the 1960s was a significant precursor of widespread Tunkaseño migration to the United States.

The United States and Mexico established the Bracero Program in 1942 to help fill the wartime labor shortages in the U.S. agricultural sector. Mexican workers were given short-term contracts (two to six months) that allowed them to enter the United States legally, provided they returned to Mexico when their contracts expired. Tunkaseños learned about the program through newspapers and in open-air meetings, and some registered with local officials. Their names were sent to Mérida, where state officials selected candidates for the program, and the state government informed the municipality which residents had been chosen to participate. Selected Tunkaseños gathered their belongings and made the 3,200-kilometer journey to a contracting center in the northwestern state of Sonora, where they received their contracts, took medical tests, and were fumigated. Tunkaseño braceros left Sonora for Mexicali and then went on to the United States.

Although Bracero Program recruitment began in Mexico in 1942, the flow of bracero labor from Tunkás did not start until 1956. The number of braceros from Tunkás, while not trivial, was never very large. According to state records, there were three Tunkaseño braceros in 1960, two in 1961, and five in 1962.[7] However, an in-depth look at the experience of braceros from Tunkás shows how the town's relatively meager participation in the program provided the impetus for today's extensive migration to the United States.

---

[7] Archivo General del Estado de Yucatán. Poder Ejecutivo, Vol. 1, Expedientes 1224 and 1228 from 1960 and 1961; Vol. 2, Expediente 1228 from 1962.

Former braceros we interviewed in Tunkás had worked in California, which today receives more Tunkaseños than any other U.S. state.[8] José left Tunkás as a bracero and for ten years traveled back and forth between Yucatán and the United States. After working legally in Texas, he went to California without authorization in search of higher wages. He lived in Santa Ana, California, where a large community of Tunkaseños has settled, and saved money to provide for his family in Tunkás. After working in a Southern California metal factory for several years, he returned, now a grand economic success, to Tunkás to help his wife raise their family. Returned braceros like José served as a model for potential migrants. Their experiences signaled that migration could be an economically viable alternative to staying in Tunkás.

The experience of Arcenio, who left Tunkás in 1960 to harvest strawberries in San Jose, California, also follows this model. Arcenio left "to get to know the United States and because here there was no work." He was able to complete five bracero contracts in different parts of California before the program ended in 1964. During his final contract period, Arcenio learned that legal entry into the United States would soon be closed off, so he remained in California for several years without authorization, working agricultural jobs in northern California and commercial jobs in Los Angeles. He worked until he saved enough money to purchase land in Tunkás and subsequently to establish a butcher shop. Arcenio is another successful returned migrant serving as an example of the opportunities that migration offers to Tunkaseños.

Arcenio contributed to the burgeoning flow of migration from Tunkás in a more concrete way. After returning to Tunkás, he found that other Tunkaseño men wanted to go to the United States. Absent the Bracero Program, there was little hope of legal entry, so Arcenio became the first in a chain of *coyotes*, or people smugglers, who have since become part of the social fabric of Tunkás and its satellite communities in California. He connected fellow Tunkaseños to a third party in the United States, who arranged tourist visas that allowed would-be migrants to enter legally and then search for work with employers

---

[8] We were able to interview only four surviving former braceros in Tunkás. Two had traveled to California to fulfill their work contracts; the others were unable to recall where in the United States they had worked.

willing to hire individuals without work documents. Through his early knowledge of a transnational U.S.-bound migration network, Arcenio serves as a direct link between the Bracero Program and the first wave of sustained migration from Tunkás to the United States in the 1970s.

During the 1970s, internal migration also began to affect Tunkás. Developers in Cancún and Quintana Roo who needed labor to construct the massive tourist resorts on Mexico's east coast turned to the largely Mayan population of the Yucatán Peninsula as a source of labor (Re Cruz 2003: 496). Tunkaseños left for wage-paying jobs in Cancún and its neighboring areas beginning in the early 1970s. While economic opportunities in the resort areas originally impeded the flow of Tunkaseños to the United States, the two migration systems have since stabilized and now work in concert (see chapter 4).

The origins of Tunkaseño migration are consistent with a comprehensive analysis of the numbers of Tunkaseños entering the United States (figure 2.3). Influenced by the success of Arcenio, José, and other braceros, migration from Tunkás to the United States began in volume during the 1970s. The number of migrants leaving Tunkás for the United States remained relatively constant during the 1970s and 1980s but jumped during the 1990s as Cancún established itself as a "school of migration," increasing the number of Tunkaseños who venture to *el norte*.

Figure 2.3 First Migration from Tunkás to the United States, by Year

N = 800.

In Tunkás, as elsewhere in rural Mexico, the most important force pushing migrants from their home communities is the lack of adequately paid job opportunities (Mines 1981: 59–65; Gaytán et al. 2007). But on the Yucatán Peninsula, weather also plays a role in the decision making of potential migrants. Hurricanes have destroyed local agriculture on numerous occasions, pushing people from Tunkás to the United States. For example, the devastation caused by Hurricane Carmen in 1974 was associated with a wave of out-migration to the United States and to destinations elsewhere in Mexico. Similarly, Hurricane Mitch, which hit Tunkás in 1998, was followed by a sharp increase in migration to the United States in the two following years. Over three times as many people left in 2000 as in 1998. Not all hurricanes push Tunkaseños from their town, but particularly devastating hurricanes do seem to increase the flow of people exiting the town.

In 2005, Hurricane Wilma wreaked havoc on Cancún. Although it missed Tunkás, emigration from the town increased as Tunkaseños went to the resort areas to take jobs in the reconstruction effort. As Wilma demonstrates, hurricanes can also serve as a pull factor for internal migration by creating jobs domestically. Wilma's indirect impact on Tunkás was so pronounced that when inaugurating the town's annual fiesta in January 2006, the mayor welcomed returned migrants from the United States and "our brothers who have gone to Cancún to help rebuild the homes of our countrymen."

INFRASTRUCTURE AND PUBLIC SERVICES

Improvements to rural infrastructure are intended to help those living in the countryside, but they may also accelerate out-migration from rural areas. As roads and communication systems connect small rural communities to urban centers, rural dwellers find it easier to leave their villages in search of wage-paying jobs (Rhoda 1983: 54). Improvements in health and sanitation services lower mortality rates, thereby augmenting the population and forcing more people to compete for already scarce resources. Competition places increased stress on the village economy until the pressure is relieved through emigration (Cornelius 1976: 17). And while infrastructure projects often create short-term employment opportunities, mostly in construction, only permanent, wage-paying jobs provide a viable long-term alternative to emigration (Alarcón 1995: 51).

The Valladolid–Mérida railroad line linked Tunkás to urban centers beginning in the first decade of the twentieth century. The train served an important commercial purpose by transporting the ejido's timber, as discussed above, but it also connected the townspeople to the larger population centers. The first migrants to the United States—the braceros who left in the 1960s—traveled to Mérida on this train line. Passenger service was discontinued in the early 1990s, however, and bus service is now Tunkás's only connection to the state capital. A paved road connects Tunkás with Izamál to the west and with Valladolid to the east, and busses cover this route several times a day. The road is frequently used by internal migrants who continue on to Cancún. Table 2.1 summarizes the development of major infrastructure and public services in Tunkás.

Table 2.1   Year of Introduction of Public Services and Infrastructure in Tunkás

Service	Year Introduced
Public school	1930
Electricity	1968
Road	1968
Phone	1975
Medical clinic	1992
Train	1906

The Tunkás municipio is heavily dependent on federal aid to fund its annual budget. Revenues generated in the municipio provide only 2 percent of its budget, compared to 9 percent from the state government and 89 percent from the federal government. Much of this money is disbursed directly to poor citizens through welfare or rural development programs.

The average education level among Tunkaseños is six years of elementary school (*primaria*). The town's schools—two kindergartens, four primary schools, and one secondary school—bring teachers on short-term contracts from urban centers (usually from Mérida). There is also a technical agricultural management program, established in 1987, that corresponds roughly to a high school education, but the program is relatively small, with fewer than 200 students, many from outside Tunkás. The nearest postsecondary schools are in neighboring Motul (a technical finishing school) and Mérida (the state university), each a two-hour drive from Tunkás. Very few Tunkaseños take advantage of these higher educational opportunities.

COMPARISONS WITH OTHER MIGRANT-SENDING COMMUNITIES

Tunkás differs in a number of ways from rural communities in Mexico's traditional migrant-sending regions, most of which have sent migrants to the United States for generations. In this section we compare Tunkás to Tlacuitapa, Jalisco, in west-central Mexico, whose outmigration has been studied since 1975 (Alarcón 1995; Cornelius 1976, 1990, 1998; Cornelius and Lewis 2007).

According to Mexico's 2000 census, the municipio of Tunkás has a population of 3,528, of whom 2,890 (82 percent) live in the county seat (*cabecera*), where our fieldwork was conducted. Tlacuitapa, a town of fewer than 2,000 residents, falls within the municipio of Unión de San Antonio, which has 15,000 residents (INEGI 2002). While Tunkás and Tlacuitapa are roughly comparable in size, there is a sharp contrast between the indigenous composition of Tunkás and the mestizo character of Tlacuitapa, as well as in the religious identification of the residents.

Ann Craig (1983: 13) describes the Los Altos de Jalisco region, where Tlacuitapa is located, as having "an overwhelmingly *mestizo* population." Indeed, according to the 2000 census, only thirty-three people in all of Unión de San Antonio reported speaking an indigenous language. Tunkás, however, is decidedly indigenous. Many homes are constructed in the traditional Mayan form, with walls of rough-hewn wooden poles and roofs of palm fronds. These huts provide a sharp contrast with more durable homes of concrete, which are generally owned by migrants. These two home styles—the traditional and the modern—exist side by side throughout Tunkás. Extended families frequently construct multiple dwellings on a single house lot, both to pool resources and to preserve the extended family, a unit of great importance in Mayan culture (Brown 1999: 327–31).

This Mayan influence permeates more than patterns of home construction in Tunkás. Although Spanish is now the dominant language in Tunkás, roughly two-thirds of town residents still speak Mayan and nearly three-quarters understand it, according to our survey. At the beginning of the twentieth century, Spanish was hardly spoken among the town's mostly indigenous residents, and it is not uncommon for people to refer to themselves as *mayeros*,[9] while also reaffirming their identity as Mexican citizens. The interplay between Tunkás's indigenous identity and migration is discussed further in chapter 9 of this volume.

Also notable is the presence and strength of Protestant churches in Tunkás. According to the 2000 census, 26 percent of Tunkaseños self-identified as *evangélicos*, versus 68 percent as Catholic (INEGI 2002). By comparison, in the nation as a whole, only 5 percent of Mexicans responding to the 2000 census identified themselves as *evangélicos*, versus 77 percent as Catholic. The six traditional sending states identified above—Jalisco, Michoacán, Guanajuato, Zacatecas, Durango, and San Luis Potosí—are even more uniformly Catholic (nearly 95 percent on average). While the various churches of Tunkás coexist in relative harmony, each has its own way of coping with the emerging culture of migration that is solidifying in Tunkás. Chapter 10 discusses the different churches of the town and the relationship between religion and migration in Tunkás.

Tunkás is also considerably poorer than traditional migrant-sending communities. Mexico's National Population Council (CONAPO) categorizes Tunkás as a highly marginalized community, while Tlacuitapa is in a municipio of medium marginalization (CONAPO 2000).[10] Within the state of Yucatán, Tunkás ranks as the thirty-seventh most marginalized municipality, out of 106. The town ranks 814 nationally among the

---

[9] *Mayero* is an ethnic categorization assigned to persons whose native tongue is Maya (Gutiérrez Estévez 1992).

[10] CONAPO's marginalization index takes into account issues such as access to public services, average wage, and education levels.

most marginalized municipios, out of 2,437; by contrast, the municipio in which Tlacuitapa is located ranks 1,534 (CONAPO 2000).

Tunkaseños who choose not to migrate earn less than their counterparts in traditional sending communities. Over 90 percent of Tunkaseños earn less than US$8 per day (the minimum wage in Yucatán is $4 a day). By contrast, only 50 percent of people in the municipio of Unión de San Antonio earn less than $8 daily (CONAPO 2000). The economic alternatives to migration are clearly bleaker in Tunkás than in Tlacuitapa.

The relative wealth of many small towns in Mexico's west-central plateau region can be explained by many decades of heavy migration to the United States. Tlacuitapa is in a better economic position because generations of migrants have built a modest level of economic prosperity in these towns through their remittances. In a 2005 study, Canto and Shaiq (2007) found that migrants from Tlacuitapa and Las Ánimas, Zacatecas, sent home a median monthly remittance of US$300. U.S.-based migrants from Tunkás, by comparison, have a median monthly remittance of $200. Migrants from traditional sending communities are able to remit more money to relatives at home, thus allowing these communities to better offset the lack of local economic development.

Though Tunkás differs substantially from traditional migrant-sending communities in central Mexico, it is typical of new migrant-sending communities in Yucatán. In his ethnography of Tetiz, Yucatán,[11] Paul Eiss (2002: 296–97) notes that high poverty levels and a lack of employment opportunities have greatly increased migration from Tetiz to the United States. We note similar poverty levels and a lack of employment opportunities in Tunkás (see chapter 8). The pervasive poverty in Yucatán, high even by Mexico standards, serves as an important motivating factor for potential migrants.

Rachel Adler's case study of Yucatecan migration from "Kaal" reveals a town very similar to Tunkás in terms of both demographics and migration history (Adler 2004: 7–28). "Kaal" (a pseudonym) and Tunkás both have indigenous populations that actively self-identify as Maya in their home community. Language, clothing, family structure, and hous-

---

[11] Tetiz also ranks as a highly marginalized community on the CONAPO index.

ing arrangements are all influenced by indigenous customs. Mayan speakers are proud of their indigenous language, though they note that it has been heavily influenced by Spanish. Members of both communities see their local culture as a blend of Mayan traditions and contemporary Mexican customs.

The towns' migration histories are also very similar. U.S.-bound migration from both communities began with the Bracero Program, and contemporary migration can be directly linked to these pioneer migrants. Migrants from both "Kaal" and Tunkás settle in tight-knit communities in the United States. Large concentrations of migrants from "Kaal" can be found in Dallas, Texas, and San Bernardino, California, while Tunkaseños concentrate in Anaheim, Santa Ana, and Inglewood, California—three communities of the Los Angeles/Orange County metropolis. Both towns also have experience with internal migration to the Cancún beach resort area and have established a complex interface between internal and U.S.-bound migration. The similar migration patterns of "Kaal" and Tunkás have been shaped by many common factors, including the historical isolation of the Yucatán Peninsula, the Bracero Program, the opportunity to migrate to Cancún, and traditional family structures identified with Mayan culture.

CONCLUSION

Given its stagnant economy, its poverty, and its vulnerability to natural disasters, Tunkás quickly became dependent on migration for economic survival, despite having sent its first migrants to the United States only a half-century ago. Returned braceros demonstrated that migration to *el norte* was a winning economic strategy, and thus helped develop a culture of migration that has come to dominate the social structure of Tunkás. Internal migration opportunities have reinforced this culture by de-stigmatizing the migrants' social position in the town. As chapter 3 explores in detail, patterns of migration from Tunkás have become stronger over the last decade, and 38 percent of Tunkaseño households have some experience with out-migration.

Because there are so few local opportunities for economic advancement in Tunkás (see chapter 8), new migrants leave for the United States almost daily. The pioneers of international migration who participated in the Bracero Program have now been replaced by a younger generation of migrants, like 17-year-old Antonio, who at the time of our fieldwork was planning his first trip to the United States. His views underscore the lack of opportunities in his town, which pushes migrants toward the United States:

> Those who cross the desert face a lot of danger. You can die of starvation and dehydration, and there are also poisonous animals. But it is necessary to take these risks to cross to the other side.... I want to have my own home, like my brother, have everything I want, and not depend on anyone.... You have to face these risks, you must walk across mountains. And there are some who run out of water in the desert, but this does not affect me at all.

Although aware that trying to enter the United States clandestinely is increasingly dangerous, Antonio believes he must make the journey to achieve some measure of economic prosperity in Tunkás. The price of a coyote and the probability that he will have to make repeated crossing attempts are known burdens, but Antonio's determination mirrors that of many Tunkaseños who increasingly view migration to the United States as the only viable option for personal success.

References

Adler, Rachel H. 2004. *Yucatecans in Dallas, Texas: Breaching the Border, Bridging the Distance*. Boston, MA: Pearson.

Alarcón, Rafael. 1995. "Transnational Communities, Regional Development, and the Future of Mexican Immigration," *Berkeley Planning Journal* 10: 36–54.

Brown, Denise F. 1999. "Espacios mayas de familia y comunidad: una relación de interdependencia," *Mexican Studies* 15, no. 2 (Summer): 323–42.

Canto, Brisella, and Fawad Shaiq. 2007. "Migration and Local Development." In *Impacts of Border Enforcement on Mexican Migration: The View from Sending Communities*, ed. Wayne A. Cornelius and Jessa M. Lewis. La Jolla, CA: Center for Comparative Immigration Studies, University of California, San Diego.

Cardoso, Lawrence. 1980. *Mexican Emigration to the United States, 1897–1931: Socio-economic Patterns.* Tucson, AZ: University of Arizona Press.

CONAPO (Consejo Nacional de Población). 2000. "Marginalization Index, Appendix B." Mexico City: CONAPO.

Cornelius, Wayne A. 1976. "Outmigration from Rural Mexican Communities." In *The Dynamics of Migration: International Migration*, ed. Shirley Sirota Rosenberg. Washington, DC: Smithsonian Institution.

———. 1990. "Labor Migration to the United States: Development Outcomes and Alternatives in Mexican Sending Communities." La Jolla, CA: Center for U.S.-Mexican Studies, University of California, San Diego.

———. 1998. "Ejido Reform: Stimulus or Alternative to Migration?" In *The Transformation of Rural Mexico*, ed. Wayne A. Cornelius and David Myhre. La Jolla, CA: Center for U.S.-Mexican Studies, University of California, San Diego.

Cornelius, Wayne A., and Jessa M. Lewis, eds. 2007. *Impacts of Border Enforcement on Mexican Migration: The View from Sending Communities.* La Jolla, CA: Center for Comparative Immigration Studies, University of California, San Diego.

Craig, Ann L. 1983. *The First Agraristas: An Oral History of a Mexican Agrarian Reform Movement.* Berkeley, CA: University of California Press.

Crksson, Hiliborne T. 1892. "Phonetic Value of the Ch'I Glyph in the Maya Graphic System," *Science* 20, no. 498 (August): 101–102.

Durand, Jorge, and Douglas Massey. 2003. *Clandestinos: migración México–Estados Unidos en los albores del siglo XXI.* Mexico City: Universidad Autónoma de Zacatecas.

Eiss, Paul K. 2002. "Hunting for the Virgin: Meat, Money, and Memory in Tetiz, Yucatan," *Cultural Anthropology* 17, no. 3: 296–97.

Fernández, Francisco. 1995. "Celebrar a los santos: sistema de fiestas en el nor-occidente de Yucatán," *Alteridades* 5, no. 9: 51–61.

Gaytán, Seidy, et al. 2007. "The Contemporary Migration Process." In *Impacts of Border Enforcement on Mexican Migration: The View from Sending Communities*, ed. Wayne A. Cornelius and Jessa M. Lewis. La Jolla, CA: Center for Comparative Immigration Studies, University of California, San Diego.

Gutiérrez Estévez, Manuel. 1992. "Mayas y mayeros: los antepasados como otros." In *De palabra y obra en el nuevo mundo.* Vol. 1, *Imágenes interétnicas*, ed. M. León Portilla, M. Gutiérrez Estévez, G. H. Gossen, and J. J. Klor de Alba. Madrid: Siglo Veintiuno de España.

INEGI (Instituto Nacional de Estadística, Geografía e Informática). 2002. *XII Censo general de población y vivienda. Principales resultados por localidad, Yucatán.* www.inegi.gob.mx.

INFDM (Instituto Nacional para el Federalismo y el Desarrollo Municipal). 2002. *Enciclopedia de municipios de México–Yucatán.* Mérida, Yucatán: Gobierno de Yucatán. http://www.yucatan.gob.mx/estado/municipios/31097a.htm. Accessed June 16, 2006.

Johnson, Nancy L. 2001. "Tierra y Libertad: Will Tenure Reform Improve Productivity in Mexico's 'Ejido' Agriculture?" *Economic Development and Cultural Change* 49, no. 2 (January): 291–309.

Joseph, Gilbert M. 1986. *Rediscovering the Past at Mexico's Periphery: Essays on the History of Modern Yucatán.* University, AL: University of Alabama Press.

Mann, Arthur J. 1973. "The Economic Organization of the Ancient Maya," *The Americas* 30, no. 2 (October): 209–28.

Mines, Richard. 1981. *Developing a Community Tradition of Migration to the United States.* Monograph Series, no. 1. La Jolla, CA: Program in United States–Mexican Studies, University of California, San Diego.

Padilla, F., et al. 1992. "Bees, Apiculture, and the New World," *Archivos de Zootecnia* 41, no. 154 (extra): 563–67.

Re Cruz, Alicia. 2003. "Milpa as an Ideological Weapon: Tourism and Maya Migration to Cancún," *Ethnohistory* 50, no. 3 (Summer): 489–502.

Rhoda, Richard. 1983. "Rural Development and Urban Migration: Can We Keep Them Down on the Farm?" *International Migration Review* 17, no. 1 (Spring): 34–64.

Traditional *casa de paja* in Tunkás, constructed of sticks with palm frond roof.

Casa de mampostería, made of concrete, being built by a returned migrant.

3 The Contemporary Migration Process

ALPHA MARTELL, MARIBEL PINEDA, AND LUIS TAPIA

This chapter focuses on the demographic profile of Tunkaseño migrants to the United States and their motivations for migration. We also examine migrants' labor market experiences in the United States, their choices of destination, and their interactions with Tunkaseños and other groups in their U.S. host communities. Using transnationalism as a conceptual framework, we explore the transnational social networks that channel Tunkaseños to particular destination cities, neighborhoods, and workplaces. The chapter concludes by discussing the role of gender in U.S.-bound migration from Tunkás.

Migration from Tunkás to the United States is a relatively recent phenomenon compared to outflows from traditional migrant-sending communities in Mexico's central-western states of Jalisco, Zacatecas, and Michoacán. Nevertheless, the density of Tunkás residents with U.S. migratory experience is quickly approximating the levels found in more established communities of migration. In the thirty-six migrant-sending communities surveyed by the Mexican Migration Project (MMP) between 1998 and 2002—most of which were located in the traditional states of origin for Mexican migration to the United States—the population with U.S. migration experience in 1990 averaged 15 percent. Despite the relatively late onset of large-scale Tunkaseño migration to the United States, we also found that 15 percent of the population had U.S. migration experience.

As transborder social networks become more deeply embedded, Tunkaseño migration will likely increase. Over a fifth of the migrants sampled said they wanted to settle permanently outside Tunkás. In a follow-up question asking where they planned to move, two-thirds answered, "the United States." Individuals with no migratory experience to the United States were asked the same question, and 22 percent answered that they planned to move permanently from Tunkás to the United States.

MIGRANTS' DEMOGRAPHIC PROFILE

The demographic attributes of migrants exiting Tunkás are similar to those of migrants from traditional labor-exporting areas. U.S.-bound migration from Tunkás follows the traditional male-dominant pattern, with men accounting for 65 percent of those with U.S. migration experience. The median age of Tunkaseño migrants to the United States is 36 years, indicating that the town's migrants are spending their most economically productive years in the United States (see table 3.1).

Table 3.1 Demographic Profile of Tunkaseños with U.S. Migration Experience

Median age (years)	36
Males	65%
Married	71%
Number of children (mean)	3.1
Years of education (mean)	6

One of the principal attributes affecting migration to the United States is marital status. In Tunkás, 71 percent of migrants with U.S. experience were married, with an average of 3.1 children. These characteristics are similar to those of migrants to the United States from Tlacuitapa, Jalisco, and Las Ánimas, Zacatecas, where nearly three-fourths of experienced migrants were married and had an average of 2.7 children (Cornelius and Lewis 2007). As discussed in the following section, the economic incentives for migration are compounded when potential migrants have families to support.

MOTIVES FOR MIGRATION

Tunkaseños identified economic pull factors in the United States as more important than push factors in Mexico for their decision to migrate. The pull factors are the same as those identified in previous research, most importantly, the lure of higher wages in the United States (see table 3.2).

Table 3.2 Reasons Given for Most Recent Migration to the United States

Better pay in the United States	25%
Home construction, debt repayment, or starting a business in Mexico	16%
More job opportunities in the United States	15%
Family reunification	12%
Low salaries in Yucatán	11%
Vacation	8%
Returning to the same job in the United States	3%
Legalize status	2%
Purchase land	1%
Other	7%
Total	100%

N = 397.

Vicente, a migrant observes:

> Over there [in the United States] you work and you get to eat from that. Better said, your whole family eats. Here, you work hard in hard jobs and sometimes you don't see any food come out of it. There are always dry spells in the job season that leave us with no money.

Better working conditions and the opportunity to earn additional income through overtime are also significant attractions to the United States. Don Clemente, another experienced U.S. migrant, explains:

> In the United States I enjoyed having a set schedule and much better working conditions. I easily got used to working eight-hour shifts. Another benefit of working in the United States was the overtime hours, which I always took advantage of, of course.

While the wage and employment differential between Tunkás and the United States was the most important pull factor for a plurality of Tunkaseño migrants, family ties to the United States were also a strong determinant of migration decisions. We found that 12 percent of Tunkaseños had migrated to the United States on their most recent sojourn primarily because of a desire to reunite with family members and friends living there. As discussed below, family networks play a key role in locating jobs for migrants.

As shown in table 3.2, many Tunkaseños have gone to the United States to fulfill some specific economic goal: to construct a home, repay debts, or start a business in Mexico. Building a new home (or expanding an existing one) is a necessary investment for growing families, which for many is possible only with income earned in the United States. In a rural town like Tunkás, where the poorest live in *casas de paja* constructed of sticks and palm frond roofs, a *casa de mampostería*—a home made of concrete—is a dream. The typical casa de paja costs approximately US$2,500 to construct. A casa de mampostería costs $8,000. Because it is nearly impossible to save enough money to build one of these homes through the subsistence wages earned from agricultural labor, those desiring a sturdier and more prestigious dwelling are forced to migrate. The hardship of living in a casa de paja vulnerable to the elements is illustrated by the wife of a migrant:

> We had a *palapita [casa de paja]*. We lived there together
> and when the rain came my children would get wet.
> We never thought we would have a little house, but
> thank God we have it now.

By migrating to the United Status as a bracero, the woman's husband was able to accumulate enough money to achieve his dream of constructing a small cement home for his family.

Another long-term migrant, Don Arcenio, explained how he used migration to finance his home as well as his business:

> My land and this house were bought with the money I
> would send. The money I earned in the United States
> gave me capital to work and establish our own business.
> With that money I bought bees, and thanks to the profits
> that I earned, I was able to build this house.

One of the biggest dreams of migrants is to use capital accumulated in the United States to open their own business. While businesses founded by former U.S. migrants in Tunkás do not generate much employment for other residents (see chapter 8), such businesses can eliminate the need for further migration by those who establish them (Massey 1987). Arcenio, who went to the United States in 1960 as a 30-year-old bracero, explains: "What I have now, I owe to Los Angeles, where I worked and saved money.... I have my little ranch, I have my hogs, I have my house, and I have my butcher shop"— the only one in Tunkás.

Underemployment is a potent push factor for some Tunkaseños. Don Gregorio, an experienced migrant to the United States, explains, "In the countryside, we used to work six days a week, and now there is only work for three days. What are we supposed to do with eighteen dollars a week?" Don José, who has lived in the United States for forty years, explains how low wages cannot sustain a decent lifestyle in Yucatán:

> I have another brother who lives in Valladolid [a nearby city in Yucatán]. He is working and is earning what an agricultural worker earns in a day. Here they pay five dollars a day. What is a person to do with five dollars? Nothing. Here the people do not work five days of the week; they can only work two or three days. So what are [Tunkaseños] going to do with $15?

Both migrants express the common distress of individuals working in Mexican rural communities where it is not open unemployment as much as underemployment that drives emigration.

In previous research, perceptions of relative deprivation have been found to influence decisions to migrate from rural Mexico (Stark and Taylor 1990). However, we found little difference in perceptions of economic well-being between migrants and nonmigrants in Tunkás. When asked, "On a scale from 1 to 10, with 10 being the family with the best living conditions in this town and 1 being the family with the poorest conditions, where would you put yourself and the family?," the median response for Tunkaseños with U.S. migration experience was 6. For those lacking U.S. migration experience, the median rank was 5. Even though the difference in relative perceived wealth is small, we found that those who have migrated have a more positive view of local economic conditions than those who have not migrated. Sixty-three percent of interviewees with U.S. migration experience felt that Tunkás's economy had improved in the last year. Nevertheless, three-quarters of the migrants perceiving an improving economy still believed that it is necessary for an individual to leave the town in order to succeed.

Lastly, most migrants go into debt to finance their first migration to the United States, and many Tunkaseños incur major debts when a family member becomes ill. Due to the lack of credit available to most residents of Tunkás (see chapter 8), the only source of income for debt repayment is migration to the United States. Celmy explained the shortcomings of her husband's earnings while in Tunkás:

> At that time he earned very little, and we would spend the money on food. Sometimes at midweek he would ask the man he was working with for money. On Saturdays when they would pay him, the *patrón* would discount what he owed him. And my husband would say, "See, there is no money for food or other things; if our son gets sick and we have to take him to the doctor, we do not have enough to pay for the debt." Instead he told me he was going to leave [for the United States]. Then he came back, and we were even able to build our little home.

A noneconomic push factor in Tunkaseño migration to the United States is the value system that has been created in the community as a consequence of migration. Based on fieldwork in migrant-sending communities in Jalisco, Michoacán, and Zacatecas, Cornelius (1990: 24) has defined this culture of migration as "a set of interrelated perceptions, attitudinal orientations, socialization processes and social structures, including transnational social networks, growing out of the international migratory experience, which constantly encourage, validate and facilitate participation in this movement." Cohen (2004: 5) has characterized the culture of migration in Oaxacan sending communities as follows: "First, migration is pervasive—it occurs throughout the region and has a historical presence that dates to the first half of the twentieth century. Second, the decision to migrate is one that people make as a part of their everyday experiences. Third, the decision to migrate is accepted by most Oaxacans as one path toward economic well-being."

In the case of Tunkás, the first contributors to a local culture of migration were the braceros who began going to the United States for short-term agricultural employment in the early 1960s. They returned with new expectations, for example, of what a decent house should look like. In Tunkás today, numerous concrete-block houses have been built or are being remodeled by returned migrants from the United States. Most nonmigrants are unable to build such houses.

As the incidence of U.S. migration experience increases among Tunkaseños, the "migrant agendas" that lead to first-time migration decisions are expanding. Adler (2004: 61) defines migration agendas as "a complex set of ideas and values that includes the goals and motivations for migration, plans for migration, and the coordination of life goals with migration." In Tunkás, we found that experienced migrants have motives for returning to the United States that differ from those of individuals who have not yet made the journey. Fourteen percent of our interviewees who had no U.S. migration experience said they were considering migrating to the United States in the next twelve months, compared to 35 percent of experienced migrants. The difference is most likely attributable to the fact that experienced migrants have established social ties in the United States that will facilitate their migration, job seeking, and housing needs. This explanation is consistent with the fact that 13 percent of experienced migrants said that they planned on returning to the United States for family reunification, and another 21 percent planned on returning because they had jobs waiting for them in the United States (see table 3.3). The primary reason given by both experienced migrants and potential first-time migrants planning to go to the United States in 2006 was higher U.S. wages, but potential first-timers appear to be even more sensitive to the real-wage differential than are experienced migrants.

Among potential first-timers, 28 percent reported that their main reason for migrating was more plentiful job opportunities in the United States, compared with only 17 percent of experienced migrants who cited this as their main reason for repeat migration. The most obvious explanation for this difference is that many experienced migrants who had returned to Tunkás only to be present for the annual town fiesta (when we interviewed them) intended to return to their most recently held job in the United States and did not expect to live permanently in Tunkás. Twenty-one percent of experienced migrants said that they had jobs waiting for them in the United States, compared to only 12 percent of potential first-time migrants. Among nonmigrants, 16 percent stated that building a better home was their primary reason for planning to go to the United States, compared with only 5 percent of experienced migrants. This illustrates the urgency of home construction as a motive for first-time migrants.

Table 3.3 Motives for Prospective Migrants Planning to Go to the United States in 2006

Reasons Migrants Gave for Planning to Migrate	Experienced Migrants (N = 86)	Prospective First-time Migrants (N = 32)
Higher wages in the United States	35%	41%
More jobs in the United States	17%	28%
Job waiting in the United States	21%	12%
Reunification of family	13%	3%
Build better home	5%	16%
Vacation	3%	0%
Other	6%	0%
Total	100%	100%

These results reflect the changes in migration agendas that come with increased migration experience. Experienced migrants have family and work responsibilities in the United States that draw them back there. As the original goal for migration is achieved, the individual's motives for subsequent migration change accordingly. For example, building a better house is a key motive for migration among potential first-time migrants, but it is less important among experienced migrants who have already used their U.S. earnings to finance home construction.

MODELING THE DECISION TO MIGRATE TO THE UNITED STATES

A logistic regression analysis helps to isolate the various factors that have affected Tunkaseños' decisions to go north. The dependent variable for our analysis is having migrated to the United States one or more times, with the reference category being nonmigrants. Our first hypothesis is that younger males are more likely to migrate, both because of their need to accumulate capital to start families and build houses, and because of the increased physical risk of clandestine border crossings that would favor fit and healthy migrants, who tend to be younger. The results of the logistic regression confirm that an increase in a person's age has a significant, negative effect on the likelihood of migrating to the United States when both the age and age-squared variables are considered. In addition, males are more likely than females to migrate to the United States, holding other factors constant (see table 3.4).

Table 3.4 Determinants of Having Migrated to the United States

Determinant	β	Standard Error	Significance
Age	1.108***	0.329	**0.001**
Age^2	−0.108***	0.039	**0.005**
Male	0.649***	0.233	**0.005**
Married	0.206	0.197	0.296
Education	−0.007	0.022	0.758
Household members who migrated to U.S.	0.740***	0.098	**0.000**
Constant	−3.888***	0.695	**0.000**

N = 663. Chi-squared = 81.39. *** 99% confidence interval.

Our second hypothesis is that years of education has a negative effect on the probability of migrating, due to the high level of inequality in Mexico. Individuals with higher levels of education benefit from inequality by obtaining higher-wage employment that is inaccessible to individuals with lower levels of education. Because higher education is scarce in Tunkás, those who have achieved a post-secondary level of education are able to earn higher wages in Mexico and thus are less likely to migrate. The logistic regression, however, fails to find any statistically significant effect of the level of education on the likelihood of migrating from Tunkás to the United States.

Third, we analyze whether marital status has an impact on the propensity to migrate. Whether due to social networks or increased financial responsibility, we would hypothesize that married individuals are more likely to migrate to the United States than are their single counterparts. However, the results in table 3.4 show that there is no statistically significant difference between married and single persons in terms of their likelihood to migrate to the United States.

Finally, we examine the effect of social networks, operationalized as the number of household members who have migrated to the United States. We find that having household members who have previously migrated to the United States contributed significantly to the likelihood that an individual has migrated to the United States.

A second logistic regression shows the factors that affect the propensity to migrate to the United States *in the next twelve months*. Table 3.5 summarizes the results. As with the previous model, this regression model suggests that age has a negative effect on the propensity to migrate, when considering both the age and age-squared variables. Males are more likely than females to migrate. Marital status and education are again not significant statistically. A person's legal status and number of household members in the United States both have a significant, positive impact on the respondent's stated intent to go north during the coming year.

Interestingly, there is a strongly gendered difference in the effects of age on stated intention to migrate. Figure 3.1 shows stated intention to migrate in the next year by age and gender. For men, there is a negative correlation between age and intended migration. For women, there is no correlation between age and intended migration until around age 40, when a positive correlation appears. This difference may be attributed to the fact that, unlike their male counterparts, older women are more likely to be family-reunification migrants than labor migrants.

Table 3.5 Determinants of Intent to Migrate in 2006

Determinant	β	Standard Error	Significance
Age	1.029**	0.502	**0.040**
Age^2	−0.166***	0.063	**0.008**
Male	0.710**	0.337	**0.035**
Education	−0.004	0.030	0.889
Married	−0.445	0.293	0.128
Legal status	1.989***	0.533	**0.000**
Household members who migrated to U.S.	0.444***	0.114	**0.000**
Constant	−3.069***	0.971	0.002

N = 467. Chi-squared = 38.76. *90%, **95%, ***99% confidence levels.

Figure 3.1 Intention to Migrate by Age and Gender (N = 481)

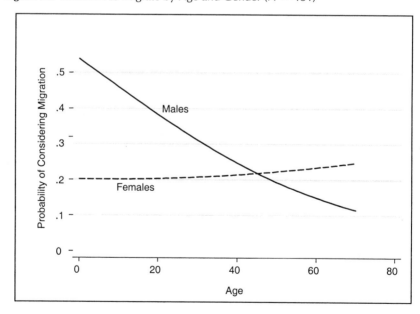

CHOICE OF A U.S. DESTINATION

California is the primary destination of Tunkaseños in the United States. Ninety percent of our interviewees went to California on their first trip to the United States, with the largest concentrations in Los Angeles and Orange counties (see table 3.6).

Table 3.6 U.S. Destination of Tunkaseño Migrants

Destination	First Trip (N = 527)	Most Recent Trip (N = 207)
Orange County	46%	49%
Los Angeles County	31%	19%
Northern California	1%	1%
Other California	12%	11%
Texas	1%	5%
Minnesota	3%	3%
Colorado	2%	2%
Oklahoma	1%	0%
Florida	1%	1%
Wisconsin	0%	1%
Other	3%	7%
Total	100%	100%

We found that 93 percent of Tunkaseño migrants chose their U.S. destination based on the presence of family or friends living in that area. Having relatives or friends with experience living in the destination decreases the social and economic costs of relocating for newly arrived immigrants (Portes and Rumbaut 1990). The major immigrant gateways of California are particularly attractive for migrants with low levels of education. Nogle (1997) finds that the U.S. foreign-born population with low levels of education and English fluency are more likely to choose traditional immigrant-receiving states like California. Similarly, Bauer, Epstein, and Gang (2005) find a link between poor English skills and higher probabilities of choosing locations with large Mexican populations. Finally, large metropolitan areas like Los Angeles–Orange County provide a degree of invisibility for unauthorized migrants (Zúñiga and Hernández-León 2005: xvi).

At a national level, Mexican immigrant destinations diversified following the 1986 Immigration Reform and Control Act (IRCA). IRCA granted permanent legal residence to 2.3 million Mexicans (Durand, Massey, and Capoferro 2005: 2). Legalization allowed freedom of mobility among Mexican immigrants without fear of deportation. The large-scale legalization program, combined with a sharp recession in California and increasing anti-immigrant sentiment, provided an atmosphere leading to a deflection of immigrants to other states in nontraditional destinations of the Midwest and eastern seaboard regions (Durand, Massey, and Capoferro 2005: 16).

Tunkaseño migration mirrors the broader diversification of Mexican migrant destinations. Small numbers of Tunkaseños are settling in nontraditional immigrant-receiving regions like Minnesota, Florida, Colorado, and Wisconsin. On their first trip to the United States, 31 percent of Tunkaseño migrants arrived in Los Angeles County, compared to 19 percent of migrants on their last trip. The traditional receiving state of Texas is becoming an increasingly important destination for Tunkaseño immigrants. On the first trip to the United States, only 1 percent of respondents reported arriving in Texas, compared with 5 percent on their most recent trip. The growth in migration to new destinations can be attributed to greater employment opportunities, a lower cost of living, and the freedom of mobility allowed by the IRCA legalizations. Chano, a Tunkaseño resident with U.S. migration experience, explains:

> People have already gone to other areas. They go to Minnesota, Boston, San Mateo [in northern California], Oregon, Washington, Texas, and Atlanta. They go because of the quality of life or for work. For example, when an individual is a ranch worker and someone tells him that they are paying better in another area, he leaves for that area. The cost of living is also cheaper in other areas; Minnesota is one of those areas, I believe.

Like immigrants to the United States in general, Tunkaseño migrants are responding to market conditions that affect income, and they tend to locate to areas with higher wages and lower rates of unemployment (Jaeger 2006: 22).

U.S. LABOR MARKET EXPERIENCE

The primary source of employment for first-time migrants from Tunkás tends to be the service sector in the Inglewood and Anaheim areas of greater Los Angeles. Twenty percent of Tunkaseños worked in a car wash on their first trip to the United States. Other key service-sector occupations for Tunkaseño migrants have been in the restaurant industry, where 13 percent were cooks, 10 percent were dishwashers, and 2 percent were waiters. Less than 6 percent worked in agriculture on their first trip to the United States, and only 2 percent worked in construction. As table 3.7 shows, there was little variation between first and last trips in terms of the sectors where Tunkaseños worked.

Table 3.7 Sector of U.S. Employment among Tunkaseño Migrants

Employment Sector	First-time Migrant Occupation (N = 711)	Most Recent Migrant Occupation (N = 284)
Agriculture	2%	0%
Services	57%	60%
Construction	6%	7%
Manufacturing	11%	11%
Professional	3%	4%
Other	6%	6%
Non-wage labor	15%	13%
Total	100%	100%

The types of occupations held by Tunkaseño migrants are comparable to the profile of recently arrived unauthorized immigrants of all nationalities in the United States (Passel 2006), with one exception: only 7 percent of the Tunkaseño migrants we interviewed had been employed most recently in the construction industry, compared to 20 percent of the estimated U.S. population of undocumented migrants. We speculate that this is due to the existence of previously established social networks that connect Tunkaseños to specific places of employment in the service sector (such as car washes). Eighty percent of the Tunkaseño migrants had been referred to their current U.S. employer by a relative or friend. Only 9 percent had asked the employer directly for work, while 6 percent had sought work on the street, usually at a gathering site for migrant day laborers, and 1 percent searched in the newspaper or listened to the radio for job opportunities. Only 2 percent of Tunkaseño migrants sought assistance from a temporary employment agency. Informal, hometown-based labor recruitment mechanisms work efficiently for them, so there is little need to search outside of their social networks.

BUILDING TRANSNATIONAL SOCIAL NETWORKS

In *Return to Aztlan*, Massey and colleagues (1987) found that once international migration begins, social networks develop to make foreign employment increasingly accessible to all classes in a sending area. Social networks based on kinship, friendship, and community origins ease the cost of migration. Glick Schiller, Basch, and Blanc Szanton (1992) have termed these ties and networks "transnational" to describe how migrants maintain or build multiple networks of connection to their country of origin while at the same time settling in a new country. Transnational connections take many forms. Among Tunkaseño migrants, 40 percent send money home for public fiestas in Tunkás. Many undocumented Tunkaseños interviewed in Southern California maintain close ties to their homeland through phone calls, letters, and remittances. Forty percent of them call their family twice a month.

Luis is a 33-year-old Tunkaseño who has been living in California for almost twenty years. He does not feel American and describes himself as a Yucatecan. Because he has no legal document that would allow him to reenter the United States, he is one of the many Yucatecans who cannot go home every January to march through the streets of Tunkás with the Gremio de Braceros, the organization of Tunkaseño migrants to the United States and their relatives (see chapter 10). Instead, he sends an annual monetary contribution for the Mass and fiesta celebrating Santiago Apóstol, the patron saint of Tunkás. His children, who are U.S. citizens, usually travel with their grandparents back to Tunkás to become acquainted with Yucatecan traditions. Though migrants like Luis may leave Tunkás and settle in the United States permanently, they routinely engage in various transnational behaviors. In the case of Luis, such behaviors include sending money and gifts to relatives in Tunkás and occasionally attending meetings convened by various organizations that conduct activities in both the United States and Mexico.

Thirty percent of Tunkaseño migrants participate in a U.S.-based organization consisting of migrants from their hometown—a notable proportion, considering the relatively recent onset of U.S.-bound migration from the town. Hometown associations (HTAs) often raise funds in the United States to assist community development projects back home. The Mexican government's 3 x 1 Program promotes the creation of HTAs and provides matching funds from the federal, state, and municipal governments to pursue local development projects (see Fernández de Castro, García Zamora, and Vila Freyer 2006). Most of the Tunkaseños who have donated money through this program are undocumented and send the collected money through a representative they choose, someone who regularly travels back and forth (see chapter 8).

Transnational social networks also present business opportunities on both sides of the border. Richard Mines argues that communities with successful "pioneer migrants" have the best potential to develop migration networks, because the returning pioneer can help relatives cross the border and find work (Mines 1981: 37). One pioneer from Tunkás is 50-year-old Olivia, who has been living in Anaheim, California, since 1976. She became a U.S. permanent resident in 1986 and is now the manager of the apartment complex where she lives. Pioneer migrants like Olivia are key advisers for Tunkaseño newcomers; they have helped fellow Tunkaseños cross the border and find work, lodging, and food. Olivia prepares Yucatecan food daily in her apartment in Anaheim to sell to young Yucatecan men at the end of their workday. She travels to Tunkás every two or three months to buy Yucatecan spices like *recado negro* and *chimole* to prepare her ethnic recipes. In Tunkás, Olivia has her own business, selling U.S. baseball hats, clothing with English lettering, imitation Converse shoes, cosmetics, and Chinese-made jewelry. Her business trips and commercial exchanges permit the consolidation and reproduction of her transnational networks.

GENDERED MIGRATION

In this section we evaluate how gender influences the U.S. migration experience of Tunkaseños. Previous studies in other migrant-sending communities have shown that men and women experience migration differently in terms of their motives to migrate, border crossing experiences, and roles in the labor market and household (Aysa and Massey 2004; Donato and Patterson 2004; Itzigsohn and Gioruli-Saucedo 2002). In particular, it has been shown that Mexican women are less likely than men to migrate illegally to the United States (Donato 1993; Kanaiaupuni 2000). Our results are consistent with this general pattern. From 2000 to 2006, 84 percent of Tunkaseño male migrants were undocumented, versus only 69 percent of women migrants.

Legalized men can sponsor their wives as legal immigrants, and even undocumented women can draw upon male resources to ensure a safer crossing. For example, Olivia left Tunkás at 20 years of age to reunite with her husband after the birth of her second child. "I didn't want my children to grow up with no father," she said. She crossed the border with the help of a *coyote*.

Luin Goldring (2001) has observed that Mexican migrants' participation in transnational activities is strongly gendered. Her study of Mexican migrant organizations from the state of Zacatecas finds that these organizations are mostly arenas of male action that allow immigrant men to claim a social status denied to them in their new host society. Women participate in these organizations as beauty pageant contestants or as helpers. Itzigsohn and Gioruli-Saucedo (2002) also argue that institutional and public transnational activities among Latin American immigrants are mostly a male-dominated arena, with women typically investing their resources in the subsistence of their households before directing them to other ends, such as transnational activities. This pattern holds in the case of Tunkás. For example, Tunkaseña migrants hold fund-raising parties—*quermeses*—among Tunkaseños and help in preparing and serving the food. Only 9 percent of the Tunkaseños who participate in their HTA are women, and men are nearly twice as likely as women to participate in the HTA. A third of Tunkaseño men participate, compared to only 17 percent of the women.

In Tunkás, women generally care for their children and home. A very small percentage of women in Tunkás engage in some type of remunerated work, such as weaving hammocks or preparing food for sale. Many Tunkaseñas criticize the position of women in their community. Young women like Berenice and Lolita complain about being assigned a passive social role. In many cases, parents tell their daughters that educating them is a waste of resources, because they will likely get married at an early age. There are also cases of arranged marriages. Domestic violence against women is common, especially when the husband is under the influence of alcohol.

The relative autonomy that we observed among Tunkaseña migrants in Southern California shows a transformation in social perception. Women reported noticing changes in relations with spouses or partners that result from the women's involvement in work outside the home and from the employment of some males in "women's" work, as in restaurant kitchens. For example, men now occasionally prepare the *cochinita pibil* (a traditional Yucatecan dish) for family gatherings. Nevertheless, the submissive behavioral pattern of Yucatecan woman is still strong, a product of their close ties to the home country and culture.

For Tunkaseño husbands, life in the United States means a loss of power—both within the family and in the receiving society, where the male migrant is viewed as a second-class citizen. Armando, age 40, spends half of the year in Tunkás and half in Anaheim. He does not like women who migrate to *el norte*.

> When women go to California they change a lot. For example, I cannot hit my wife in California because she knows she can call the police. Here in Tunkás, if she shouts at me I calm her, saying, "stop it or I'll slap you." In Tunkás we men can do whatever we want, but not in California. The women feel more independent there because they work, they earn money, they buy their clothes and stuff. Men do not influence them that much. Women feel free when they earn money. Here in Yucatán there are no temptations. Indigenous women are poor, humble, and innocent; and as long as they don't have money they are docile. Money transforms our culture.

Armando also complains that Tunkaseña women who live in the United States advise each other to go to parties and clubs and to dress more provocatively:

> They tell each other, "let's go dancing, let's go here,
> let's go there." At that point the cultural distortion
> starts. Many of my fellow Tunkaseños have divorced
> because of too much freedom.

Women who come to the United States to reunite with family have
the advantage of a preestablished social network. Such networks facilitate accommodation to the new social and economic order and provide
women with emotional and psychological support. Our data show that
96 percent of Tunkaseña migrants came to the United States because
they had relatives already living here. Yet the transnational community
can be a source of both support and oppression for migrant women
(Clifford 1994: 314). According to one of her friends, Olivia is an object
of envy among some people in Tunkás, due to her success in business.
Although she suffered domestic violence for years, she still allows her
husband to act as the head of the household. As Olivia explained: "I did
not want to divorce him because I was thinking about my children. If I
get married to another man, he won't take care of them. Women of
today are different; they don't put up with bad treatment."

CONCLUSION

Mexico's yawning wage gap with the United States is the primary motivation for out-migration from Tunkás, as it is for the Mexican population more generally. The lack of local economic development has
prompted 15 percent of the population of Tunkás to emigrate. The
demographic profile of these U.S.-bound migrants is consistent with
that found in previous studies of Mexican migration to the United
States. Migrants tend to be young, married, male household heads with
children, who migrate to provide for their families in the sending community.

Tunkaseños continue to follow the traditional settlement pattern
focused on California and other southwestern states, though some migrants leaving since the early 1990s have dispersed themselves, choosing destinations in the eastern seaboard states and the Midwest. An
analysis of the motives that propel Tunkaseños into the migration
stream shows that family reunification is more important for experi-

enced migrants than for potential first-time migrants. The labor market experiences of Tunkaseño immigrants follow the broader trends of Mexican immigrant labor in the United States, except in the case of the construction industry, where Tunkaseños are underrepresented. Tunkaseños concentrate mostly in the service sector, with the majority working in either a car wash or a restaurant.

Transnational social networks are the key to border crossing and coping with life in the United States among Tunkaseños. Such networks explain the channeling of Tunkaseños to particular destination cities and neighborhoods and to specific workplaces, as well as the perpetuation of migration to the United States. Tunkaseña women are migrating through these networks in increasing numbers, but their decision making is still constrained by patriarchal norms and gender-linked power differences. Women generally follow their husbands and sons, whose resources they draw upon to ensure a safe crossing, and they depend heavily on their social network contacts in the United States to adjust to life in the host country.

References

Adler, Rachel H. 2004. *Yucatecans in Dallas, Texas*. Boston, MA: Pearson/Allyn and Bacon.

Aysa, María, and Douglas S. Massey. 2004. "Wives Left Behind: The Labor Market Behavior of Women in Migrant Communities." In *Crossing the Border*, ed. Jorge Durand and Douglas S. Massey. New York: Russell Sage Foundation.

Bauer, Thomas, Gil S. Epstein, and Ira N. Gang. 2005. "Enclaves, Language and the Location Choice of Migrants," *Journal of Population Economics* 18, no. 4: 649–62.

Clifford, J. 1994. "Diasporas," *Cultural Anthropology* 9, no. 3.

Cohen, Jeffrey H. 2004. *The Culture of Migration in Southern Mexico*. Austin, TX: University of Texas Press.

Cornelius, Wayne A. 1990. "Labor Migration to the United States: Development Outcomes and Alternatives in Mexican Sending Communities." Final Report to the Commission for the Study of International Migration and Cooperative Economic Development, Washington, DC.

Cornelius, Wayne A., and Jessa M. Lewis, eds. 2007. *Impacts of Border Enforcement on Mexican Migration: The View from Sending Communities*. La

Jolla, CA: Center for Comparative Immigration Studies, University of California, San Diego.

Donato, Katherine M. 1993. "Current Trends and Patterns of Female Migration," *International Migration Review* 27, no. 4: 748–71.

Donato, Katherine M., and Evelyn Patterson. 2004. "Women and Men on the Move: Undocumented Border Crossing." In *Crossing the Border*, ed. Jorge Durand and Douglas S. Massey. New York: Russell Sage Foundation.

Durand, Jorge, Douglas S. Massey, and Chiara Capoferro. 2005. "The New Geography of Mexican Immigration." In *New Destinations: Mexican Immigration in the United States*, ed. Víctor Zúñiga and Rubén Hernández-León. New York: Russell Sage Foundation.

Fernández de Castro, Rafael, Rodolfo García Zamora, and Ana Vila Freyer, eds. 2006. *El Programa 3x1 para Migrantes*. México, DF: Instituto Tecnológico Autónoma de México, Universidad Autónoma de Zacatecas, Miguel Ángel Porrúa.

Glick Schiller, Nina, Linda Basch, and Cristina Blanc Szanton, eds. 1992. *Towards a Transnational Perspective on Migration: Race, Class, Ethnicity, and Nationalism Reconsidered*. New York: New York Academy of Sciences.

Goldring, Luin. 2001. "The Gender and Geography of Citizenship in Mexico-U.S. Transnational Spaces," *Identities* 7, no. 4: 501–37.

Itzigsohn, José, and Silvia Gioruli-Saucedo. 2002. "Immigrant Incorporation and Sociocultural Transnationalism," *International Migration Review* 36, no. 3: 766–98.

Jaeger, David A. 2006. "Green Cards and the Location Choices of Immigrants in the United States, 1971–2000." IZA Discussion Paper No. 2145. Bonn: Institute for the Study of Labor (IZA).

Kanaiaupuni, Shawn M. 2000. "Reframing the Migration Question: An Analysis of Men, Women, and Gender in Mexico," *Social Forces* 78, no. 4: 1311–48.

Massey, Douglas S. 1987. "Understanding Mexican Immigration to the United States," *American Journal of Sociology* 92, no. 6 (May): 1372–1403.

Massey, Douglas, Rafael Alarcón, Jorge Durand, and Humberto González. 1987. *Return to Aztlan: The Social Process of International Migration from Western Mexico*. Berkeley, CA: University of California Press.

Mines, Richard. 1981. *Developing a Community Tradition of Migration to the United States: A Field Study in Rural Zacatecas*. Monograph No. 1. La Jolla, CA: Program in U.S.-Mexican Studies, University of California, San Diego.

Nogle, June Marie. 1997. "Internal Migration Patterns for US Foreign Born, 1985–1990," *International Journal of Population Geography* 3: 1–13.

Passel, Jeffrey S. 2006. *The Size and Characteristics of the Unauthorized Migrant Population in the United States: Estimates Based on the March 2005 Current Population Survey.* Washington, DC: Pew Hispanic Center. http:// pewhispanic.org/files/reports/61.pdf.

Portes, Alejandro, and Rubén G. Rumbaut. 1990. *Immigrant America: A Portrait.* Berkeley, CA: University of California Press.

Stark, Oded, and Edward Taylor. 1990. "Relative Deprivation and Migration, Evidence and Policy Implications." In *Unauthorized Migration: Addressing the Root Causes.* Hearings before the Commission for the Study of International Migration and Cooperative Economic Development, 1987–1990. Washington, DC: The Commission.

Zúñiga, Víctor, and Rubén Hernández-León, eds. 2005. *New Destinations: Mexican Immigration in the United States.* New York: Russell Sage Foundation.

Now-unused railroad tracks that once carried Tunkaseño migrants to Mérida and other urban centers.

4 The Interface between Internal and International Migration

ANDREA RODRÍGUEZ, JENNIFER WITTLINGER, AND
LUIS MANZANERO RODRÍGUEZ

Unlike Mexican communities with strong traditions of labor migration north across the border but little internal migration, Tunkás sends people to both international and national destinations. Today, as the United States increases in popularity as a work destination for Tunkaseños, more people are confronting the decision to stay within Mexico or migrate internationally. This chapter examines the relationship between internal and international migration from Tunkás. To date, internal migration patterns have not been studied adequately, especially in how they relate to Mexican migration to the United States. We question whether internal migration deflects or facilitates U.S.-bound migration. In doing so, we look at associations between internal and international migration and examine the factors that contribute to a migrant's choice of destination.

We begin with a brief overview of the context of migration from Tunkás to national destinations, followed by an explanation of how migration to internal destinations affects the propensity to migrate to international destinations. Lastly, we provide an analysis of the major determinants of internal versus international migration. Based on this analysis, we argue that while internal migration continues to occur, rather than deflecting U.S.-bound migration as it did in the past, it now promotes migration to international destinations.

THE HISTORICAL CONTEXT OF INTERNAL MIGRATION

Cancún and the Quintana Roo Tourist Belt

The paucity of historical connections between Tunkás and the United States, combined with the pull that domestic tourist destinations exert on would-be migrants in Tunkás, largely explains the recentness of this town's emergence as a source of international migrants. Internal migration has long been the more attractive migration alternative, with abundant employment opportunities close to home. Internal migration from Yucatán to the neighboring state of Quintana Roo began in the early 1970s, driven by a demand for wage laborers in the growing hotel industry in what would become the booming tourist center of Cancún.

Tropical forests, coral reefs, pristine beaches, transparent coastal waters, and close proximity to Mayan archaeological ruins made the Quintana Roo coastline an ideal location for the construction of a center for tourism. Massive public investments in infrastructure made Cancún the first tourist center integrally developed by the Mexican government:

> The original plans for Cancún were part of a national program to develop vacation resorts throughout Mexico that would appeal to an international clientele. The purpose of this program was to attract hard foreign currency that could be used to pay off Mexico's international debt (Haydt 1994: 199).

To this end, the Mexican government encouraged both national and international investment in the hotel industry, a core component in the growth and development of Cancún as a center for tourism and in the area's emergence as a destination for internally migrating laborers (Re Cruz 1994: 56). The workforce for this construction boom came in large part from neighboring Yucatán.

Quintana Roo is among the top five states in Mexico in terms of wages, and this state receives 72 percent of all internal migrants. The first laborers to migrate from Tunkás to Cancún were drawn by offers of employment published in the Mérida press and by labor contractors. Faustino, one of the first Tunkaseños to migrate to Cancún, in 1971, explained, "When they began building a hotel [the investors] solicited people through the newspaper. For those who wanted a job, there were jobs. You went there, and they hired you." Migrants to Cancún traveled to hiring stations where contractors were waiting to hire laborers. In addition, labor contractors from Cancún arrived in Tunkás and other rural Yucatecan communities and offered employment. Due to Cancún's distance—a three-hour drive from Tunkás—labor contractors made employment more attractive and accessible to Tunkaseños by bussing them back and forth weekly. As Manuel, who first migrated to Cancún in 1986, described the process:

> We simply went contracted. A labor contractor or em-
> ployer came to Tunkás to recruit people and take people
> to work in Cancún. They took us to Cancún weekly, they
> paid us on Saturdays, and then they brought us back to
> Tunkás. They told us they would come back at four in the
> morning on Sunday and take us to Cancún again. I didn't
> find my job through a family member, but rather through
> a labor recruiter that came to Tunkás.

As word spread of abundant employment, more Tunkaseños migrated to Cancún. Over the next decade, the combination of job advertisements in the press, the in-town presence of labor contractors, and endorsements by returning migrants sustained migration between Yucatán and the nascent Quintana Roo tourist belt. Although the migrants' employment in Cancún was initially limited to the construction sector, over time their employment opportunities spread to the service sector as tourist facilities opened.

Ultimately it was the social networks formed between Tunkás and Cancún that sustained the migration. As anthropologist María Bianet Castellanos relates, "Migrants informed their younger brothers, sisters, and cousins of the shifting employment trends in Cancún's service industry" (Castellanos 2003: 112). As news of employment opportunities were spread by word of mouth, migration patterns to Cancún solidified further. When asked how she learned about Cancún, María, a migrant who has now settled there, recalled: "I knew a lot of people that went there. They would come back and say that there were a lot of jobs and that they paid well. They encouraged us, and we went." Although labor contractors continued to recruit through the 1980s, they were eventually rendered unnecessary by the development of social networks between Tunkás and the Quintana Roo tourist belt.

The consolidation of migration patterns to Cancún is evidenced by the significant jump in the number of internal migrants leaving Tunkás in the second half of the 1980s. From 1980 to 1984, 48 Tunkaseños migrated to a destination within Mexico; between 1985 and 1990, the number of internal migrants rose to 122, more than double the earlier number. "By the 1980s, Cancún was known throughout the peninsula and the country as the place with abundant work opportunities for all" (Castellanos 2003: 128).

Cancún's tourist industry and migration to Cancún have continued to expand in tandem. The area's popularity stimulated the creation of other tourist—and therefore migrant—destinations along the Mexican Riviera. Playa del Carmen is now the third-most-popular internal migration destination for Tunkaseño migrants, who are drawn by two decades of construction of hotels, nightclubs, restaurants, and other labor-hungry, tourist-related industries there (Bever 1999: 131).

Mérida

While the majority of migrants from Tunkás continue to work in Quintana Roo, 26 percent of internal migrants, the second-largest contingent, migrate within the state of Yucatán. Of these, the majority travel to the capital city of Mérida, a two-hour bus ride from Tunkás. Due to its proximity to Tunkás, many of those who choose to work in Mérida commute home weekly. Although Tunkaseño migration to Mérida began in the 1960s, a more significant flow began in the 1980s as a consequence of the henequen crisis (see chapter 1, this volume), and this flow has continued to the present. Contemporary migration patterns to Mérida resemble those to other internal migration destinations. Forty-three percent of migrants to the capital are female, a significantly greater proportion than found among their international counterparts. The high number of female migrants is partly the result of their widespread employment as domestics in Mérida, an employment niche that accounts for nearly 8 percent of migrant jobs there. Another explanation for the high representation of females is the increased migration of family units. Men are more likely to bring their families with them when they are migrating to destinations within Mexico. However, even though the number of female migrants to Mérida is comparatively high, males still compose the majority. They typically find work in construction or in the service sector, as store clerks, chefs, or waiters. However, not all migrants to Mérida are low-skilled. Six percent of Tunkaseños working in Mérida are professionals, unlike the flow to Cancún, which is made up almost exclusively of laborers. Mérida's proximity and its importance as the state capital lure skilled and unskilled migrants alike.

SCHOOL FOR MIGRATION?

Stepwise Migration from the Quintana Roo Tourist Belt to the United States

Because of the continued flow of migrants from Tunkás to destinations within Mexico, it can be argued that internal migration continues to suppress migration to the United States. By providing opportunities for economic advancement in locations much closer to home, internal destinations absorb migrants who would otherwise move northward in search of opportunities. Internal destinations hold the further advantage of being legally accessible and offering a cultural milieu that is easier to navigate. One migrant to Cancún related: "Many young men I have known in Cancún have had good jobs in the hotels and such. Then they leave. To go there [to the United States] to wash cars? No, it's not worth it." Thus opportunities within Mexico sometimes outweigh those in the United States, deterring international migration.

While the proximity of internal destinations may have deflected U.S.-bound migration in the past, we argue that internal migration no longer suppresses international migration, but rather complements and propels it. The success that Tunkaseños achieved through migration to Quintana Roo and other destinations in Mexico encouraged them to look toward the United States as a new migratory destination, one that may offer even better economic prospects. Internal migration became a trampoline to the United States, and internal destinations now serve as "migration schools" for potential migrants to the United States. For example, 64 percent of people with migratory experience in both the United States and Mexico first migrated to locations within Mexico. This idea of "stepwise" migration supports the hypothesis that migration within Mexico positively affects a person's propensity to migrate across the border.

Figure 4.1 depicts migration flows out of Tunkás to both internal and international destinations from 1970 to 2006. Migration patterns to both destinations generally track well together from the 1980s onward.

Figure 4.1 Historical Patterns of Migration Flows, 1970–2006

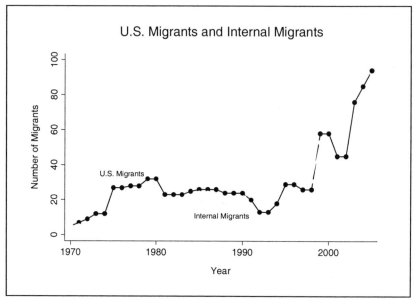

N/US = 1124.

N/MEX = 854.

Note: The points in the figure have been moderately smoothed to capture long-term trends rather than short fluctuations.

While this figure lends support to our claim that internal and international migrant flows are correlated, it also presents an anomaly to our argument by showing a lower volume of internal migration than international migration through the early 1980s. We suspect that an unavoidable methodological problem explains this anomaly. The survey data from Tunkás may less accurately capture the true flows of internal migrants during the earlier period than they do flows of contemporary migrants. If whole families left Tunkás, there was no one left to report on their migration histories at the time of the 2006 survey in Tunkás. The greater presence of women in internal migration versus international migration suggests that whole family migration is probably more prevalent in internal than in international migration. Historical evidence from other Mexican towns with internal rural-to-urban migration patterns in the 1970s also indicates that migrants were more likely to settle permanently in their internal destination and weaken ties with their hometown than were their international counterparts during this era (Cornelius 1976a; Fitzgerald 2006).

There is little doubt as to the significance of Cancún as a migrant destination, regardless of the levels of Tunkaseño migration during this decade. The mayor of Tunkás discussed this massive outflow of internal migrants: "The impact of Cancún was huge. When it was being constructed, they took everyone, all kinds of people: carpenters, construction workers, professionals, everyone."

Despite the anomaly in the data for the 1970s, the interdependence of internal and international migration is illustrated through the relatively similar trends witnessed in subsequent decades. Internal migration is not only complementary to international migration, but it actually facilitates and encourages it.

One possible explanation for this complementary relationship is that internal migration allows rural-origin migrants to ease into the migration experience, rather than have to confront the risks and shocks associated with international migration unprepared. Based on his research in rural Mexico, García España (1992: 116) found that "once an individual has migrated anywhere he or she is more likely to cross the northern Mexican border." In this scheme, internal destinations expose migrants to environments and situations somewhat similar to those found abroad. With internal migratory experience, people are more likely to chance international destinations. Prior experience gives increased knowledge and understanding of the lifestyle of migration, minimizing the cost and risk of international moves.

Many parallels can be drawn between the migrant experience in national destinations and in the United States. By leaving the security of Tunkás for a job in any urban location, migrants are confronted with drastic changes in lifestyle. For numerous reasons, "the Maya peasants envision Cancún as a kind of United States" (Re Cruz 1996: 3). When in Cancún or another Mexican urban center, rural migrants are in fact adapting to a lifestyle similar to what they would encounter in the United States. Employment is wage-based in both types of location and often is to be found in similar industries. For example, the three most common occupations for internal migrants are chef, carpenter, and construction worker. The three most common occupations for migrants to the United States are as a worker at a car wash, chef, or dishwasher. The fact that chef is one of the most common occupations in both settings supports the idea that internal migrants use skills gained in internal migratory employment once they migrate to the United States. In both internal and international migratory contexts, more than two-thirds of Tunkaseño migrants find employment in either the service sector or construction: 67 percent in Mexico and 72 percent in the United States.

Aside from the introduction of new occupations, working conditions in either urban setting are often radically different from previous, often agricultural, work in Tunkás. Many migrants have little control over their own schedule and work methods in their new wage-based occupations. Work in urban locations typically means answering to someone else in the form of a boss or foreman and adhering to a strict weekly schedule. This new experience translates across the border, as narrated by José, a migrant to the United States:

> It's a habit we have in Tunkás.... We are used to working three or four days a week, and that's it. We were not taught to have a regular work schedule; to work eight hours a day, five days a week, and rest Saturday and Sunday. We are not used to it here in the *pueblo*.

Time spent in internal migratory destinations introduces potential migrants to the United States to the structure of wage labor. Thus experience as paid laborers within Mexico gives migrants a better notion of how the U.S. labor market functions.

In addition to higher incomes through wage labor, the new urban destinations, in both Mexico and the United States, also bring new financial responsibilities. The relative affordability of Tunkás morphs into a life where migrants have to pay much more for food, transportation, rent, and utilities, leaving little for savings (Castellanos 2003: 146).

This new reality can be harsh. As Manuel, a Tunkaseño migrant to Cancún, explained: "When you are in Cancún, you are only living to pay the rent, food, clothes, that's all. You buy a television, a radio, you always have this debt. What you earn stays in Cancún."

Learning how to mange money well enough to cover all expenses and still send money home—a primary motivation for migration—is a crucial skill for the successful migrant. Migrants gain valuable practice in financial accountability in internal urban destinations, and these skills then translate to international migratory destinations as well. When asked to compare his experience in Cancún with that in the United States, Miguel, a migrant with extensive work experience in both destinations, told us: "It's the same in both settings. If you know how to keep track of your finances, you keep track of them; if not, you don't." Miguel is not only referring to rent, utilities, and remittances, but also to the new social pressures of the urban lifestyle that can drain the wallets of many migrants.

Due to Cancún's status as an international tourist destination, migrants to this city are "exposed to a transnational economy dedicated to conspicuous consumption, and are constantly bombarded by goods produced in the global economy" (Castellanos 2003: 212). Again, this is a radical change from Tunkás and very similar to the migrants' experience in the United States, where they develop new expectations. Consumer goods become status symbols as "migrants learn that one is defined by what one owns" (Castellanos 2003: 198). The strong influence of the global capitalist market evokes new desires in migrants who are otherwise accustomed to the subsistence economy of Tunkás.

Apart from its role in acclimating migrants to the global economy, Cancún often offers internal migrants the opportunity to develop English language skills. Many Tunkaseños who work in Mexico's hospitality and tourist industries are exposed to English-speaking tourists on a daily basis. Migrants in tourist locations like Cancún quickly recognize the economic rewards of English language skills, and some opt to develop their English conversation skills through courses at a language school (Castellanos 2003: 117). English not only aids migrants in internal destinations, where English is often the lingua franca for tourists from countries around the world, but it also allows potential U.S.-

bound migrants to familiarize themselves with the language of *el norte*. In a self-reported English competence assessment among Tunkaseños, international migrants with prior internal migratory experience reported a consistently higher level of proficiency in speaking English than those who migrated directly to the United States. Besides breaking down the language barrier, English language skills reduce the migrant's culture shock and increase his or her propensity to migrate internationally.

The role that Cancún and other internal migration destinations play in facilitating international migration can also be seen in the amounts that migrants remit to the families or home communities. Migrants who have migrated both internally and then internationally remit a median amount of US$349 a month. This contrasts sharply with the amount remitted by migrants who ventured directly to the United States without previous internal migration experience; they remit a median amount of only $200 a month. Experience in the internal "school for migration" appears to have a clear economic payoff. Migrants learn how to successfully navigate an environment that is comparable to the United States in many ways. The combination of strict work schedule, new financial responsibilities, a consumer culture, and development of English language skills provides a training ground in which prospective international migrants can become accustomed to a lifestyle similar to that found in the United States.

DETERMINANTS OF INTERNAL VERSUS INTERNATIONAL MIGRATION

Regardless of the United States' emerging importance as a migrant-receiving destination for Tunkaseños, potential migrants continue to face the decision of whether to migrate internally or across the northern border. A number of factors contribute to the choice of internal versus international destination. One determinant is a migrant's previous migration history. Internal migration experience increases the propensity to migrate to the United States. Other factors in the decision-making process are the costs and risks associated with border crossing, potential earnings, and, most importantly, social networks.

Eighty-nine percent of Tunkaseño migrants entered the United States clandestinely on their first trip to that country, and the difficulties and dangers associated with international migration are well understood throughout the town. A higher percentage of internal migrants perceive border crossing to be very dangerous or impossible when compared with migrants who have migrated to the United States. Rather than face the dangers of border crossing, Tunkaseños often choose to migrate to internal destinations, especially when moving as a family unit. When asked why she and her family decided to migrate to Cancún instead of the United States, Urbi responded, "It was the prospect of the risk to go to the United States. By going to Cancún we didn't face that danger. It is better to go to Cancún; it's easier for us to go to Cancún." Thus the perceived danger of going to the United States acts as a catalyst for internal migration, where there is no need to cross a border. This is especially applicable to migrants lacking social contacts in the United States, for migrants often rely on social networks to help facilitate their border crossing.

The Influence of Wage Disparities

The main factor driving Tunkaseño migration to both internal and international destinations is the wage differential. The median income for a head of household in Tunkás is far below the average wage in most migrant destinations, so employment in Quintana Roo, Mérida, or the United States offers the possibility of wages much above those available at home. The median salary for nonmigrant Tunkaseños is $25 per week, versus $47 for internal migrants and $200 for migrants to the United States. By migrating to an internal destination, migrants are able to double their wages, and by going to the United States migrants can earn eight times more than the local wage. When asked to rank themselves economically on a scale of 1 to 10, with 10 being the best-off compared to other families in Tunkás, internal migrants reported a mean of 4.4, compared to a mean of 6.3 reported by international migrants. The higher wages to be earned abroad give migrants the opportunity to save more of their earnings after covering their subsistence costs.

The Impact of Social Networks on Choice of Destination

The higher wages in the United States clearly lure migrants across the border, but wage disparities alone cannot explain why people choose the international option. A principal determinant of migration destination is the migration history of a migrant's family and friends. Table 4.1 shows that each additional household member who has migration experience in the United States increases the likelihood that a nonmigrant Tunkaseño will migrate internationally. Although not as significant, the same holds true for internal migrants. Tunkaseños who have family in migrant destinations elsewhere in Mexico are more likely to first migrate internally. Consequently, both internal and international migrants rely heavily on existing relationships in their choice of destinations (see also García España 1992: v). Social networks are the gateways to housing, employment, and other contacts needed for survival in the new environment. Such social networks serve the same function in facilitating migration from Yucatán to Cancún today as they did in the 1970s, when Cancún was being constructed. Urbi, the wife of a migrant, explained:

> When we went to Cancún, my husband went first and I stayed in Tunkás. My husband went for one month. Then he came back to get me and brought me to Cancún because he had a cousin there, and she told him, "Why do you leave your wife in Tunkás? Bring her here and she can help you by making a little place where she can work in a paid laundry service, so that you can save up a little bit." So he took me there and we stayed there for eight years. We lived with my husband's cousin. She is also from Tunkás and she moved to Cancún in the 1980s.

Thus social networks in internal migratory destinations serve the same function as they do in U.S. destinations, helping migrants adjust to life in the new location. Although important in the process of adaptation to an internal migrant destination, social networks prove especially influential in the decision to migrate across the border. Internal destinations present fewer obstacles to success than do international destinations, because internal destinations are usually more familiar. Internal migration also poses less of a financial and personal risk, making it more accessible to migrants who have no contacts in any destination. When asked why more people do not choose to go to the United States to work, Luis, who has been to the United States twice, responded: "Because they don't have friends or relatives in the United States to help them. The people that don't go to the United States, it isn't because they don't want to, it's because they don't have family there." The costs of clandestine border crossing and the need for contacts through whom to find employment and housing are addressed through social network contacts abroad. Without such support, both the costs and risks associated with international migration may appear prohibitively high.

Table 4.1 Propensity to Migrate to the United States[a]

Determinant	β	Standard Error	Significance
Age	−0.089***	0.011	**0.000**
Male	0.890***	0.294	**0.002**
Married	1.160***	0.251	**0.000**
Education	−0.442***	0.153	**0.004**
Prior internal migration	1.276***	0.227	**0.000**
Relatives that migrated to U.S.	1.083***	0.142	**0.000**
Relatives that migrated in Mexico	−0.391***	0.104	**0.000**
Constant	0.155	0.498	0.756

N = 670. Chi-squared = 126.36. *** 99% confidence interval.
[a] Reference category is nonmigrants.

THE INTERACTION BETWEEN INTERNAL AND INTERNATIONAL MIGRATION

The logit regression summarized in table 4.1 estimates the impact of a prior history of internal migration on the decision to migrate internationally, while holding constant basic demographic and social network factors. The dependent variable measures whether the individual has a history of U.S. migration. The independent variables are number of persons in the household with migratory experience in the United States, number of persons in the household with migratory experience in Mexico, gender (male), marital status, years of education, age (migrant's age at the time of migration), and prior migratory experience in Mexico. The reference categories are the general demographic characteristics of the nonmigrant respondents.

All of the independent variables are statistically significant in determining the probability of international migration. The variables indicating males, married, the number of people per household with migratory experience in the United States, and prior migratory experience in Mexico correlate positively with the dependent variable, demonstrating an increased likelihood that a Tunkaseño will migrate to the United States, controlling for other demographic factors, if the person has previous internal migratory experience.. Education, age, and households with larger numbers of people with migratory experience in Mexico are negatively correlated with U.S. experience. Using the findings of table 4.1, we created a "first difference" table to calculate the probability of international migration given prior internal migratory experience. We found that having prior migratory experience within Mexico increases the probability of U.S. migration by 28 percent.

Further evidence that internal migration increases the propensity to migrate internationally comes from Tunkaseños' statements of intention to migrate. When asked whether they were planning to migrate to the United States in the next year, 43 percent of respondents with internal migratory experience answered yes, compared to only 11 percent of nonmigrants.

CONCLUSION: AN EVENTUAL END TO INTERNAL MIGRATION?

Tunkaseños are leaving home in growing numbers. Of Tunkaseños with migratory experience, 49 percent migrated within Mexico, 12 percent have migratory experience in both the United States and Mexico, and 40 percent migrated directly to the United States. According to our analysis, these numbers will continue to change in favor of the United States, as internal migration promotes future international migration. One result of the growing numbers of international migrants will be the expansion of social networks linking Tunkás and the United States. Assuming that migration to the United States continues to develop, it is possible that in Tunkás, as in small Mexican towns with longer traditions of international migration, internal migration may eventually fade.

For example, in much of the Los Altos region of Jalisco, internal migration from rural communities to Mexican urban centers dried up as international migration gained momentum and transnational networks matured. For many years Los Altos exported workers to cities like León, Guadalajara, and Mexico City, but with the introduction of the Bracero Program in 1942 this internal migration declined sharply (Cornelius 1976b). When the Bracero Program ended in 1964, former braceros continued to migrate to the United States, illegally, and began settling there permanently. By the 1970s internal migration to neighboring cities in Mexico had been replaced by direct migration to the United States. The increased security created through transnational social networks, coupled with the opportunity of higher-paying jobs in the United States, made the pull from abroad significantly stronger than that of any internal destination.

While most northern and central Mexican towns in the post-bracero era were building migration networks that linked them ever more tightly to the United States, Tunkaseños still had relatively little international migratory experience, a consequence of very limited participation in the Bracero Program. In contrast to how international migration replaced internal migration in Tlacuitapa, a town in Los Altos, the lack of network connections kept the majority of Tunkaseños in Mexico. However, this trend is now shifting as more migrants are venturing north; network connections between Tunkás and the United States are strengthening with each new trip northward. As narrated by María, a potential first-time migrant to the United States: "I, too, want to go to the United States. I want to leave Cancún. I want to go to Los Angeles because Cancún isn't the same anymore." Migrants once distracted by closer internal destinations from the lure of economic opportunity in the United States are now refocusing their gaze.

References

Bever, Sandra. 1999. "Migration Household Economy and Gender: A Comparative Study of Households in a Rural Yucatec Maya Community." PhD dissertation, UMI Dissertation Services.

Castellanos, María Bianet. 2003. "Gustos and Gender: Yucatec Maya Migration to the Mexican Riviera." PhD dissertation, University of Michigan.

Cornelius, Wayne A. 1976a. "Mexican Migration to the United States: The View from Rural Sending Communities." Working Paper Series. Cambridge, MA: Center for International Studies, Massachusetts Institute of Technology.

———. 1976b. "Outmigration from Rural Mexican Communities." In *The Dynamics of Migration: International Migration,* ed. Shirley Sirota Rosenberg. Washington DC: Smithsonian Institution.

Fitzgerald, David. 2006. "A Nation of Emigrants? How Mexico Manages Its Migration." Manuscript. La Jolla, CA: Department of Sociology, University of California, San Diego.

García España, Juan Felipe. 1992. "Determinants of Internal and International Migration from Rural Areas of Mexico." PhD dissertation, UMI Dissertation Services.

Haydt, Marly. 1994. *Amplitud histórica, social, económica, y sus perspectivas en México: Cancún-Tulum.* Mexico: Policromia.

Re Cruz, Alicia. 1994. "Lo sagrado y lo profano de la identidad maya entre los emigrantes en Yucatán," *Nueva Antropología* 14, no. 46: 56.

———. 1996. *The Two Milpas of Chan Kom: Scenarios of a Maya Village Life.* Albany, NY: State University of New York.

Procession of Tunkaseños honoring the town's patron saint and migrants to the United States, a highlight of the annual fiesta.

5 Impacts of U.S. Immigration Policies on Migration Behavior

ANN KIMBALL, YESENIA ACOSTA, AND REBECCA DAMES

> *We don't care if we have to walk eight days or fifteen days; the danger we are in doesn't matter. If and when we cross alive, we will have a job to give our families the best.*— Miguel, an experienced 28-year-old Tunkaseño migrant.

Politicians, the media, and the general public continue to debate how to control the inflow of undocumented migrants to the United States, but usually without regard to the effects that various enforcement measures are actually having on migratory behavior. How have heightened border controls, worksite enforcement, and proposed immigration law reforms affected migrants' decision making and migration strategies? Our findings support earlier research showing that tightened border enforcement in the post-1993 period has not kept undocumented migrants from entering the United States, nor has a higher probability of apprehension by the Border Patrol discouraged potential migrants, despite the increasing danger of clandestine entry. To evade apprehension by the Border Patrol and reduce the risks posed by natural hazards, migrants increasingly turn to people-smugglers (*coyotes* or *polleros*), allowing them to charge more for their services. And by making clandestine border crossings an increasingly expensive and risky affair, U.S. border enforcement policy has unintentionally encouraged undocumented migrants to remain in the United States for longer periods.

THE IMPACT OF ENFORCEMENT ON APPREHENSIONS AND DETERRENCE

Beginning in 1993, the Clinton administration introduced a strategy of "prevention through deterrence," aimed at discouraging clandestine border crossings through four concentrated border enforcement operations: Operation Hold the Line in Texas, launched in 1993, Operation Gatekeeper in San Diego in 1994, Safeguard Arizona in 1995, and Rio Grande in Texas in 1997. Fortifications in each area included a primary 10-foot-high steel fence, closely spaced concrete poles, high-intensity lighting, video surveillance, an increased number of Border Patrol agents, and a computerized fingerprint identification system. Policy makers believed that fortifying the four main corridors of clandestine entry in these ways and making apprehension more likely would discourage migrants—assuming that people would not attempt to cross via the unfortified desert and mountain areas. These areas present a range of physical hazards, including subfreezing temperatures in winter and triple-digit heat in summer (Cornelius 2005: 778–79).

As early as 1994, research showed that apprehension by the Border Patrol did not stop immigrants from eventually entering the U.S. labor market. Apprehensions were followed immediately by new border-crossing attempts (Espenshade 1994: 875). "Voluntarily repatriated" migrants quickly reunited with their coyote and kept on trying to cross the border until they were successful. Rudy, an experienced migrant from Tunkás, explained the ritual of apprehension, deportation, and the next attempt: "I have to wait until they deport me, and then I meet up again with the same people, with the same pollero. I get in contact and organize another trip across the border." A 1992 study by Donato, Durand, and Massey found that "the number of attempts was always one greater than the number of apprehensions; that is, all migrants simply tried until they succeeded" (cited in Espenshade 1994: 872).

Tunkaseños appear to be extremely adept at clandestine border crossing. On their most recent trip to the United States, 74 percent of undocumented Tunkaseños whom we interviewed were able to cross without being detected on the first try. Of the remainder, the majority were only apprehended once or twice, and an impressive 97 percent ultimately entered the United States on the same trip to the border. Thus, repeated apprehensions discouraged only 3 percent of unauthorized crossers from trying until they succeeded—an even lower proportion than found in 2005 among undocumented migrants from Tlacuitapa, Jalisco, and Las Ánimas, Zacatecas, 8 percent of whom were ultimately unsuccessful at entering the United States on the same trip (Cornelius and Lewis 2007: 11). This evidence suggests that even though Tunkás is a relatively new sending community, its migrants have already mastered the game of clandestine entry to the United States. This is a crucial finding, because migrants from relatively new sending communities like Tunkás have not yet developed the extensive transnational social networks that traditional sending communities have built over time and which provide information and contacts useful to would-be illegal entrants.

Figure 5.1 shows that the average number of apprehensions for Tunkaseños actually declined among those who migrated most recently in the 2000–2006 period. This accords with data from the Mexican Migration Project, which found that the rate of border apprehensions climbed with the introduction of more Border Patrol officers and then declined as migrants turned to coyotes for assistance (Massey, Durand, and Malone 2002: 57). For Tunkaseños, the average apprehension rate was higher during the 1994–1999 period, while migrants and coyotes were learning how to evade the newly enacted border enforcement programs, but by 2000–2006 it is clear that Tunkaseños and the coyotes they hire had learned how to avoid the Border Patrol.

If Border Patrol tactics are not effective in stopping migrants at the border, does the threat of apprehension deter people from deciding to migrate? Policy makers have assumed that if potential migrants are made aware of the increased difficulty of evading the Border Patrol, they will be discouraged from making the attempt. But the opposite effect surfaced in our interviews with some Tunkaseño migrants. When we asked Rudy, an experienced migrant, if he would attempt to cross the border again, given all the information he now possesses, he responded, "Yes, because now I go with less fear. The obstacles are familiar, including the Border Patrol itself. Someone who has never gone is not very sure about what he will encounter, but when you know it, it isn't so surprising."

We asked Tunkaseños who had migrated to the United States at least once whether they had known about stepped-up Border Patrol operations to curb illegal immigration prior to their first trip; 75 percent answered that they did. One migrant recalled his feelings during his second U.S. trip: "I was nervous and thinking, 'what if we arrive, then they toss us back, after all that walking?'" More than two-thirds of our survey respondents reported that crossing the U.S.-Mexico border is difficult. Sixty-eight percent of experienced migrants said that it was very difficult to evade the Border Patrol, and 63 percent of potential first-time migrants said the same.[1] Nevertheless, fewer than 1 percent of those lacking U.S. migration experience cited the Border Patrol or the lack of legal documents as the reason why they did not plan to migrate to the United States in 2006.

Figure 5.1 Mean Number of Apprehensions on Most Recent Trip to the U.S.

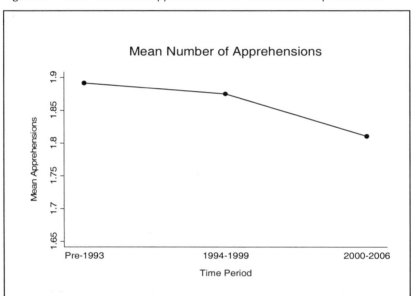

These findings are consistent with data collected in a 2005 study of migration from Las Ánimas, Zacatecas, and Tlacuitapa, Jalisco (Cornelius and Lewis 2007: chap. 4). In those longtime sending communities, 80 percent of surveyed migrants reported they were informed about

---

[1] Of undocumented migrants from Tlacuitapa and Las Ánimas, 61.5 percent stated that crossing the border undetected was "*much* more difficult" than in previous years.

Border Patrol efforts to intercept unauthorized migrants, yet only 20 percent claimed that it would influence their decision to migrate again. Analyzing the same dataset, Cornelius and Salehyan (2007) found that "individuals who report being well-informed about current Border Patrol efforts are *more* likely to cross." They offer the explanation that "persons considering migration seek information about Border Patrol operations in order to avoid capture." Whether they acquire this information through family and friends who have preceded them to the United States or by actively seeking it out, migrants preparing to cross the border illegally regard this knowledge as a tool for success.

THE IMPACT OF BORDER ENFORCEMENT ON ENTRY LOCATION

Tighter border enforcement in the urbanized San Diego–Tijuana region since 1993 has pushed most illegal entry attempts eastward into the Arizona desert. A 2005 survey among migrants from Jalisco and Zacatecas revealed a drop in California crossings from 74 percent pre-1993 to 46 percent since 1993 (Cornelius and Lewis 2007: chap. 4). But among undocumented Tunkaseños on their most recent trip to the border, over 83 percent arrived initially in the San Diego–Tijuana region before crossing into the United States (see figure 5.2). Only 10 percent said they took the Calexico–Mexicali desert route, and fewer than 4 percent responded that they came first to the Arizona desert. These responses are consistent with a recent rise in Border Patrol apprehensions in the San Diego sector, up 43 percent in the October 2005–March 2006 period, compared with the same period a year previously (Berestein 2006). Despite stronger border enforcement in San Diego–Tijuana, Tunkaseños have been choosing the increased probability of apprehension over the high risks associated with a trek through the Arizona desert.

A 2004 study asked migrants staying temporarily in Tijuana's Casa del Migrante, a refuge for people apprehended crossing the border and then repatriated, about the dangers involved in reaching the United States. Although 67 percent claimed to know of a death at the border, 70 percent had no personal connection to the victims (Sherry 2004: 82–83). Rather, they had become aware of deadly crossings through news media reports, from others in their hometown, and via information at the Casa del Migrante itself.

Figure 5.2 Initial Point of Arrival on Most Recent Trip to United States

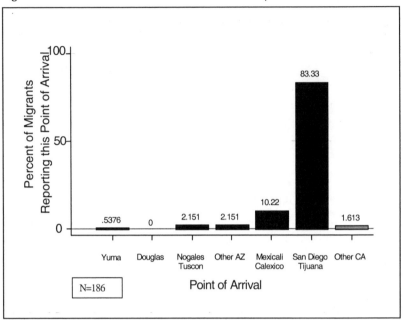

In our study, we asked Tunkaseños whether they personally had known someone who died attempting to cross the border, and over 87 percent of them—both migrants and those with no migration experience—responded that they did not. But many had heard stories of deaths at the border from other townspeople, which contributed to their perception of danger. Eighty-four percent of those who had not yet migrated to the United States felt that it was very dangerous to cross the border without documentation, and an additional 16 percent considered it somewhat dangerous. Of those who had been to the United States within the previous twelve months, 81 percent considered it to be very dangerous to cross the border without documents, and another 18 percent believed it to be somewhat dangerous. Thus, experienced migrants and those who have not yet migrated have a similarly keen perception of the danger of crossing the border clandestinely. For those who have never experienced a crossing, the high perception of risk could be explained by stories spread among Tunkaseños by word of mouth.

To determine what other factors may be influencing Tunkaseños' perception of danger, we asked whether migrants had seen or heard announcements on television or radio warning about the dangers of clandestine border crossings prior to their most recent trip to the United States and, further, how this information influenced their decision to migrate. Over 90 percent of migrants said that the media announcements did not have any impact on their decision. This suggests that Tunkaseños are well aware of the dangers involved in crossing the border without documentation, but this perception does not stop most of them from migrating. Rather, they try other routes, seek out knowledge about crossing conditions, and hire people-smugglers to assist them. Some Tunkaseño migrants are also choosing to cross through official crossing points to avoid the physical risks of a desert or mountain crossing. Among our undocumented interviewees, 9 percent reported that they did no walking during their most recent crossing into the United States, suggesting they entered as passengers in a vehicle or as pedestrians using false or borrowed documents to pass through legal ports of entry. A surprising one-fourth of the unauthorized migrants we interviewed reported walking between 0 and 2 hours, confirming that a substantial number had avoided the days-long hike characteristic of desert crossings.

Manuel, a 27-year-old migrant who lived in California for eight years without documentation, described why he preferred to cross through an official port of entry at Tijuana with borrowed papers, rather than risk the desert: "My uncle lent me his birth certificate, and I memorized everything on it and used it to cross.... I wasn't nervous at all because it was an easier way to cross." He went on to say that he was glad not to have to worry about the dangers of crossing through the desert, like so many other migrants.

Miguel, a Tunkaseño who had migrated to the United States illegally three times, described the hardships and risks that other migrants are now trying to avoid by going even further east, away from the deserts of Arizona. Just before embarking on a 72-hour trek through the Arizona desert, Miguel's group was robbed at the border by armed bandits, people he believes were working in collusion with his coyote. He recounted the agony of going without food for the three days and rationing what little water he had. Another Tunkaseño migrant, Máximo, was stuffed into a vehicle with eighteen others at a pickup point after hours of walking through the desert. Only minutes after leaving the pickup point, the vehicle caught fire (all the migrants managed to escape). Such experiences explain why more Tunkaseños may be choosing the risk-reduction strategy of crossing in the urbanized sector of San Diego–Tijuana.

Celmy, a 28-year-old mother of two young children and one of the many wives who remain in Tunkás while their partners go north, described the struggles of her husband, José, to get to the United States. On his first trip, he had to walk for over sixteen hours before finally making it to a pickup point away from the border. On his most recent trip, he opted to cross the border smuggled inside a truck. Celmy described how her husband was shoved under a stack of mattresses in the bed of the coyote's pickup. Although it was an uncomfortable ride, Celmy's husband did not regret his choice. The decision to pass through the official crossing point is risky due to frequent Border Patrol inspections, but increasingly migrants from Tunkás reason that being apprehended once or twice in an urban area is a minor inconvenience compared to the risk of dying from dehydration in the desert.

If stepped-up border enforcement were effective in influencing the decision to migrate (as contrasted with the choice of a border-crossing strategy) among Tunkaseños, we would expect variables such as difficulty in evading the Border Patrol, level of information on rising enforcement, and perceptions of danger and death in clandestine entry to correlate negatively with intent to migrate. No such relationships appeared among our Tunkaseño interviewees (see table 5.1). The logistic regression model tests whether our dependent variable—stated intent to migrate to the United States within the next twelve months—is influenced by the perceived difficulty of border crossing, level of information about border enforcement, perceptions of danger, and a dichotomous variable showing whether the respondent knew someone who died trying to cross the border. Controls for standard demographic variables of gender, age, marital status, education, and legal status were applied. We ran our models using a maximum-likelihood logit estimator and robust standard errors.

Crucial to assessing the efficacy of the "prevention through deterrence" strategy, models 2 and 4 show that the perceived difficulty of evading the Border Patrol and awareness of the physical dangers of clandestine crossings do not have a statistically significant effect on the propensity to migrate. Similarly, knowledge of Border Patrol operations does not substantially influence the decision to attempt a crossing, as model 3 in table 5.1 shows. The only statistically significant factors that contribute to a person's intention to migrate are age, marital status, and legal status. Our results from Tunkás suggest that the post-1993 border enforcement buildup has yet to create an effective deterrent to illegal entry.

IMPACTS OF BORDER ENFORCEMENT ON PEOPLE-SMUGGLING

As U.S. border policy increases the physical danger of border crossing and raises the likelihood of apprehension, more migrants are relying on professional people-smugglers to guide them across the border. *Coyotaje* is common among migrants seeking to enter the United States illegally. Although migrants understand that hiring a coyote is illegal, many view it as necessary to evade apprehension and to mitigate the danger of crossing clandestinely. Coyotes' services typically include the purchase of airline tickets to points of entry near the border; guides who accompany the migrants, evading the Border Patrol and the criminal gangs that operate on the border; lodging at safe houses in border communities; and delivery to a U.S. employer (Spener 2005: 53, 55). As we have seen, the post-1993 strategy that militarized heavily transited segments of the U.S.-Mexico border has shifted migrants' points of entry, but it also accounts for the large proportion of migrants who hire a coyote to navigate a clandestine entry.

In Tunkás, about 90 percent of unauthorized migrants who crossed most recently in the 2000–2005 period had used a coyote (see figure 5.3), a small increase over the 1994–1999 period. But the vast majority of undocumented Tunkaseños had been using coyotes even before the border buildup, probably because Tunkás's transborder social networks are relatively undeveloped and fewer of the town's migrants have personal experience in border crossing.

Table 5.1 Logistic Regression Models of Intent to Migrate among Undocumented Migrants from Tunkás

	I	II	III	IV	V	VI
Border Patrol Difficulty	—	0.493	—	—	—	0.501
		(0.411)				(0.494)
Border Patrol Information	—	—	0.065	—	—	0.316
			(0.405)			(0.451)
Danger	—	—	—	0.302	—	-0.154
				(0.469)		(0.561)
Death	—	—	—	—	-0.010	0.086
					(0.492)	(0.520)
Male	-0.203	-0.175	-0.213	-0.178	-0.202	-0.256
	(0.523)	(0.531)	(0.527)	(0.554)	(0.527)	(0.573)
Age	**-0.034****	**-0.031****	**-0.034****	**-0.033****	**-0.034****	**-0.033****
	(0.015)	(0.016)	(0.015)	(0.016)	(0.015)	(0.017)
Married	**-1.077*****	**-1.176*****	**-1.066*****	**-1.059****	**-1.058****	**-1.054****
	(0.412)	(0.420)	(0.417)	(0.429)	(0.423)	(0.455)
Education	-0.026	-0.023	-0.028	-0.007	-0.029	-0.012
	(0.046)	(0.050)	(0.047)	(0.047)	(0.047)	(0.051)
Legal Status	**1.828*****	**1.829*****	**1.826*****	**1.637*****	**1.805*****	**1.747*****
	(0.510)	(0.557)	(0.510)	(0.523)	(0.519)	(0.573)
Constant	**1.787***	1.282	**1.764***	1.415	**1.789***	1.213
	(0.953)	(1.042)	(0.967)	(1.082)	(0.952)	(1.18)
N	186	177	186	177	184	168
Chi-squared	37.41	36.68	37.44	35.41	35.23	34.74

90%, **95%, ***99% confidence levels; standard errors in parentheses.

Figure 5.3 Undocumented Migrants' Use of Coyote on Most Recent Trip to United States

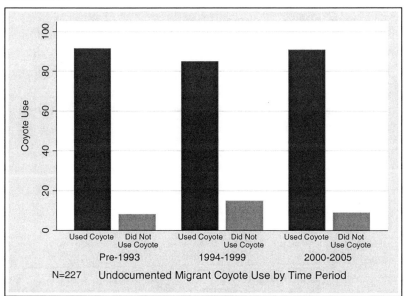

As figure 5.4 indicates, Tunkaseños find coyotes in a variety of ways. On their most recent trip, 57 percent found their coyote through family or friends, mostly based in the United States. One former coyote from the town explained how she helped fellow Tunkaseños contract and pay for the services of other coyotes:

> I would travel with them from Tunkás to Mérida and leave them in Tijuana with the pollero—my friend, a *paisano* from Yucatán. After they paid $2,000 dollars and I recommended that he treat them as one of my family, he would help them to cross the border.

David Spener (2005: 64) refers to such coyotes as "socially embedded," based in migrant-sending or migrant-receiving communities, rather than free agents operating in Mexican border cities. A substantial minority of Tunkaseño migrants (42 percent) obtained their most recent coyote by searching in a border city, rather than through referrals from relatives and friends. Tunkás differs from older sending communities like Tlacuitapa in this way. According to data collected in Tlacuitapa and Las Ánimas in 2005, only 31 percent contracted with a coyote at the border (Fuentes et al. 2007). Tunkaseños typically have little trouble finding a coyote at the border. In border cities like Tijuana, the market is saturated with coyotes wishing to capitalize on the migrant journey. Miguel describes being accosted by coyotes trolling for clients: "As you are stepping down from the plane, they say, 'Listen, do you want to cross the border? I am a smuggler, I'll take you.'"

Figure 5.4 How Undocumented Migrant Contacted a Coyote

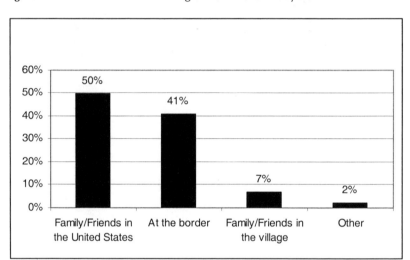

In the case of migrants from Tunkás, the main impact of tougher border enforcement since 1993 has been on the fees that they must pay for a coyote-assisted crossing. While the median fee paid to a coyote before 1993 was less than $400, the median fee for Tunkaseños who crossed between 2000 and 2006 had quadrupled to nearly $1,600 (see figure 5.5).

There are few migrants who can save enough cash to cover the coyote's fee, purchase a plane ticket from Mérida to a U.S.-Mexico border city, and pay for food and lodging during the trip. As shown in figure

5.6, by January 2006 the median total cost of an undocumented crossing was approaching US$1,800. Forty percent of all undocumented Tunkaseño migrants reported receiving loans for these expenses from relatives already in the United States. Miguel left for the United States to help support his growing family, but he lacked the money to pay a coyote. A friend in the United States offered to pay for the trip, charging Miguel no interest on the loan "because in case he [the friend] returns to Mexico and I [Miguel] stay to work in the United States, I will have to pay for his trip back to the United States."

Figure 5.5 Coyote Fee Paid on Most Recent Trip to United States

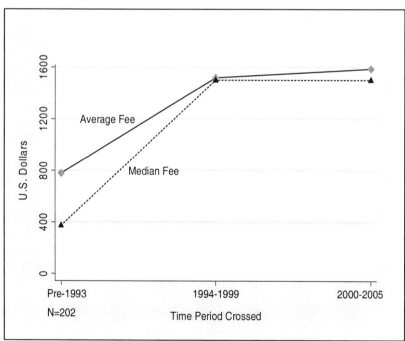

Coyotes usually collect the bulk of their payment away from the border area, once the migrant has safely reached his or her final destination. Payment is generally made by a family member or friend. Prior to the mid-1990s, coyotes typically collected fees from migrants at the border prior to crossing. In his historical account of *coyotaje*, Spener describes a few cases of cash-on-delivery arrangements prior to this time, but with the escalation of coyote fees following the concentration of border enforcement, C.O.D. payment became the established practice. Traveling with large amounts of cash with which to pay a coyote made migrants vulnerable to robbery, so payment in full at the destination helps protect them from attack or extortion. The C.O.D. payment arrangement also encourages coyotes to transport their clients safely, so that they will receive full payment (Spener 2005: 62).

Figure 5.6 Total Cost of Most Recent Undocumented Crossing

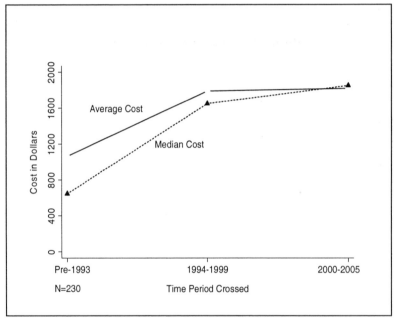

Nevertheless, migrants are at risk of abuse by coyotes or robbery by gangs. Twenty-two migrants out of 201 undocumented respondents whom we interviewed reported being assaulted or robbed while crossing. On his third trip to the United States in 2003, Miguel was robbed. Like many Tunkaseños, for each trip Miguel used a different coyote that he found at the border. Miguel's coyote led the group to a remote location where "the robbers were waiting for us.... There were three of them, with their faces covered [and wielding pistols]. I imagine that they were friends of the coyote, because nobody else knew we would be crossing there." Many migrants know they may be robbed and prepare for it ahead of time. Miguel was able to pay his coyote when he arrived in Boulder, Colorado, because he had hidden $700 in the lining of his backpack.

EFFECTS OF WORKSITE ENFORCEMENT ON MIGRATION BEHAVIOR

The employer sanctions provisions of the Immigration Reform and Control Act of 1986 (IRCA) were designed to curb undocumented immigration by eliminating the pull of U.S. jobs. IRCA made it illegal for employers to hire individuals not authorized to work in the United States and also established the process by which employers are to verify the employment eligibility of new hires. However, sanctions have failed to deter employers from hiring unauthorized workers. Most experts ascribe this failure to competing missions within the INS, the ready availability of fraudulent documents, and the extremely limited resources allocated for enforcing IRCA's employer sanctions (Brownell 2004; Magaña 2003: 39–46).

Under IRCA, employers are to complete an I-9 form for every new employee to confirm the individual's identity and his/her eligibility to work in the United States. This process is imperfect because, according to Marc Rosenblum, "as many as half of all undocumented workers are hired by employers who fully comply with I-9 requirements." Some employers are intentionally noncompliant, but others simply lack the expertise to identify fraudulent documents. All employers, though, are protected from serious investigations and fines as long as they complete an I-9 form for every employee (Rosenblum 2005). In 2004, fines were levied against only three employers in the entire country (GAO 2005: 14).

Enforcement of sanctions never reached a level where it effectively deterred employers from hiring unauthorized workers or altered the migration decisions of undocumented immigrants. Among our interviewees in Tunkás, 81 percent of migrants identified opportunities in the United States as their reason for migrating. For migrants such as José, U.S. policy is not an important factor in the migration decision since it is "not for pleasure that one moves away and leaves one's family, but out of necessity." Once in the United States, the likelihood that a Tunkaseño migrant will be deported because of employer sanctions is negligible.

Initially the INS strategy for implementing sanctions was based on targeting industries and regions that traditionally employed unauthorized workers. As post–9/11 policy discourse shifted from immigration to national security, however, enforcement efforts were refocused on workplaces vulnerable to terrorism, such as airports and nuclear plants (Brownell 2004). Considering that 19 percent of Tunkaseño migrants worked as cooks and 14 percent were last employed at car washes, the current trend in worksite enforcement is unlikely to directly affect their employment prospects. In fact, no migrant from Tunkás was employed in an industry of significance to national security. The focus of the current system leaves businesses like restaurants, hotels, car washes, construction companies, and gardening operations open to undocumented workers. Some employers even pay the travel and coyote costs for their employees. For example, José worked at a Los Angeles car wash that hired undocumented employees. Celmy, his wife, explained that his employer loaned him money (at interest) to pay the coyote.

Nevertheless, undocumented migrants are vulnerable to mistreatment by their employers. Many lack English skills and are unaware of the legal protections available in the workplace. For instance, Eduardo said that his employer, a Chinese restaurateur in Minnesota, exploited migrant workers by extending their hours and failing to pay overtime:

> At first we were paid well, but later the owner wanted us to work longer and longer for the same pay. It's not fair. She did not want to pay us. We began at eight o'clock in the morning and left at ten or twelve at night. And I told her that there are laws. She thought that since we didn't have papers she could mistreat us. What does it matter to me that I don't have papers? I can work someplace else. Everybody left that job. Nobody stayed.

Thus, despite their undocumented status, Eduardo and his co-workers were able to abandon an abusive employer without worrying about finding another job.

The current system for demonstrating that one is legally entitled to work in the United States has spurred a growing industry that produces fraudulent documents for undocumented migrants. The easy availability of counterfeit documents undermines the effectiveness of the I-9 process, even for employers who wish to comply with the law. Olivia, an important contact for new migrants in Los Angeles, explained that she would tell migrants where to go to buy bogus identification cards and Social Security numbers: "I also suggest where to get a job as a gardener or car washer. I advise them which employers ask for documents and which don't." Among our interviewees, only 2 percent reported that it was "very difficult" or "impossible" for a migrant without papers to obtain work in the United States. On their most recent trip to the United States, 73 percent of Tunkaseño migrants said their employer required them to show some type of identification, and 17 percent of these were asked only for a Social Security number. This means that over a quarter of employers did not ask for any identification document. These employers are either unaware of IRCA's requirements (improbable) or believe the risk of being investigated or fined is minimal (much more probable).

ACCESS TO U.S. SOCIAL SERVICES AND DECISIONS TO MIGRATE

In 1994 California Governor Pete Wilson, running for reelection, embraced an anti-immigration movement that led to the passage of Proposition 187. Had it been enacted,[2] this law would have denied undocumented immigrants access to public services, such as schools and hospitals. Prop. 187 was designed to deter illegal immigration, following the logic that many people migrate to the United States specifically to use social services. Though the measure was never enacted in California, it inspired the federal-level Illegal Immigration Reform and Immigrant Responsibility Act and the Personal Responsibility and Work Opportunity Reconciliation Act, both passed in 1996. These laws assumed that if illegal migrants—and sometimes legal immigrants as

---

[2] The proposition was immediately challenged in court and was ultimately declared unconstitutional.

well—were denied social services, they would be less likely to come in the first place. The two laws prohibited illegal (and sometimes legal) immigrants from receiving Social Security benefits, food stamps, or other means-tested social programs, and they also limited undocumented immigrants' access to educational benefits (Massey, Durand, and Malone 2002: 95–96).

For these policies to act as effective deterrents, migrants must base their migration decisions at least partially on access to U.S. public services. But our research shows that people do not migrate to the United States purposefully to use welfare or other tax-supported services. Fewer than 1 percent of experienced migrants we interviewed reported that their last U.S. trip was motivated by a desire to use some social service. Of the nonmigrants who reported that they were considering going to the United States in 2006, not one reported access to social services as their reason for migrating. Among undocumented interviewees, only 8 percent reported using food stamps during any of their stays in the United States; 5 percent had received some form of welfare assistance; and 26 percent had sent their children to public schools in the United States (see figure 5.7). Fifty-nine percent said they preferred to educate their children in Yucatán.

Figure 5.7 Migrant Use of Social Services, by Documentation Status

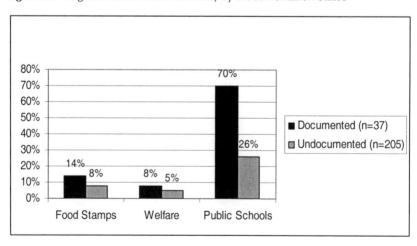

IMPACT OF BORDER ENFORCEMENT ON SETTLEMENT BEHAVIOR

Because it is now more difficult and costly than in the past to cross the border clandestinely, we wanted to determine if the increased cost and risk had affected the circularity of migration flows between Tunkás and the United States. We found that legal status has a strong impact on length of stay in the United States. While a significant portion of undocumented Tunkaseño migrants report that they stayed in the United States longer on their most recent trip than on their first trip, the opposite is true for documented migrants. Sixty-three percent of documented migrants reported that they return to Tunkás more frequently, with 70 percent attributing the higher frequency of return to their legalized status. When undocumented Tunkaseños were asked if they returned to Tunkás more or less often than they used to, 56 percent said that they return less often. Of those, 32 percent explained that they return home less often because crossing the border is too dangerous, and 23 percent said that the financial costs of migration prohibit more frequent returns.

As discussed earlier, coyote fees are the single largest migration expense, for which migrants often incur large debts that take years to repay. Faustino, a 26-year-old father of two, described his debt situation:

> When you arrive and don't know anyone, it's a real shock. I didn't have clothes, nothing. The person who lent me the money included an extra amount to buy me clothes and my first groceries, and, of course, a fake ID. People who lend the money do not do it because they want to help; it's because they make money off of people like me. They even charge a high interest rate. So instead of sending money to our households, we have to start paying off our enormous debt.

Faustino typifies the many migrants who must remain in the United States longer than they intended in order to repay debts incurred in migration and then to save money to send home (Reyes 2004: 316).

Even though high costs and physical risks do not stop Tunkaseños from migrating to the United States, these factors do limit the number of times people are able to undertake the migration journey. Celmy, the Tunkaseña wife left behind by her migrating husband, José, tells about his hesitation to return to Tunkás: "'To return,' he says, 'and to suffer again like I did to get there [to the United States], I don't want to.'" After three years, José did return to Tunkás to get acquainted with his young son, who was born while he was in the United States. Fifty-two percent of our respondents said they knew someone who had remained in the United States rather than run the risks associated with a return to their hometown. Thus, as other scholars have also noted, the result of increased border enforcement has been longer trip durations, less circular migration, and a parallel shift toward permanent settlement in the United States (see, for example, Massey, Durand, and Malone 2002: 131–33). Increased border enforcement has not kept undocumented migrants out of the United States, but it has kept them in and encouraged settlement (Cornelius and Lewis 2007: chap. 5). While pre-1990s Mexican migration was often of short duration and migrants traveled frequently between Mexico and the United States, today's undocumented migrants must choose their return trips wisely.[3]

AWARENESS ABOUT U.S. IMMIGRATION REFORM PROPOSALS AND ITS EFFECT ON MIGRATION BEHAVIOR

In January 2004, President George W. Bush proposed a new temporary foreign worker program that would grant three-year visas (renewable for a total of six years). Supporters of Bush's proposal argued that by creating a pathway for workers to enter the United States legally, it would reduce the necessity for clandestine entry. Critics countered that creating a large-scale temporary worker program would only increase the undocumented immigrant population, due to the migrants' belief that, once in the United States and in possession of a guestworker visa, they would become eligible for permanent legal residence; in short, they would not go home.

---

[3] For a more detailed discussion of the U.S. settlement process, see chapter 6 in this volume.

However, our findings suggest a much less dramatic influence on migrating behavior than supporters of the Bush proposal and its critics have predicted. In Tunkás, three-fifths of those who had previously migrated to the United States knew about the Bush proposal. Of these, 83 percent believed, correctly, that the main thrust of the proposal was to provide temporary permits to work in the United States; only 13 percent thought that the proposal mainly involved legalization of un-documented migrants. And regardless of their view of the proposal, most did not see it as a reason for migrating: 69 percent of migrants said that such an initiative would not influence their decision to return to the United States. Furthermore, only 1 out of 397 Tunkaseños with U.S. migration experience cited the Bush proposal as the principal motive for their most recent trip to the United States. However, given that we asked interviewees to specify their *primary* reason for migrating, the hope of obtaining a temporary work visa could still be a secondary reason for migrating among some respondents.

When Tunkaseños who had not yet migrated to the United States were asked whether they were familiar with the Bush proposal, 73 percent answered that they were not. These results are not unexpected, given that only 12 percent of nonmigrants had relatives living in the United States—a key source of information about possible changes in U.S. immigration policy—compared with 80 percent of those who had some U.S. migration experience. Despite the disparity in knowledge about immigration policy, a majority of those with no prior U.S. experience who did know about the proposal said that it would not have any effect on their probability of migrating to the United States for the first time.

CONCLUSION

Although debate continues over stepped-up immigration control efforts focusing on physical barriers at the border and more Border Patrol manpower, the evidence from Tunkás supports the growing consensus among academicians that such measures are ineffective in reducing unauthorized migration to the United States. Tunkaseños have increasingly sought out coyotes to guide them through or around existing fortifications. Instead of following dangerous desert routes, Tunkaseños are finding ways to cross through legal ports of entry, primarily through Tijuana–San Diego.

Our research demonstrates that migrants are undeterred by their awareness of physical danger and heightened risk of detection. Our data also confirm that the increasing costs of circumventing these obstacles are contributing to longer stays by migrants once they reach the United States. The lack of worksite inspections by government agents is reflected in the ease with which migrants find U.S. jobs and in their lack of concern about worksite enforcement when making migration decisions.

Our research in Tunkás has shown that, contrary to common belief, access to welfare and other social services is not a significant factor in the decision to migrate. With regard to the impact of the U.S. debate over immigration reform, we found that migrants' knowledge of President Bush's guestworker proposal was not a key determinant of their intent to migrate to the United States in the near future. One of our migrant interviewees shared his opinion on why people risk everything and continue to migrate despite the obstacles: "They can expand the border fencing, but they will never stop the flow of people…. If I had stayed in Mexico these past ten years, I likely would have nothing to show for it. People want to work and have something to offer their families. That's something no government seems to understand."

References

Berestein, Leslie. 2006. "Border Arrests Surge in S.D. Region. Increased Enforcement in Arizona Pushing Illegal Immigrants West," *San Diego Union-Tribune*, April 15. http://www.ccis-ucsd.org/news/SDUT-4-16-06.pdf.

Brownell, Peter. 2004. "The Declining Enforcement of Employer Sanctions." Washington, DC: Migration Policy Institute.

Cornelius, Wayne A. 2005. "Controlling 'Unwanted' Immigration: Lessons from the United States, 1993–2004," *Journal of Ethnic and Migration Studies* 31, no. 4: 775–94.

Cornelius, Wayne A., and Jessa M. Lewis, eds. 2007. *Impacts of Border Enforcement on Mexican Migration: The View from Sending Communities.* La Jolla, CA: Center for Comparative Immigration Studies, University of California, San Diego.

Cornelius, Wayne A., and Idean Salehyan. 2007. "Does Border Enforcement Deter Unauthorized Immigration? The Case of Mexican Migration to the United States," *Regulation & Governance* 1, no. 2: 139–53.

Espenshade, Thomas. 1994. "Does the Threat of Border Apprehension Deter Undocumented US Immigration?" *Population and Development Review* 20, no. 4: 871–92.

Fuentes, Jezmin, Henry L'Esperance, Raúl Pérez, and Caitlin White. 2007. "Impacts of U.S. Immigration Policies on Migration Behavior." In *Impacts of Border Enforcement on Mexican Migration: The View from Sending Communities*, edited by Wayne A. Cornelius and Jessa M. Lewis. La Jolla, CA: Center for Comparative Immigration Studies, University of California, San Diego.

GAO (U.S. General Accountability Office). 2005. "Immigration Enforcement: Preliminary Observations on Employment Verification and Worksite Enforcement Efforts." Washington, DC: GAO. http://www.gao.gov/new.items/d05822t.pdf.

Magaña, Lisa. 2003. *Straddling the Border*. Austin, TX: University of Texas Press.

Massey, Douglas, Jorge Durand, and Nolan Malone. 2002. *Beyond Smoke and Mirrors*. New York: Russell Sage Foundation.

Reyes, Belinda. 2004. "U.S. Immigration Policy and the Duration of Undocumented Trips." In *Crossing the Border: Research from the Mexican Migration Project*, ed. Jorge Durand and Douglas Massey. New York: Russell Sage Foundation.

Rosenblum, Marc R. 2005. "Policy Brief: Reforming the Employer Sanctions System." New Orleans, LA: Migration Policy Institute and University of New Orleans, September.

Sherry, Adam. 2004. "Foundations of U.S. Immigration Control Policy: A Study of Information Transmission to Mexican Migrants and the Role of Information as a Deterrent at the Border." CCIS Working Paper No. 95. La Jolla, CA: Center for Comparative Immigration Studies, University of California, San Diego. http://www.ccis-ucsd.org/PUBLICATIONS/wrkg95.pdf.

Spener, David. 2005. "Mexican Migration to the United States, 1882–1992: A Long Twentieth Century of Coyotaje." La Jolla, CA: Center for Comparative Immigration Studies, University of California, San Diego. http://www.ccis-ucsd.org/PUBLICATIONS/wrkg124.pdf.

A baseball team in Anaheim, California, consisting of migrants from Tunkás.

6 Tunkaseño Settlement in the United States

ANGELA GARCÍA AND ALEX BARRENO

> *I said, "I'll be back in a year," and I stayed. I liked it.... I had a steady job, a paycheck. I sent money back to my mom. I liked it a lot, and I wasn't thinking much about my hometown. I started to forget. It's normal, you know—to leave, to forget.*—Máximo, a 39-year-old Tunkaseño settler in the United States.

In his seminal book *Birds of Passage*, Michael Piore (1979) distinguishes between immigrant sojourners, or target earners, and settlers. In his conceptualization, sojourners return to their country of origin after accumulating a certain amount of money, while settlers are immigrants who intend to stay in the destination country. Piore's elaboration of the differences between these two groups of migrants has influenced the scholarly debate on settlement, with many academics favoring his definition of the settled migrant as simply one who has the intention of remaining in the receiving community. In this chapter, settlement by Tunkaseño migrants is defined by the migrants' perception of the United States as their place of primary residence. Because migrants who consider themselves based principally in the United States are more likely to settle there than are those who view Tunkás as their main residence, we use place of primary residence as a proxy for settlement. However, a variety of additional factors indicating and influencing settlement will also be discussed in our analysis of Tunkaseño settlers. These factors include migration by entire family units, nonseasonal employment, use of U.S. institutions, documentation status, social participation, and English proficiency. While both adults and minors may be settlers, this chapter focuses on adults because these are the individuals who are directly responsible for migration decisions.

The distinction between sojourners and settlers is neither static nor absolute. While sojourner or circular migration often—but not always—evolves into settlement, settlement itself can never be deemed permanent with complete certainty. Conscious decisions to settle permanently are rare among migrants. Instead, settlement often happens as the unintended consequence of a series of decisions about events as mundane as buying a washing machine or as serious as bringing children to the United States. An awareness of the uncertainty surrounding settlement behavior is the starting point for our discussion of Tunkaseños in the United States.

MEXICAN MIGRATION TO THE UNITED STATES AND THE "SETTLED" TUNKASEÑO

The end of the Bracero Program of contract labor importation in 1964 marked the close of a significant chapter in Mexican migration to the United States. For about a decade after the end of the program, post-bracero migration consisted of a circular flow of mostly undocumented, unaccompanied young men—many of them former braceros—working seasonally in agriculture and returning home at the end of the season. The shift to "a more socially heterogeneous, year-round, de facto permanent Mexican immigrant population" became apparent in the 1980 U.S. census, which depicted far more settlement than circular migration (Cornelius 1992: 156, 171, 157). In 1986 the Immigration Reform and Control Act (IRCA) gave new impetus to whole-family migration and family reunification in the United States (Cornelius 1989: 698–99), while the launch of concentrated border enforcement programs like Operation Gatekeeper in 1994 began to add greatly to the cost and danger of unauthorized border crossings (Cornelius 2001).

Undocumented migrants' reluctance to continue circular migration patterns under these harsh border conditions has led to a major unintended outcome of the militarization of the U.S.-Mexico border—the deepening of Mexican migrant settlement in the United States (Reyes, Johnson, and Van Swearingen 2002: 25). Graciano, an experienced Tunkaseño sojourner, noted that "many, many stay [in the United States].... They say, 'it was hard enough for me to cross; much worse having to come back [to Tunkás] and cross all over again.'" Indeed, as documented in the previous chapter, increased border enforcement has contributed to growing Tunkaseño settlement and whole-family migration to the United States.

A demographic profile of the typical settled migrant helps us to understand the factors that contribute to settlement. Of Tunkaseños with migratory experience in the United States, approximately 28 percent are adult settlers. Most have been living in the United States for over 7 years (see figure 6.1). The majority of adult Tunkaseño settlers are between 25 and 34 years of age. This age range for settlers is consistent with the traditional life cycle of Mexican migrants to the United States: individuals are more likely to migrate before or during—rather than after—their economically productive years (Marcelli and Cornelius 2001: 114).

Figure 6.1 Number of Years Tunkaseño Settlers Have Lived in the United States

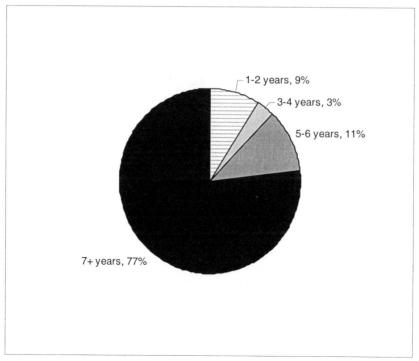

1-2 years, 9%

3-4 years, 3%

5-6 years, 11%

7+ years, 77%

N = 138.

As shown in figures 6.2 and 6.3, both settled and non-settled Tunkaseño migrants work in year-round industries such as restaurants (as cooks, dishwashers, and busboys); in the service sector (as car washers, landscapers, and domestic employees); and in skilled trades (as plumbers, painters, and general construction workers). Only 3 percent of settled migrants from Tunkás are employed in agriculture or other seasonal work, compared with 4 percent of non-settler Tunkaseños. Thus there must be other factors that differentiate migrants who settle in the United States from those who return to their hometown.

Figure 6.2 Current Occupations of Tunkaseño Settlers in the United States

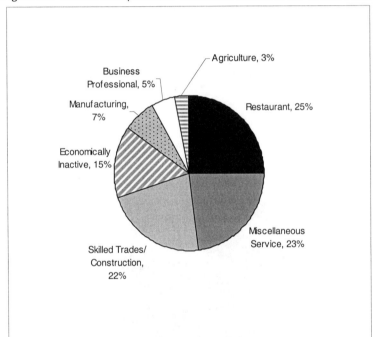

N = 197.
Note: "Economically inactive" includes retired, unemployed, and handicapped Tunkaseños, along with minors, students, and housewives.

The shift away from seasonal employment among both settler and non-settler Mexican migrants is confirmed by other studies. According to labor economist Philip Martin, migrants with other job options in the

United States tend to leave farmwork for jobs with higher wages, more hours, better benefits, and opportunities for upward mobility (personal communication, May 2, 2006). Though migration scholars struggle with a wage-data lag in their analyses, reports of farmworker shortages are not uncommon. For example, in January 2006, the *Sacramento Bee* reported that fewer Mexican workers were crossing the border to harvest winter vegetables. Reports of labor shortages in the San Joaquin Valley also abound, including the November 2005 assertion by Manuel Cunha, Jr. of the Nisei Farmers League that raisin growers were lacking 40,000 of the 50,600 workers needed for the harvest (*Rural Migration News* 2006: 1). In 2005 Tom Nassif of the Western Growers Association illustrated the competition for migrant labor: "You've got construction companies standing at the edge of the fields offering higher wages," he reported (*Rural Migration News* 2006: 1). Indeed, the continuing dispersion of Mexican migrants beyond the agricultural sector is "one of the most conspicuous features of the current wave of Mexican immigration to the United States" (Cornelius 1992: 186).

Figure 6.3 Occupations of Non-settled Tunkaseño Migrants in the United States

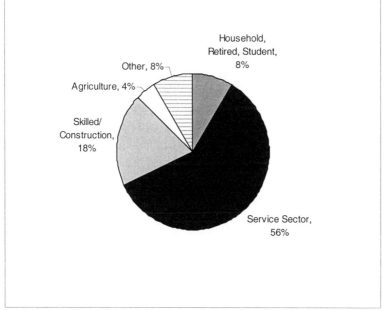

N = 75.

Settlers are much more likely than non-settlers to be in the United States legally. Forty percent of settled migrants from Tunkás reported having U.S. residency or citizenship during their most recent trip to the United States; even so, more than half (53 percent) of settlers said that they were undocumented on their last trip to the United States (see figure 6.4). Only 7 percent of Tunkaseño sojourners claimed to be legal residents of the United States during their most recent trip, while 83 percent entered without documents (see figure 6.5).

Figure 6.4 Documentation Status of Tunkaseño Settlers during Most Recent Stay in the United States

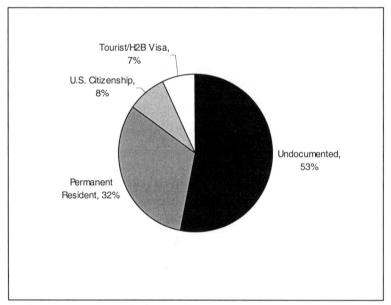

N = 59.

Although a considerable number of settlers from Tunkás are undocumented, comparison of the documentation status of Tunkaseño settlers on their first and last trips is revealing. This analysis indicates a trend toward legalized status for migrants who are long-term settlers: while 88 percent of settlers reported crossing the border without documentation during their first trip to the United States, only 53 percent entered illegally on their most recent trip to the United States. In addition, 48 percent of settlers indicated an interest in obtaining documentation in order to stay in the United States legally. Finally, when asked if they would like to become U.S. citizens, 67 percent of Tunkaseño settlers answered affirmatively; 24 percent said that they had already completed the naturalization process. Because settlement increases migrants' exposure to amnesties and legalization through family or "chain" migration, it is reasonable that the longer Tunkaseños spend in the United States, the more likely it is that they attain legal status.

Figure 6.5　Documentation Status of Tunkaseño Sojourners on Most Recent Trip to the United States

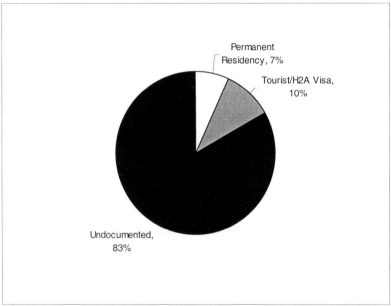

N = 81.

GENDER, THE NUCLEAR FAMILY, AND MIGRANT SETTLEMENT

According to Marcelli and Cornelius (2001: 111), a gradual feminization of the Mexican migrant flow began in the early 1970s and accelerated greatly in the 1990s. In his national-level estimates of undocumented immigration to the United States, demographer Jeffrey Passel has not found a rising percentage of women in the migration flow in recent years, but he does estimate that 35 percent of the stock of undocumented migrants in 2005 were adult females (Passel 2006: 1). Our 2006 data from Tunkás indicate increasing numbers of female migrants to the United States over the last two decades. While there was only one woman from Tunkás who migrated to the United States for the first time in the 1960s, forty-six Tunkaseña women crossed into the United States in each of the following decades. In the 1990s, eighty-seven women migrated to the United States, with twenty-five of them leaving for the United States in 1995 alone (see figure 6.6). Moreover, female migrants are more likely to be settled in the United States than their male counterparts (see figure 6.7).

Figure 6.6 Growth in Female Migration from Tunkás to the United States

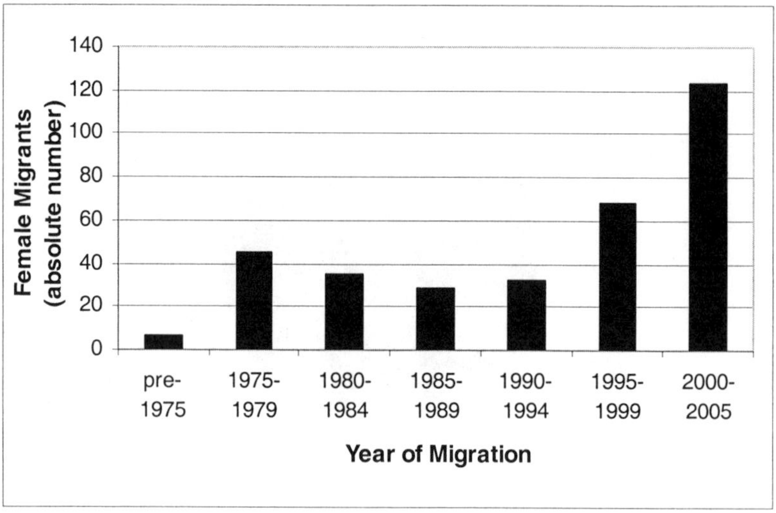

N = 257.
Note: Data include multiple migrations by some respondents.

Female migration is closely associated with the increasing frequency of whole-family migration (Hondagneu-Sotelo 1995: 22). Female Mexican immigrants in the United States tend to be married mothers, many with both Mexican- and U.S.-born children (Chávez 1988: 101). This is true of female migrants from Tunkás as well. Olivia, one of the first women to migrate from Tunkás and an important person in the network of U.S.-based Tunkaseños, observed that most women from Tunkás migrate with their husbands. Our research shows a total of 130 children born in the United States who have at least one parent from Tunkás, while there are 373 Tunkás-born children currently living in the United States. Having children present in the United States, regardless of their birth country, is strongly correlated with permanent settlement.

Figure 6.7 Gender of Tunkaseño Settlers and Sojourners

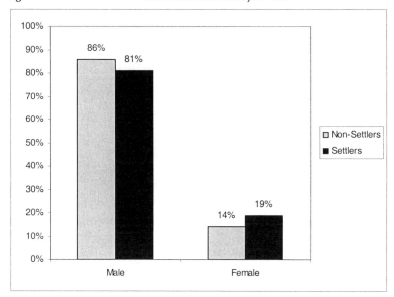

Settlers: N = 231; Sojourners: N = 177.

The ways in which family formation and whole-family migration contribute to immigrant settlement are diverse. Cornelius notes that immigrant teenagers are attracted to the lifestyles of U.S. youth, while women experience a lightening of their domestic chores. Adults of both genders give weight to the accumulation of financial obligations in the receiving community (Cornelius 1992: 176). However, these factors promoting settlement can be offset by others, such as the problems migrant parents encounter as they struggle to raise their children in a foreign land. Long work hours, problems with English, the strangeness of urban environments, and different cultural approaches to child rearing contribute to Tunkaseño parents' frustration with both their Mexican- and American-born children. One female settler expressed disappointment with minors who take advantage of the protections offered them under the U.S. legal and child welfare systems: "There [in the United States] children threaten their parents, saying, 'if you hit me, I'm going to call the police, so that they take you away.'... Because where I am [in Anaheim, California], if kids are seen even with a scratch, the police come to get you and they judge you and lock you up," she warned.

The belief that the United States is a better place than Yucatán to raise a child is associated with settlement. Sixty-eight percent of non-settled U.S. migrants interviewed in Tunkás or in U.S. destination communities said that it is better to raise children in Yucatán, while only 41 percent of settled migrants preferred Yucatán. The accumulation of experience in the United States may allow settlers to identify advantages to raising children there that are perhaps not immediately apparent to temporary migrants. Indeed, 48 percent of Tunkaseño settlers believe that children raised in the United States enjoy more opportunities, more support, and better nutrition than they would in Tunkás, compared to only 25 percent of non-settlers. Graciano, a migrant sojourner, drew an important distinction between the environments of Tunkás and California in terms of parenting: "Here in Tunkás, if I have a child, I can control him; I teach him a very different way. But if I take my child to California, he'll start school there and he'll learn another way of living, another way of carrying himself—changes in clothing, earrings, tattoos, hairstyle." Facilitated parental control such as Graciano references—avoiding gangs, drugs, and family disintegration—is more frequently cited by non-settlers (31 percent) than by settlers (17 percent) as a primary reason why it is preferable to raise children in Yucatán rather than in the United States. Varying convictions about the best atmosphere for child rearing factor significantly into patterns of settlement and sojourner migration.

Hondagneu-Sotelo argues that immigrant women, in addition to contributing to family reunification, also advance settlement by "creating patterns of permanent, year-round employment" (1995: 29). Our data reflect the contribution of women's labor to the household. Forty-nine percent of settled female migrants from Tunkás are employed outside the home, all in nonseasonal industries. Interestingly, while the median monthly wage of Tunkaseño settlers in general is US$1,280, women settlers earn slightly more, approximately $1,560. This difference could be due to higher rates of informal work situations (housecleaning, child care) among women settlers, in which taxes are not withheld from "under-the-table" pay. Regardless, the combination of two salaries in a household is powerful, and it is very likely that whole-family settlement would be less feasible without women's incorporation into the U.S. labor force.

USE OF U.S. INSTITUTIONS AND THE SETTLEMENT PROCESS

Increasing female and whole-family migration have important implications for the use of public services and institutions in the United States. In general, women tend to interact more than men with churches, schools, and other U.S. institutions, both "provisioning resources for daily family maintenance and reproduction and building community life" (Hondagneu-Sotelo 1995: 25). These experiences often serve to root life in the United States. For example, a female migrant settled in the United States for over two decades recounted how she sought out and received assistance for her Tunkaseño family shortly after arriving to California: "I went to the St. Bonifacio Church in Inglewood, and I asked for help.... Well, the children of God helped me and gave me shoes, a television, blankets to cover up with.... That donation they gave me, I still carry it with me even today." While our data show significant levels of Tunkaseño use of public schools and hospitals in the United States, the opposite is true of their use of public assistance, such as welfare and food stamps (see chapter 5, this volume).

The correlations between settlement and use of U.S. institutions follow logical temporal patterns: longer stays lead to increased utilization of institutions and social services. As whole families begin to migrate, Tunkaseño migrants initiate engagement with schools in the United States. Sixty-seven percent of settlers said they had enrolled their children in public schools; only one Tunkaseño settler sent his child to a private school. If there is indeed a gradual trend toward whole-family migration and U.S. settlement among migrants from Tunkás, public education will become an even more significant resource for migrant families with school-age children in the United States.[1]

Likewise, a more heterogeneous immigrant population—with higher proportions of female migrants and children—inevitably requires more hospital and clinic visits for childbirth and children's illnesses. Twenty-eight percent of 232 adult Tunkaseño settlers reported having received medical attention in a U.S. hospital or clinic. Twelve percent of those settlers who had been treated in a U.S. hospital or clinic paid for the service themselves, while 53 percent covered the cost of care with employer-provided health insurance or with money from family members. Medi-Cal or a similar government-funded program paid for 32 percent of Tunkaseño settlers' medical treatment. By contrast, only 14 percent of Tunkaseño sojourners reported receiving public assistance when paying for health care. What is most striking about the heath care data is that, while a significant portion of settlers who received medical attention received government assistance to pay for it, the number of settlers who reported actually receiving treatment in any U.S. hospital or clinic is very low. This may be related to the high cost of medical attention, fear of authorities, or lack of information concerning available health care services and facilities. Chapter 11 in this volume explores the issue of health care for migrants more extensively.

While all migrants—regardless of documentation status—have the right to send their children to public schools and have at least limited access to health care in the United States, unauthorized migrants and authorized entrants lacking U.S. citizenship often do not qualify for many other social services available to U.S. citizens (Reyes, Johnson, and Van Swearingen 2002: 72–73). For example, the 1996 Personal Responsibility and Work Opportunity Reconciliation Act (PRWORA) dramatically curtailed noncitizens' access to welfare (Tumlin and Zimmermann 2003: 9). During their last trip to the United States, 92 percent of settlers from Tunkás did not have U.S. citizenship. This may explain their low rates of utilization of some restricted institutional services in the United States, especially welfare (Temporary Assistance for Needy

---

[1] The U.S. Supreme Court's 1982 ruling in *Plyer v. Doe* guaranteed the right of undocumented children to attend U.S. public schools without payment of tuition.

Families, or TANF) and food stamps. Only 11 percent of settled adult Tunkaseños stated that they or someone in their family received welfare, and 7 percent said they or a family member had used food stamps. Tunkaseños' use of this sort of public assistance appears to be based far more on individual and familial socioeconomic situation than on settlement per se.

Figure 6.8 Contributions to U.S. Federal and State Tax Revenues by Settled Tunkaseño Migrants

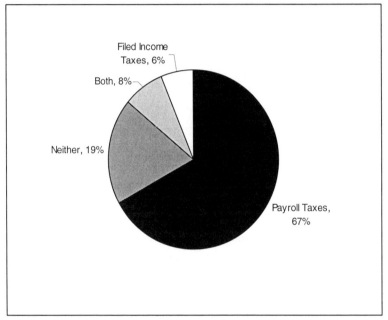

Filed Income Taxes, 6%

Both, 8%

Neither, 19%

Payroll Taxes, 67%

N = 100.

Although Tunkaseño settlers have relatively little recourse to public assistance programs like welfare and food stamps, they do engage frequently with U.S. financial and tax institutions. Fifty-two percent of settlers from Tunkás report that they had a U.S. bank account during their last U.S. trip. Most also pay income taxes, viewing this as a normal part of life in the United States. Approximately 81 percent of settled Tunkaseños paid income taxes in the United States, either through direct withholding from their pay, by filing yearly tax returns with the

Internal Revenue Service, or a combination of the two (see figure 6.8). Settlers are more likely than non-settlers to pay income tax. Finally, 14 percent of settlers from Tunkás reported owning their own home in the United States and were paying property taxes. Each of these indicators points to a process of gradual settlement, though, as the following section argues, that transition is rarely easy.

URBAN DESTINATIONS, RURAL ROOTS: TUNKASEÑO SETTLEMENT AND THE AMERICAN CITY

Tunkás is decidedly rural, and its day begins early. Hammocks are gathered and fastened to walls while roosters crow, church bells chime the hour, and announcements are made over loudspeakers: Señora Alma is selling fresh fish starting at 11 a.m., the Tuc family will offer tacos at midday. Many Tunkaseños express a strong affinity with the traditional environment of their pueblo, highlighting the important mixture of a sense of belonging and the safety inherent in rural communities. Indeed, when nonmigrating Tunkaseños were asked why they had not left Tunkás, 21 percent replied that the town's atmosphere was what most influenced their decision to stay. When asked what he liked best about Tunkás, Gustavo, an *ejidatario* with no migration experience but with two children in the United States, explained, "I feel like here, where you find me, this is my space.... Here you can return home late at night, at midnight or at one in the morning.... It's calmer here, more peaceful." Manuel, a young ex-migrant who lived in California for eight years before losing his job and returning to Tunkás, concurs with his elderly neighbor: "People from Tunkás aren't confrontational; they're very peaceable."

Yet the majority of migrants from Tunkás reside in the urban areas of Los Angeles and Orange counties—a huge shift from rural-to-urban orientation, especially for those migrants without previous migration experience in Mexican cities like Cancún or Mérida. When asked for his impressions of the environment of his destination community, Jesús noted that it was not excessively difficult for him to become adapted to life in Orange County because of his previous urban experience: "I had worked in Cancún ... and in Cancún there are many Americans, Brazilians, Cubans, all kinds of people." The impact of the sheer size of Los

Angeles and the cities in Orange County on newly arriving Tunkaseño migrants is strong. When asked what he thought about Los Angeles, Clemente labeled it "a bit of a shock" and commented that the noise and traffic—standard features of U.S. urban life that are absent in rural Tunkás—made it difficult for him to get around outside his apartment. Graciano expressed a similar sentiment, commenting that Los Angeles "is a city where you can easily get lost."

Issues such as gangs, drugs, crime, and violence that are inherent in the greater Los Angeles metropolitan area likewise have a powerful impact on newly arrived Tunkaseños. Máximo, a Tunkás native who has more than twenty years of experience in Inglewood, reflected on the gangs in his host community and in Inglewood schools: "I saw lots of gang members in the schools ... gangster here, gangster there. The insecurity of the schools scares me. The gangs in Inglewood control everything." These issues become particularly salient for migrants with families, who must decide whether they are willing to expose their spouses and children to the social problems they see in the American city.

Tunkaseño migrants who perceive high levels of criminality and danger in the United States are less likely to settle, and thus are less likely to have their nuclear families with them. Of Tunkaseño sojourners, 84 percent responded that "criminality" was the most difficult aspect for them in terms of living in the United States. Yet the amount of time spent in Los Angeles or Orange County influences perceptions of urban criminality and violence. Settled migrants with more experience in the United States perceive much lower levels of criminality and danger; only 15 percent of Tunkaseño settlers claimed that criminality was a primary difficulty in the United States, suggesting that perceptions of urban problems weaken over time as migrants adjust to the big-city environment. Another possible interpretation is that the financial benefit to the migrant family of living in urban America ultimately trumps the negative aspects. Finally, while the problems associated with U.S. cities can work against settlement, it is also important to note that large cities are ideal environments for the settlement process because they offer an array of relatively stable, year-round job opportunities, especially for women (Hondagneu-Sotelo 1995: 26).

SETTLEMENT AND TUNKASEÑOS' SOCIAL NETWORKS IN THE UNITED STATES

Despite the challenges of making their way in U.S. society, Tunkaseños have been able to maintain close ties with friends and family in Tunkás. While in the United States, 94 percent of Tunkaseño migrants maintain telephone contact with their families, calling Tunkás at least once a month. Migrant remittances to Tunkás are also strong; 86 percent of migrants send money home, reinforcing the ties they have with their place of origin. Our research shows that migrants maintain steady contact with their home community even as they integrate into U.S. society.

It is extremely rare for Tunkaseños to migrate to the United States without a set destination. Instead, most migrants head north toward clusters of established Tunkaseños and family members. Tunkaseño immigrant communities assist newcomers in many ways with their adaptation to the new environment. Networks of Tunkaseño migrants in California have even developed into organized clubs and sports teams.

The variety of Tunkaseño hometown groups, social clubs, and sports teams in the United States is impressive, especially considering that Tunkás is a relatively new migrant-sending community. The large community of Tunkaseño migrants in Inglewood, California, boasts two baseball teams (the "Yucatecan Twins" and the "Faisanes"), a basketball team, and a "Jarana" dance group, whose members learn and perform the traditional dances of Yucatán. Tunkaseños in Anaheim have also formed a baseball team. Participation in these groups reinforces social networks among migrants from Tunkás and from Yucatán more generally, and Mexicans from other regions sometimes participate in these organizations as well. The social acceptance inherent in U.S.-based social groups composed of Tunkaseños or Yucatecans creates a comfortable environment for migrants, helping them adjust to life in the United States.

As is to be expected, participation in Tunkaseño social associations is related to settlement in the United States. Our sample of Tunkaseños in Southern California demonstrated very strong, consistent participation in and dedication to the migrant sports groups they had formed. When asked if they participated in any local sports teams, many Tunkaseño migrants answered enthusiastically that there are games every

Sunday; rainy weather is the only thing that stops them from playing. When a game in Inglewood was cancelled on one soggy Sunday in early April, we observed that most of the team and their families nevertheless gathered to socialize. Families come to games to cheer for brothers, fathers, and cousins, and games are followed by afternoon barbecues.

¿HABLAS INGLÉS? TUNKASEÑO SETTLEMENT AND LANGUAGE

Formal and informal Tunkaseño social groups create a comfortable, familiar environment for migrants. Because the social world they inhabit in the United States is dominated by Spanish speakers, some Tunkaseño migrants do not become proficient in English. "At work, at home, and with friends, you speak Spanish," David, a settled Tunkaseño in Inglewood, made clear. Manuel, a returned migrant in Tunkás who lived in the United States for over eight years, similarly noted, "Wherever you turn [in California] there are lots of Latinos. There's always someone who speaks Spanish." English is clearly a hurdle for these migrants, and many of them struggled with the language at work. When describing a job he held at a Disneyland restaurant that was dominated by Anglo employees, one settler noted: "after hearing the same thing every day—for example, 'tomato sauce, tomato sauce'—you realize what it means.... After working there for three years I finally knew a little English." The lack of English proficiency was the second-ranked difficulty related to living in the United States, according to our Tunkaseño sample, just behind loneliness due to family separation.

A recent study by Bauer, Epstein, and Gang (2005) shows that migrants' English levels are heavily influenced by involvement in migrant enclaves. "Mexican migrants with poor English proficiency choose large ethnic enclaves while those with good English proficiency choose to migrate to relatively smaller enclaves," the authors argue (p. 6). The lack of English fluency is related to low-paying, entry-level jobs and stagnant social mobility. As Bauer and colleagues note, there is "a positive correlation between the language skills of migrants and their earnings" (p. 2). Poor English language skills can also inhibit migrants' ability to understand their rights and responsibilities in the United States and to communicate with government bureaucrats and with their children's teachers.

Although some Tunkaseño migrants surveyed in Southern California expressed ambivalence about speaking English, field observations revealed that migrants use English quite frequently, even within Spanish-speaking social groups. On the ball field, for example, Tunkaseños encouraged and admonished each other in both Spanish and English, and members of the "Yucatecan Twins" yelled and cursed in both languages. During post-game socializing, Tunkaseño team members joked with us in English, proudly displaying their linguistic skills.

Settlers are more likely than sojourners to speak English. Eighty-two percent of settlers claimed to be proficient in English, compared to only 18 percent of non-settler migrants. The effect of English proficiency on settlement is especially evident among the younger generation. As migrants form families in the United States and bring Mexico-based family members north, the drive for children to attain English proficiency is a significant consideration. Nearly 60 percent of the parents in a study by Leslie Reese stated that they wanted their children to become fluent in English (Reese 2001: 460). The small but growing second generation of Tunkaseños is learning English in American schools.

EDUCATION AND SETTLEMENT BEHAVIOR

The average adult Tunkaseño migrant, whether Mexico-based sojourner or U.S.-based settler, has received six years of primary education. This relatively low education level reduces the possibilities for acquiring a skilled job in Mexico, adding further to migration's push factors. At the same time, there is an abundance of "3-D" jobs—dirty, dangerous, and difficult—in the United States that do not require more than a minimal education. Once in the United States, a small number of Tunkaseño migrants take classes to learn English: 23 percent of adult Tunkaseño migrants have attended school in the United States, but 24 percent of these did not study English for more than a year.

The relationship between education and settlement will likely strengthen as the migrant flow from Tunkás incorporates more women, children, and whole-family units. Migrants from Tunkás commonly see education as an opportunity their children can access in the United States, propelling Tunkaseño families toward settlement. Sixty-eight percent of settlers have enrolled their children in U.S. schools, and educating children in the United States influences many Tunkaseño families' decision to settle. As one settler, Joshua, noted:

> A parent does not want his children to experience what they have lived. They educate children to grow, not to stay in poverty ... to look for a way to succeed. My children have an opportunity to study in the United States; therefore, I encourage them. If we all did that with our children, then we could compete with the Americans.

Reese uncovered a similar sentiment in Mexican immigrant homes in Southern California. Ninety percent of Reese's sample of 120 parents wanted their children to "finish school," including university (Reese 2001: 465). We predict that the formal education attained by both the U.S.-born and Mexico-born children of Tunkaseños settled in the United States will certainly surpass that of their parents.

THE INFLUENCE OF ECONOMIC PERCEPTIONS ON TUNKASEÑO SETTLEMENT

Mexican migrants commonly view going to the United States as a way to advance economically. This is especially true for those from rural communities like Tunkás, which are highly dependent on agriculture with unpredictable harvests. Because Tunkaseño migration is a relatively new phenomenon, sojourner migration remains strong. Migrants are often target-earners, seeking money to build a home, start a business, or pay debts. Tunkaseños in the United States, like other Mexican migrants, do not necessarily intend to settle permanently. However, as migrants see their income grow, especially in comparison to typical wages in Mexico, they become accustomed to a "consumer culture that inculcates new tastes and motivations that cannot be satisfied through economic activities at home" (Massey, Durand, and Malone 2002: 146).

Increasing migration flows from Tunkás to the United States affect how Tunkaseños view their family's economic standing. An overwhelming 81 percent of migrants interviewed claimed that their U.S. migrations were motivated more by the opportunities in the United States than by conditions in Tunkás. Positive perceptions of the economic advantages of the United States influence both the decision to migrate and the process of settlement in the United States.

The vast majority of migrants from Tunkás, both settlers and non-settlers, expressed a belief that their families are better off financially now than they were five years ago. However, settled migrants were least likely to consider their families worse off now than five years before. Only 2 percent of settlers viewed their current financial situation negatively in relation to the past, compared to 9.5 and 9.6 percent, respectively, for non-settlers and nonmigrants from Tunkás (figure 6.9). When asked to rank their families' financial standing on a scale of 1 to 10, with 1 representing the most humble Tunkaseño family and 10 the most prosperous, both settlers and non-settler migrants ranked themselves around the affluent pole. Only 11 percent of settlers claimed that their families lived at an economic level below the Tunkaseño average. The economic perceptions of nonmigrants were predictably much less positive, with 41 percent of nonmigrants placing themselves financially below the average Tunkaseño family. While almost any migration experience in the United States is linked to positive economic perceptions that influence settlement, settlers make the most optimistic economic assessments of their financial standing.

Figure 6.9 Perception of Current Personal Economic Situation versus Five Years Ago, by Migration/Settlement Experience

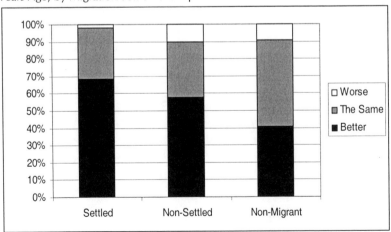

N = 517.

Many Tunkaseño migrants ultimately opt to settle in the United States rather than return to the lower living standards of their home community. There are exceptions to this trend, of course, but migration to the United States in search of better economic opportunities is generally accepted by many Mexican migrants "as a fact of life they can't imagine changing" (Stevenson 2006: 2). When Tunkaseño migrants do return home, it is often under special circumstances, such as retirement or family reunification, when an improved economic outlook is a less important factor.

WELCOME HOME: RETURN MIGRATION TO TUNKÁS

This chapter began with the observation that Mexican migration to the United States is not an inevitably linear process ending in permanent settlement. Immigrants who appear quite settled in the United States can quickly become return migrants due to personal factors such as age, illness, or homesickness. Conditions in the sending community, such as a death in the family, inheritance, or political shifts, as well as factors in the destination community, such as a negative economic climate or unemployment, can also affect the permanency of settlement. In the case of Tunkás, 29 percent of adult settlers expressed a desire to return to their village in the future, even after years of working and living in the United States. One returned migrant who had spent nearly a decade in Southern California explained his return to Tunkás: "I said to myself, 'I'm done with this.' Just as I left Tunkás quickly, I also decided to return quickly. I had been stopped by the police [in California] two times. They took my car because I didn't have documents, I didn't have a driver license. These things happen." Even seemingly simple disheartenment with the United States can trigger return migration.

Family reunification is an important reason for some Tunkaseño migrants to return to their home community. Parents of current migrants are less likely to migrate to the United States because of their age and life-long roots in Tunkás. Kanaiaupuni argues that the some elderly Mexicans with settled adult children in the United States are left "abandoned entirely or living alone" (Kanaiaupuni 2000: 11–12). The average migrant from Tunkás will still have more family members in the home community than in the United States. Reuniting with both nuclear and extended family members in Tunkás is a powerful incentive for return migration, and a clear alternative to reuniting the family in the United States.

A MULTIVARIATE ANALYSIS OF SETTLEMENT BEHAVIOR

The following logistic regression analysis systematically examines predictors of migrant settlement in the United States. The dependent variable for the model (table 6.1) is settlement, as defined by migrants' self-reporting of whether the United States or Mexico is their primary country of residence; a primary U.S. residence is scored 1. The regression analysis indicates that a migrant is more likely to settle in the United States if he holds nonseasonal employment, possesses legal status, has larger social networks, or believes that raising children in the United States is better than raising them in Yucatán. This analysis controls for the demographic variables that we found to be significant determinants of the propensity to migrate (see chapter 3, this volume). The statistical insignificance of these demographic factors in the present analysis indicates that it is the circumstances surrounding the migration experience rather than *who* migrates that most importantly influences settlement in the United States.

Table 6.1 Predictors of U.S. Settlement among Tunkaseño Migrants

	β	Standard Error	Significance
Nonseasonal employment	**1.710*****	0.374	0.000
Legal status	**0.852***	0.444	0.055
Number of relatives in United States	**0.231****	0.110	0.035
Preference to raise children in United States	**0.725****	0.326	0.026
Age	−0.015	0.014	0.290
Male	−0.194	0.437	0.657
Education	0.031	0.041	0.449
Married	−0.152	0.354	0.667
Constant	**−1.773***	0.958	0.064

N = 236; Chi-squared = 60.86; * 90%, ** 95%, *** 99% confidence intervals.

CONCLUSION

As members of a relatively new sending community, the majority of Tunkaseños have never migrated internationally. Those who do have migratory experience in the United States are often sojourners. Tunkaseño migrants who are settled enough in the United States to consider it their primary place of residence are currently a minority, but the settlement pattern of Tunkás's migrants is still emerging. Several characteristics of Tunkaseños already in the United States commonly influence settlement, including having a nonseasonal job, being documented during the last U.S.-bound trip, preferring to raise children in the United States, and having access to more social network contacts and family members. Social participation in Tunkaseño associations is also positively related to settlement. Awareness of the dangers of city life negatively affects settlement, but not to the extent of drastically changing settlement behavior. Migrants in the United States do not tend to settle to take advantage of social services or public education. Settlers have more positive perceptions of their relative economic fortunes. Optimistic financial outlooks are also strongly related to the higher wages offered in the United States, even for menial work. Economic stability is a primary motivator for settlement in the United States, although the desire to return to Tunkás for family reasons sometimes trumps the financial opportunities offered north of the border.

If Tunkás follows the pattern set by traditional sending communities, its residents will migrate and settle in the United States in growing numbers, especially if Tunkás develops a "culture of migration" similar to that found in many Mexican communities (Cohen 2004: 5). Though new immigration legislation is currently being debated in the U.S. Congress, it is too early to speculate on what policy might materialize, let alone its effects on Tunkaseño migration flows. Nevertheless, the effects of past legislation like IRCA indicate that an amnesty program would likely serve as an impetus for higher settlement rates among migrants from Tunkás. Likewise, an increasingly militarized border would likely encourage undocumented Tunkaseños to stay in the United States even longer. Barring rapid, widespread, and significant improvements in the Mexican economy, we hypothesize that Tunkaseños' northward migration will continue, with greater numbers of migrants settling in the United States in the future.

References

Bauer, Thomas, Gil Epstein, and Ira Gang. 2005. "Enclaves, Language, and the Location Choice of Migrants," *Journal of Population Economics* 18, no. 4: 649–62.

Chávez, Leo. 1988. "Settlers and Sojourners: The Case of Mexicans in the U.S.," *Human Organization* 47: 95–108.

Cohen, Jeffrey H. 2004. *The Culture of Migration in Southern Mexico*. Austin, TX: University of Texas Press.

Cornelius, Wayne. 1989. "Impacts of the 1986 US Immigration Law on Emigration from Rural Mexican Sending Communities," *Population and Development* Review 15, no. 4: 689–705.

———. 1992. "From Sojourners to Settlers: The Changing Profile of Mexican Migration to the U.S." In *U.S.-Mexico Relations: Labor Market Interdependence*, ed. Jorge Bustamante, Clark Reynolds, and Raúl Hinojosa Ojeda. Stanford, CA: Stanford University Press.

———. 2001. "Death at the Border: The Efficacy and 'Unintended' Consequences of U.S. Immigration Policy," *Population and Development Review* 27, no. 4: 661–85.

Hondagneu-Sotelo, Pierrette. 1995. "Beyond 'The Longer They Stay' (And Say They Will Stay): Women and Mexican Immigrant Settlement," *Qualitative Sociology* 18, no. 1: 21–43.

Kanaiaupuni, Shawn. 2000. "Leaving Parents Behind: Migration and Elderly Living Arrangements in Mexico." Working Paper No. 99-16. Madison, WI: Center for Demography and Ecology, University of Wisconsin–Madison.

Marcelli, Enrico A., and Wayne A. Cornelius. 2001. "The Changing Profile of Mexican Migrants to the United States: New Evidence from California and Mexico," *Latin American Research Review* 36, no. 3: 105–17.

Massey, Douglas, Jorge Durand, and Nolan J. Malone. 2002. *Beyond Smoke and Mirrors*. New York: Russell Sage Foundation.

Passel, Jeffrey. 2006. "The Size and Characteristics of the Unauthorized Migrant Population in the U.S.: Estimates Based on the March 2005 Current Population Survey." Research Report. Washington, DC: Pew Hispanic Center.

Piore, Michael J. 1979. *Birds of Passage: Migrant Labor and Industrial Societies.* New York: Cambridge University Press.

Reese, Leslie. 2001. "Morality and Identity in Mexican Immigrant Parents' Visions of the Future," *Journal of Ethnic and Migration Studies* 27, no. 3: 455–72.

Reyes, Belinda, Hans Johnson, and Richard Van Swearingen. 2002. *Holding the Line? The Effect of the Recent Border Build-up on Unauthorized Immigration.* San Francisco, CA: Public Policy Institute of California.

Rural Migration News. 2006. "Farm Labor Shortages." http://migration .ucdavis.edu/rmn/more.php?id=1110_0_4_0.

Stevenson, Mark. 2006. "Many Mexicans Say Immigration Inevitable." *Associated Press*, April 23.

Tumlin, Karen C., and Wendy Zimmermann. 2003. "Immigrants and TANF: A Look at Immigrant Welfare Recipients in Three Cities." Accessing the New Federalism Occasional Papers, no. 69. Washington, DC: Urban Institute. http://www.urban.org/url.cfm?ID=310874.

A stay-at-home octogenarian couple in Tunkás.

7 Stay-at-Homes: Why Many People Do Not Migrate

GUADALUPE CASTILLO, ZOILA JIMÉNEZ-PACHECO, AND
PATRICIA PASILLAS

This chapter seeks to explain why many Tunkaseños choose to stay in their hometown instead of migrating internally or internationally. Several factors come into play when Tunkaseños are deciding whether to abandon their hometown. An individual's stock of transferable social capital is particularly consequential. Since Tunkás is a relatively new migrant-sending community, many of its residents have little or no access to the transnational social networks that support those who migrate. Other factors influencing the decision to stay at home include socioeconomic status and the age of the potential migrant. Although these variables have an effect, we find that family circumstances and cultural traditions are the most important impediments to transnational migration of Tunkaseños.

STAYING AT HOME: THEORETICAL PERSPECTIVES

A potential migrant is tied to his or her family in numerous ways, one being the individual's contribution to the family's economic well-being. Family solidarity and family obligations exert a strong effect to keep potential migrants rooted in their hometown. The obligations may be financial or cultural—and are often both. For example, a potential migrant with aged parents may be the sole breadwinner in the household—and probably the principal caregiver as well. The cultural expression of these obligations is the assumption that in Tunkaseño households the oldest son or daughter will care for the parents when they are unable to fend for themselves. The family serves as a hometown support network, and the absence of even one member could interrupt that function. Families aspire to remain together unless it is financially imperative that a member migrate for the sake of the family's well-being. The question becomes, then, whether the increased economic contribution a family member could make by migrating outweighs the other considerations outlined above.

For Irene, a 35-year-old Tunkaseña who has never migrated, family and religion are the most important reasons why she never left her hometown. She is the eldest daughter in a family of eight children, and both of her parents became ill when she was about twelve years old. She cared for her mother and father while simultaneously helping to raise her younger siblings. When she was about eighteen, her boyfriend proposed marriage and asked her to go with him to California. She reluctantly refused, because her family needed her at home.

> I had to take care of my mother; we could not afford a nurse. I also took care of my brothers. Time flew by, and now I'm thirty-five. Once, Marcos, my boyfriend at the time, told me that I had sacrificed my life for my family. When we were young he wanted to get married, but my only goal was to take care of my mother and brothers.

Irene was able to attend school only until sixth grade. She feels that she has been blessed with a wonderful family and is also involved in her church community. Irene, her father, and her brothers are part of a musical group that performs weekly at church. Their membership in an evangelical church in Tunkás has anchored them firmly in the town. Irene is happy with her life in Tunkás and does not feel that going to the United States would make her life better. The support network she has created within her church community allows her to live the "right way" and stay close to her family.

The importance that family obligations and cultural practices hold in the decision to migrate or to stay in Tunkás is similarly illustrated by the case of 28-year-old Bernardo. He learned to appreciate the value of working in the cornfields of Tunkás, laboring alongside his father. Bernardo is the oldest of four brothers, and together with his father he has been able to provide for the household. One of his brothers died at a young age, and his sister stayed home to help their mother with household chores. Bernardo has a love and admiration for *el campo*, which dissuaded him from leaving Tunkás:

> It might have been because I was so close to my father. He worked in the field, and I wanted to work with him. I've never really thought about going to the United States. If my father had gone, my attitude toward migration would be different. If he had gone, he would have sent me money, and then I would have gotten used to having money so I would go too. But my father never migrated because he loved taking care of his ranch.

The fact that Bernardo's family had no U.S. migration experience decreased the likelihood that he would migrate. If he had already established kinship ties abroad, his decision about migration might well have been different.

The lack of family networks in the migrant-receiving country increases the costs of migration for potential first-timers. Conversely, according to Douglas Massey and colleagues, "after the first migrants have left ... the potential costs of migration are substantially lowered for friends and relatives left behind" (Massey et al. 1998: 43). We hypothesize, therefore, that the lack of ties between family members in Tunkás and others in the United States deters migration, while the presence of such ties increases the probability of future migration. There is considerable empirical support for this hypothesis from previous studies of Mexican migration to the United States. For example, in Cohen's study of eleven Oaxacan migrant-sending communities, household heads were asked to use a Likert-type scale to rank items that might hinder migration, and family circumstances were at the top of the list, followed by work obligations and community ties (Cohen 2004: 128). Cohen concludes that "social contacts based in kinship and friendship are central to the decisions of most migrants and the lack of such networks limits nonmigrants" (p. 125).

International migration results in "maintenance costs," or the cost of maintaining close ties with the people the migrant leaves behind. "Costs are economic, such as return trips, social such as trying to sustain contacts to the circle of friends and relations, cultural in practicing one's religion or other customs, and psychological in the costs of adapting to a new environment" (Faist 2000: 126). Costs are even higher for those without an already established network at their destination. Pioneer migrants from a given family or community struggle more because they have no one to guide them and facilitate their migration—a situation often seen in relatively new migrant-sending communities like Tunkás.

We also hypothesize that if a potential migrant has significant social ties to the local community, such as involvement in a religious congregation or in local government, migration will be a less attractive option. A person who remains in his hometown also acquires what can be called "insider advantages," which accumulate the longer that the individual lives and works in one place. These include social and symbolic ties and other nonmaterial resources that could be utilized in the future. Forfeiting such advantages is often a cost that the potential migrant is unwilling to accept. For example, loyalty, a "sense of obligation that arises from solidarity" (Faist 2000: 126), is a social and symbolic tie that can strongly affect the decision to migrate internationally. Even if the financial and social costs of migration are acceptable, loyalty can make the potential migrant search for other options that may not require such a drastic life change.

Those who migrate also incur adaptation costs when living and working in the United States. Adaptation costs can be viewed as the consequence of "crossing a cultural threshold" (Faist 2000: 128). Adaptation is a greater challenge for pioneer migrants who have no established resources or connections in the receiving country. To achieve success there, migrants may have to acquire competence in a new language, new cultural norms, and different attitudes toward life. People who fear having to deal with such adaptation costs are less likely to consider migration. For the Tunkaseños we interviewed who have U.S. migration experience, the worst things about life in the United States were their lack of English competence and feelings of loneliness and separation from family. Approximately 13 percent of surveyed migrants said their primary difficulty was learning the language, and about 7 percent felt that their families lost cohesiveness after they left for the United States. These migrants exemplify the adaptation costs incurred when a cultural threshold must be crossed.

The need to adapt to an environment with a high risk of violence can also discourage an individual from migrating. For many Tunkaseños, cities in the Yucatán Peninsula are synonymous with criminality and violence. Such perceptions can depress an individual's desire to migrate, both internally and internationally. For example, when visiting his daughter in Mérida, Gustavo witnessed a brutal crime that changed his mind about living outside Tunkás: "Some gangsters grabbed a woman, raped her, and then killed her. They stabbed her three times—a half-block from my daughter's house!" Gustavo attributes this sort of criminality to the urban environment, noting that in Tunkás you rarely see criminals, but "over there [in Mérida] you can't walk at night due to the violence." He recalls telling his daughter that this would be the last time he set foot in that city. The experience reminded him of another crime he had witnessed as a young man during his months as a construction worker in Cancún. One day as he walked to work, he came upon a lifeless body on the ground, apparently the victim of robbers. These experiences had a strong impact on Gustavo; he hated cities and wanted to avoid them.

Age is another factor for those making the migration decision: older adults are more likely to remain behind. And if an individual or household unit has sufficient financial resources to cover daily expenses, migration may be considered unnecessary (Cohen 2004: 126). The case of Gilberto, an 82-year-old native Tunkaseño who has worked in the cornfields of his hometown all of his life, is illustrative. Thanks to government programs to aid small farmers—PROCAMPO during the Ernesto Zedillo administration (1994–2000) and Oportunidades under President Vicente Fox (2000–2006)—Gilberto has managed to support his wife without migrating. His children have migrated both internally and internationally, and both have invited him to their new homes, but he has refused their invitations. In the 1960s, when he was a young man, Gilberto was a candidate for the Bracero Program, but he did not go because he had no wish to work outside of Mexico.

STAYING AT HOME: SURVEY EVIDENCE FROM TUNKÁS

Two-thirds of the adult population of Tunkás have never migrated internationally, and approximately 80 percent of the nonmigrant population reported that they have never considered living outside of Tunkás permanently. As shown in figure 7.1, the most important reason for not leaving Tunkás was family obligations. A positive perception of the local community environment is also important, as were not having a prearranged job in the United States or already having a job in a Yucatecan city. These findings support our hypothesis that family circumstances are the key determinant in decisions to remain in Tunkás, followed closely by satisfaction with the hometown lifestyle.

Figure 7.1 Most Important Reason Why Respondent Has Not Left Tunkás

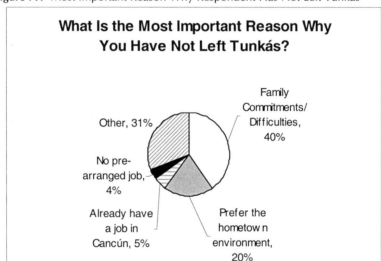

The difference between cultural traditions in Tunkás and the United States also explains why some people are more reluctant to leave Tunkás. Nonmigrants often get a negative impression from returning migrants, who have changed the way they dress, talk, and behave. When asked if migration has benefited or harmed Tunkás, majorities of both migrants and nonmigrants felt that migration has been beneficial, because it has modernized the town. However, nonmigrants were more likely to cite violent behavior, changes in style of dress, and family disintegration as negative consequences of migration (see table 7.1). Migrants returning from the United States placed more emphasis on the rising incidence of alcoholism (see chapter 11, this volume).

Table 7.1 Migrants' and Nonmigrants' Perceptions of the Negative Consequences of U.S. Migration

	Nonmigrants (N = 51)	U.S. Migrants (N = 76)
More alcoholism	20%	13%
More drug use	12%	11%
More violence	12%	8%
Changing language usage	8%	14%
Changing styles of dress	20%	13%
Little regard for agricultural work	2%	5%
Deterioration in fiestas/ ceremonies	2%	5%
Less community unity	12%	12%
Breakdown in the family	10%	8%
Other	2%	11%

When asked about differences between the educational systems in Yucatán and the United States, Rudy, a 24-year-old Tunkaseño, commented: "They become gangsters, all tattooed, head-shaven bandits with weapons.... It is very important because many say that education begins with the parents." Rudy's comment illustrates what Tunkaseños often perceive when migrants return to Tunkás with their U.S.-born children: a change in attitudes, ways of dress, and use of language. About 20 percent of Tunkaseños with U.S. migration experience agreed that the change in clothing styles was the most common way that returning migrants had been detrimental to the culture and traditions of Tunkás. Nonmigrants cite the returning migrants' language: their Spanish is not the same, and "Spanglish" has become the norm. Rudy observed:

> You can hear their accent. And they speak Spanglish. When I talk with a buddy who does not speak English, he says things like "oh yeah" and "oh sí?" He used to talk normally, but now he incorporates other words. Over here you hardly use words like "so," "yeah," "ok," and "bye."

Such language use creates a significant barrier between those who have migrated and those who have not. This divide has the ability to change values and cultural perceptions in ways that can increase or decrease the probability of migration, depending on the way that non-migrant Tunkaseños react to the difference. For example, Rudy does not intend to leave Tunkás because he wants his children to be raised and educated in Mexico; he does not want to see the changes in his children that he sees in Tunkaseños who migrate. About 60 percent of the Tunkaseños we surveyed, both nonmigrants and international migrants, stated that they preferred to raise their children in Yucatán (table 7.2). More international migrants than nonmigrants preferred that their children be raised in the United States, but this group also showed an overwhelming preference to raise their children in Yucatán, under-scoring our finding that family considerations make a substantial difference in an individual's choice to migrate.

Table 7.2 Preferred Country for Raising Children

Best Country for Raising Children	Nonmigrants (%)	International Migrants (%)	Percent of Total Cases
Yucatán	68	52	60
United States	18	36	27
Either country	14	13	13

Pearson Chi-squared (2) = 20.0983; p = 0.000; N = 491.

CONCLUSION

We have identified several key factors that explain why a large majority of Tunkaseños have not yet migrated to the United States. Because Tunkás is a relatively new migrant-sending community, many families do not yet have strong kinship ties with established migrants in the United States. We found evidence in Tunkás that the lack of such ties is a major deterrent to international migration. Family circumstances were the factor that Tunkaseños most often cited as a hindrance to migration. Because family obligations are a high priority among Tunkaseños who have decided not to leave, it is not surprising that fears about the disin-tegration of the family play a significant role in decisions to remain in the hometown. We also found that age and lack of economic need can discourage migration. For those who are doing well financially and have achieved some income stability, migration's benefits do not outweigh its costs.

Finally, our interviews in Tunkás call attention to the role of cultural practices and how migration is affecting them. Nonmigrants are sensitive to, and clearly disapprove of, the ways in which forms of dress, use of language, and family life have changed among returning migrants. As Tunkás develops as a migrant-sending community, family reunification in the United States will play a larger role in Tunkaseño life. And as the group of people opting to stay at home shrinks, so, too, may the reluctance of Tunkaseños to accept migration-related changes in cultural traditions and practices.

References

Cohen, Jeffrey H. 2004. *The Culture of Migration in Southern Mexico.* Austin, TX: University of Texas Press.

Faist, Thomas. 2000. *The Volume and Dynamics of International Migration and Transnational Social Spaces.* Oxford: Clarendon.

Massey, Douglas S., Joaquin Arango, Graeme Hugo, Ali Kouaouci, Adela Pellegrino, and J. Edward Taylor. 1998. *Worlds in Motion: Understanding International Migration at the End of the Millennium.* Oxford: Clarendon.

Nonmigrating beekeeper and his family in Tunkás.

Tunkas's only "3 x 1" project: improvements to the town's softball field.

8 Migration and Local Development

JUAN RODRÍGUEZ DE LA GALA, VANESSA MOLINA, AND DAISY GARCÍA

International migration is shaping the economies of Tunkás and similar towns in southeastern Mexico as never before. This chapter assesses the local economic opportunity structure in Tunkás for migrants and prospective migrants. We show how migration to the United States has affected available employment opportunities in three sectors of the local economy: corn cultivation, livestock-raising, and informal labor markets. We discuss the accessibility of credit for investment and development in Tunkás and apply our findings to the apiculture industry.

We also analyze the migrants' remittance behavior, including the factors that make it more likely that a migrant will send money and that determine how much is sent. We discuss the stability of remittances as an income source in Tunkás compared to other rural communities with longer migration histories. And we discuss how remittances are used in Tunkás and whether they encourage dependency or development.

Finally, we explore the ways in which the income that migrants earn in the United States might be harnessed for development projects in their hometowns, especially through the 3 x 1 Program, a government-initiated program that mobilizes contributions from U.S.-based migrants for hometown infrastructure projects. All of these issues inform our understanding of the consequences of U.S.-bound migration for sending-community development.

LOCAL OPPORTUNITY STRUCTURE

The local opportunity structure in Tunkás includes employment opportunities, the investment climate, and access to credit and other forms of capital accumulation. Residents of Tunkás see their town as deficient in most areas of economic opportunity. When asked if a young person could succeed without leaving Tunkás, 69 percent said that, to succeed, a young person must leave the town. Migrants and nonmigrants alike perceive the local opportunity structure negatively, which is why income sources have been diversified by adding wage-labor migration to the United States. Even the local authorities view money earned abroad as the only source of hope for their community. According to Elías Kuh, the current municipal president:

> Tunkás will always depend on the United States. It is very difficult for our town to develop. We've had chances to develop, but we've not managed it. There was beekeeping, but that's going now. Beekeeping declined because of Africanized bees. Those bees migrate, making the future of apiculture in Tunkás very uncertain. The cattle often get sick. We need more veterinarians. Rural extension offers classes for people who raise livestock, but it's not enough. I don't see a day when Tunkás can free itself from its dependence on remittances from the United States.

When residents were asked what it would take for fewer townspeople to migrate, over 90 percent mentioned an improved employment situation (see figure 8.1): 65 percent cited the need to create more jobs, 19 percent mentioned better-paying jobs, 6 percent wanted more non-agricultural jobs, and 1 percent saw a need for more stable jobs. These responses are similar to those of residents in two migrant-sending communities in Jalisco and Zacatecas, surveyed in 2005. The vast majority of respondents in those communities (93 percent) also cited more or better jobs as the greatest need to reduce out-migration. These data suggest that jobs—particularly nonagricultural, better-paying jobs—would be the most effective deterrent to migration from Tunkás.

Employment Opportunities

Local options for dealing with chronic unemployment and underemployment are much more limited in Tunkás than in Mexico's large urban centers, where the informal economy absorbs much of the surplus labor. For example, in 2006 there were fewer than ten street vendors, most selling food, in the entire municipality of Tunkás. Opportunities for street vendors are limited by the small population and low family incomes. Most Tunkaseños are subsistence farmers and have little disposable income. Tunkás does not have a supermarket or public market that provides employment opportunities. The town's retail sector is limited to five owner-operated convenience stores, where people can purchase a limited variety of household products at prices similar to those in supermarkets.

Figure 8.1 "What is necessary for fewer people to leave this town?"

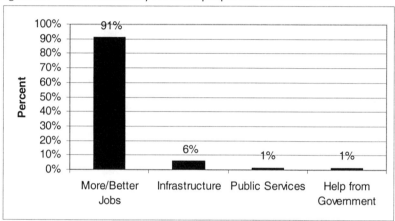

There is some labor demand in construction, however; the town's informal construction sector employs about two hundred laborers. The uptick in construction is being fueled by remittances invested in building modern concrete homes (often immediately adjacent to traditional palm-thatched houses) or remodeling or expanding existing homes of migrants working in the United States. In some cases the newly constructed homes are left empty or are lived in by relatives of the migrant abroad. And a relative of the U.S.-based migrant—a brother, father, or son—is often the construction worker. Thus migrants serve as employers, relying on social networks to transfer their money and instructions to their employees in Tunkás. One interviewee reported that his son in San Francisco, California, sent him blueprints and design sketches for a new house that has now been built in Tunkás. Local ranchers also hire temporary construction workers year-round for small-scale projects on their properties. However, employment in construction is not sufficiently significant to make an impact on out-migration.

Forty-one percent of our interviewees in Tunkás reported working in the agricultural sector, mostly in corn cultivation, even though the market for the corn grown in Tunkás is very small. Employment in the cornfields consists mainly of clearing the fields before they are burned. Day laborers earn about US$10 for a ten-hour workday in the cornfields.

Fewer than 1 percent of the migrants and potential migrants we interviewed are in livestock-raising, most likely barred from this sector by the large amounts of infrastructure and startup capital that livestock-raising requires. Thus this sector provides few opportunities for low-income Tunkaseños and has traditionally been dominated by a small group of prosperous, mostly mestizo, non–Maya-speaking ranchers. These cattlemen seem to form an elite among Tunkaseños. Some own homes in the capital city of Mérida and are able to send their children to universities in Mexico and even abroad, as does the president of the cattle association.

Informal-sector employment opportunities arise mostly during the annual week-long fiesta celebrating the town's patron saint, when migrants return and impress the locals with conspicuous displays of wealth. Tunkaseño migrants often save all year to have money to spend during the fiesta. This, in turn, elevates consumption norms and motivates others to migrate so they can have the same purchasing power as the returning migrants.[1] It is also during the fiesta that nonmigrants spend considerable money to impress their guests.

The fiesta generates a temporary spike in the demand for workers as the townspeople work to erect a temporary bullfighting ring. Laborers build stands within the bullring, each consisting of a few bleachers that are rented to bullfighting aficionados. Each family that builds a stand is able to rent out thirty seats at prices ranging from 30 to 50 pesos per show, giving some Tunkaseños an opportunity to become entrepreneurs.

---

[1] This phenomenon, common in rural Mexico, has been called the "migrant syndrome" (Reichert 1982).

Access to Credit

Investment in Tunkás is mainly at the micro level, with beekeepers and cattle ranchers reinvesting some of their profits in their businesses. The town has no factory or other large-scale business enterprise. Few residents have access to credit; the limited credit that is available comes mainly through government subsidies. Cash subsidies go primarily to cattle ranchers, while other agricultural producers only receive inputs, such as seed and fertilizer.

Formal banking does not exist in Tunkás, except for a branch of the Sistema Coopera savings association. The Coopera, which exists throughout southeastern Mexico, was established by friars in the early twentieth century to promote savings among less-educated groups. The Coopera makes loans, but the requirements exclude most Tunkaseños: a borrower must be an association member, provide proof of a stable income, have a cosigner, and pay for loan insurance. Currently 399 Tunkaseños are active members in the local Coopera. During its first four years in Tunkás, Coopera made sixty loans to members. Most of the loans paid for home construction or medical bills; health care is in fact the leading reason why Tunkaseños borrow money. All Coopera loans are personal credit lines to be used for family expenditures; the Coopera does not make business loans, further reducing Tunkaseños' options for access to capital with which to start a business.

In February 2006 Coopera began a partnership with Bansefi, a financial service institution created in 2001 by the Mexican Congress to give low-income Mexicans access to financial markets. This partnership allows Coopera to provide remittance-receiving services to its members. During the first quarter of 2006, there were twenty transfers a week on average, mainly from Inglewood and Anaheim, California. Ideally, the next step would be for Coopera to offer interest-bearing accounts. If there were some way to capture surplus remittances and lend them out as investment in income-generating projects, as opposed to consumer loans, Tunkás could be on its way to self-sustaining development. An example of this type of project would be investing remittances to add value to honey at the source. The following section provides an overview of beekeeping and its place in the Tunkás economy.

Apiculture in Tunkás: A Case Study

Apiculture is the sector with the greatest potential to provide employment and income to Tunkaseños. Given the international demand for their honey, Tunkaseños should be able to turn honey into a large-scale business.

Beekeeping, a pre-Hispanic tradition among the Maya, is thriving today in the Yucatán Peninsula. Prior to the Spanish conquest, the Maya kept bees to produce honey for use in ceremonies and as an aphrodisiac. A commercial apiculture industry began in the early twentieth century (see chapter 3 for a historical overview of beekeeping in Tunkás), and beekeeping was well established by 1960. In addition to honey, beekeeping provides *jalea real* (a rich jam-like food), wax, pollen, and a venom used locally to treat bee stings and for medical use abroad. Up to 95 percent of the honey produced in Yucatán is destined for export, mainly to Europe.

The high quality of the honey produced in Yucatán gives apiculture its strong potential to provide employment and economic returns to Tunkás. The Yucatán Peninsula accounts for 32 percent of Mexico's honey exports, bringing an estimated US$12 million into the region annually. According to a leading honey producer in Tunkás, every season the town produces over 50 tons of honey from the 435 beehive sites in the municipality. There are currently 320 beekeepers in Tunkás, each of whom has between 5 and 14 hives in one or more sites. The hives are located far from main roads (to escape car pollution) and in areas where there is sufficient flora; the bees feed entirely from the blossoms of trees and bushes that grow naturally in the region.

Bee production in Tunkás has suffered since the arrival of the Africanized honey bee (*Apis mellifera scutellata*) in 1986. Even though local beekeepers have largely adapted to the new species, they have also suffered the effects of climatological factors, especially the recurrent hurricanes that destroy hives and the flora on which the bees feed. Another problem facing beekeepers is *Varroa jacobsoni oudemans*, a parasite that increases the costs of honey production due to the treatment required. In addition, middlemen usually take the lion's share of the profits generated by honey produced in Tunkás. Because they have the international contacts, middlemen control the market. Local producers, who remain poorly organized and lack business know-how, have been unable to compete with these middlemen.

In response, half of the beekeepers in Tunkás have organized into two cooperatives, which enable them to receive government grants and aid to produce more honey and sell it on their own. During our fieldwork in Tunkás, the federal Ministry of Social Development (SEDESOL) awarded one of the cooperatives a grant to hire day laborers to clear paths to the hive sites in order to facilitate access. The Ministry of Rural Development also helps these cooperatives, but in a different manner. The cooperatives can propose projects to the Ministry, and the Ministry will lend (at low interest) 50 percent of the cost for any project that it approves.

Jorge, a young, college-educated Tunkaseño whose father has twice been municipal president, claims that Tunkás is one of the towns with the highest potential for honey production in Yucatán. He says it is a shame that the "honey culture" is being lost because young Tunkaseños want to earn "easy money" through migration to the United States. Only 3 percent of our interviewees claim to be part of the apiculture sector. The reason for migrants' low representation in this sector is the higher propensity of young people to migrate. Most workers in Tunkás's apiculture industry today are either middle-aged or older; the average beekeeper in Yucatán is a 47-year-old male of Maya descent with five years of primary schooling (Güemes-Ricalde et al. 2003).

Apiculture is a family tradition that has been on the decline due to the risks involved in working with bees and to the resulting preference of young people to migrate from Tunkás as soon as they finish high school. A typical case is that of Don Atalo, a man in his 50s who owns fourteen beehives that produce an average of 300 kilos of honey per month. At the prevailing market price of US$1.40 per kilo, he has a monthly income of about US$420 during the months of honey production (January to June). Atalo's family has been working with bees for as long as he can remember. He learned from his father, his father learned from his grandfather, and so on. Yet Atalo's son decided not to practice apiculture and instead migrated to Cancún and then, eight years ago, to the United States. Atalo and his wife used to live in a palm-roofed shack; now, thanks to remittances sent by their son, they have a modern, four-bedroom concrete house. The money Atalo earns from honey is used for food and other necessities, while his son's remittances are used to buy materials for house construction.

The community would do well to direct surplus remittances toward purchasing the center for collecting and processing honey, thereby eliminating the middlemen from honey commercialization and increasing benefits to producers. Surplus remittances could also be used to establish factories to process and label the honey produced by the townspeople, adding value and returning a substantial profit to Tunkás's beekeepers and investors. The following section will analyze remittance trends and community associations to see if such a project would be viable in Tunkás.

REMITTANCES IN THE LOCAL ECONOMY

In order to support their families, international migrants usually send much of the money they earn back home, and remittances are the main source of income for many families. The total amount of remittances that Mexican migrants in the United States sent home in 2005 has been estimated at US$20 billion, a 21 percent increase over 2004. This is more than Mexico's total tourism revenues for that year and equals 71 percent of Mexico's 2004 petroleum exports (Banco de México 2005: 43–47).

This section focuses on three aspects of remittances to Tunkás. The first is the factors that make it more likely that a migrant will send money and that determine how much money he or she will send. Second, we discuss how remittances are used in Tunkás at the household level. And third, we discuss the collective use of remittances in Tunkás through the 3 x 1 Program.

Remittance-Sending Behavior

The majority of migrants interviewed (86 percent) sent money to family members in Tunkás during their most recent stay in the United States. The typical remitter is a 30-year-old married male. The median amount sent is US$200 per month per migrant, with 55 percent of migrants remitting money at least once every two weeks. The proportion of migrants who send money home is larger in Tunkás than in two traditional migrant-sending towns—Tlacuitapa, Jalisco, and Las Ánimas,

Zacatecas—where 72 percent of migrants remitted during their most recent stay in the United States. Tunkaseños remit less per transaction than Animeños and Tlacuitapeños, but Tunkaseños send money twice as frequently as migrants from these other communities.

The amount of time a migrant spends in the United States and the level of contact maintained with family members in the home community were the strongest determinants of how much money a migrant would send to his or her hometown. To our surprise, salary was not a significant factor in determining how much money a migrant remitted. About 53 percent of all migrants who sent money home remitted $200 or less per month. This amount did not vary by income level, and remittances as a percentage of salary correlated negatively with income level. The more money a migrant makes in the United States, the lower the portion of that income is sent back home (see figure 8.2).

Figure 8.2 Remittances as Percentage of Salary Earned in United States

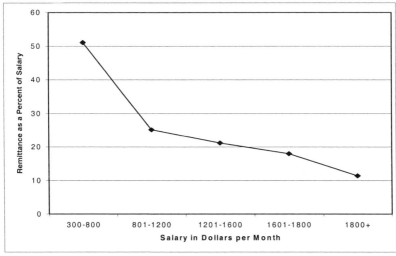

A possible explanation for this negative correlation is that migrants with shorter migration histories tend to earn less but remit more of their income because their families in Mexico have a more pressing need for this money to cover household and other expenses that sent the migrant abroad in the first place. In contrast, migrants who receive higher salaries stay in the United States longer, which suggests that they have more stable jobs, are more settled, and hence remit less. In support of this supposition, we found that the percentage of U.S.-earned income remitted by migrants who earned between US$300 and $800 a month was twice as high in Tunkás as in Tlacuitapa and Las Ánimas. Because Tlacuitapa and Las Ánimas have been sending migrants abroad for many years, their emigrants are more settled and have better-paying U.S. jobs than migrants from Tunkás.

In a cross-national survey of remittance behavior by Latin American immigrants, Briant Linsay Lowell and Rodolfo O. de la Garza (2002) found that for every 1 percent increase in time spent in the United States, the likelihood of remitting decreases by 2 percent. Table 8.1 shows that 26 percent of Tunkaseño migrants who have lived in the United States for less than three years remit more than $400 a month, while only 17 percent of those who have lived in the United States for more than seven years remit at this level. Again, the explanation seems to be that migrants who stay longer tend to have more stable jobs and are more settled, including having their families with them in the United States. According to Jorge Durand et al. (1996), a migrant is less likely to remit if he or she is accompanied by a spouse. Being unaccompanied by a spouse is a strong indicator of a short tenure and less stability in the United States and a strong indicator that a migrant is more likely to remit.

Table 8.1 Shares of Migrants Remitting at Different Levels, by Time in United States (percentages)

Time Lived in United States	Monthly Remittances (US$)		
	$1–$200	$201–$400	$401+
0–3 years	57%	17%	26%
4–6 years	45%	27%	28%
7+ years	60%	23%	17%

N = 239; p = 0.446.

Another indicator of a short stay—and a high probability to remit more—is the level of contact with family members back home. Migrants who are not accompanied by spouses usually contact their hometowns more frequently than do accompanied migrants, and those who maintain more frequent contact tend to remit more (see table 8.2). Of those migrants who contact their families once a week, 32 percent remit more than $500 a month, whereas only 6 percent of migrants who contact their families once a month remit more than $500 a month.[2]

Table 8.2 Shares of Migrants Remitting at Different Levels, by Level of Contact with Family in Tunkás

Level of Contact	Monthly Remittance Amount (US$)			
	$1–250	$251–500	$501–750	$751+
Once a week	32%	36%	7%	25%
Every two weeks	65%	21%	4%	10%
Once a month	79%	15%	1%	5%

N = 322; p = 0.00.

Use of Remittances and Local Development

Scholars have long argued whether out-migration promotes dependency or development in migrants' home communities. Central to this argument is the use of remittances. Those who argue that out-migration creates dependency suggest that remittances are used to purchase consumer goods and to cover the costs of daily life, and therefore do not contribute to local economic development. Alternatively, those who argue that out-migration spurs development in hometowns that receive remittances focus on the impact that remittances have on investment and small businesses within the town (Cohen 2004: 101).

In Tunkás, the use of remittances seems to follow the dependency pattern. Nearly three-quarters of households that receive remittances use these funds primarily for household expenses and sustenance. Only 13 percent of households that receive remittances use them mainly for construction of a new home or renovation of an existing home (see figure 8.3). Even though new construction creates jobs, these jobs are temporary and do not generate sustainable, long-term employment for residents. As mentioned above, jobs in construction are not sufficient in number to alter the pattern of migration to the United States.

---

[2] The majority of migrants (84 percent) contact their families by telephone.

Figure 8.3 Primary Use of Remittances

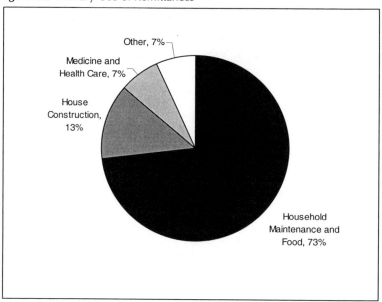

However, remittances used for consumption do generate positive effects in the communities. Remittances ease the financial constraints households face because of underdeveloped markets and the lack of well-paid jobs in their communities. Also, remittances are often instrumental in paying for education and health care, thus improving human capital (United Nations 2006). In Tunkás, 7 percent of respondents stated that remittances were used mainly for health care, while only 2 percent of households used the bulk of their remittances to cover education costs. Of course, recipients who use remittances in this way become accustomed to an enhanced supply of goods and services, and this creates continuing dependence on money earned abroad.

Furthermore, fewer than 1 percent of households in Tunkás use most of their remittances to establish a business. The businesses we found in the town included a boutique, an Internet café, a water purification service, and an in-home butcher shop. Unfortunately, we were not able to gather information on any of the businesses except for the butcher shop. This shop is owned by Arcenio, a 76-year-old former bracero, who recalled his time in the United States:

> I sent about 100 dollars home every week via money or-
> der. That money bought this lot and built this house. The
> money I earned in the United States gave me the capital
> to build up our business. With that money, I bought some
> bees, and thanks to the success of my bee business, I built
> this house. I eventually had 180 hives.

Within one year of investing in apiculture, Arcenio was able to build his home and establish his butcher shop. He eventually stopped work-ing as a beekeeper and focused entirely on the butcher shop. However, despite his economic success, Arcenio's investment has had little im-pact on local economic development.

Collective Use of Remittances: The 3 x 1 Program

The 3 x 1 Program goes beyond the traditional use of remittances to households in Tunkás. This national program, which began in Zacate-cas in the mid-1980s, uses remittances collectively to support basic infrastructure development in migrants' home communities. The pro-gram began as a joint effort between migrants and their hometown municipal governments, but it has now grown to include the state and federal levels of government as well. Under the program, each dollar a migrant contributes toward approved projects is matched by the mu-nicipal, state, and federal governments.

The 3 x 1 Program reached Yucatán in 2004 through a collaboration with the migrant services department of the Institute for Development of Maya Culture (Instituto para el Desarrollo de la Cultura Maya del Estado de Yucatán, or INDEMAYA). During its first year, five pro-grams were established in the state that focused on constructing schools, roads, and hospitals. In Tunkás, in contrast, the program has developed a recreational facility (a softball field) rather than basic infra-structure.

Only 33 percent of the migrants we interviewed knew about the 3 x 1 Program in Tunkás (though 70 percent of these knew about the softball field). Participation in the program was even lower; only twenty-seven Tunkaseños had filed a formal application to participate in it.

The first 3 x 1 project proposed in Tunkás was a cultural center, suggested by migrants' family members who remained in Tunkás. However, because the Tunkaseño migrants in Los Angeles and Anaheim failed to make a formal petition to initiate the project, it did not go forward. Then in 2005, migrants' families suggested a softball field. This suggestion was approved by municipal authorities and taken to INDEMAYA, which promoted the project to the migrants in California. Twenty-seven Tunkaseños decided to participate and filed the formal application for matching funds.

The total cost of the field, US$118,000,[3] was divided equally between the migrants/migrant families and the federal, state, and municipal governments. In order to amass the community's share, migrant remittances were supplemented with monies raised through fund-raisers, raffles, and church festivals in both Tunkás and California. Because this 3 x 1 project focused on recreation, its impact on job creation and infrastructure development was much weaker than the effects seen in towns that focused their 3 x 1 efforts on infrastructure. However, the softball field has been a great success, and hopefully in the future the 3 x 1 Program will be used in a way that generates jobs in Tunkás and thus reduces out-migration to the United States.

CONCLUSION

Our data demonstrate that Tunkaseños' negative perceptions about their local opportunity structure influence their decisions to migrate internationally. Nearly all Tunkaseños believe that a more plentiful supply of jobs would encourage would-be migrants to remain in Tunkás. We believe that the best strategy to this end would be to focus government efforts on making Tunkás a honey production center. A key step would be to establish a technical school in the town, where young people could learn how to increase local agricultural productivity. The government could support this construction and also offer scholarships to Tunkaseños to study business and marketing principles

---

[3] This amount included leveling the ground, constructing bleachers and restrooms, paving the roads around the field, and installing sprinklers, public lightning, and turf.

in the state capital that could then be applied in the honey business. Given the international demand for its honey, Tunkás, unlike some other new migrant-sending communities, has significant potential to develop without migration.

Tunkaseños could benefit greatly from access to an in-town financial institution. The government and Coopera could conduct financial literacy seminars to educate the townspeople to make best use of financial services. Surplus remittances deposited in savings accounts could support business loans to other Tunkaseños (not necessarily Coopera members), creating an investment climate that would begin turning the wheels of development by creating jobs and maintaining a money flow.

Through remittances, Tunkaseños can ease financial constraints and live more comfortable lives. Remittances increase human capital and purchasing power in Tunkás. With remittances, families can build better homes or cover their costs of living. Yet despite these positive effects, remittances have created a sense of dependency in the town as recipients of remittances grow accustomed to the goods and services they now consume with money earned abroad. A viable option for helping the Tunkás economy would be to invest remittances in job-generating projects that might allow people to remain in their home community.

References

Banco de México. 2005. *Informe Anual*. http://www.banxico.org.mx/eInfoFinanciera/DoctosBM/{B98D5BE6-A6AE-469F-B375-307D69123262.pdf.

Cohen, Jeffrey. 2004. *The Culture of Migration in Southern Mexico*. Austin, TX: University of Texas Press.

Durand, Jorge, William Kandel, Emilio A. Parrado, and Douglas S. Massey. 1996. "International Migration and Development in Mexican Communities," *Demography* 33, no. 2: 249–64.

Güemes-Ricalde, Francisco J., Carlos Echazarreta-González, Rogel Villanueva-G., Juan Manuel Pat-Fernández, and Regino Gómez-Álvarez. 2003. "La apicultura en la península de Yucatán: actividad de subsistencia en un entorno globalizado," *Revista Mexicana del Caribe* 8, no. 16: 117–32. http://www.recaribe.uqroo.mx/recaribe/sitio/contenidos/16/4guemes.pdf.

Lowell, Briant Lindsay, and Rodolfo O. de la Garza. 2002. "A New Phase in the Story of Remittances." In *Sending Money Home*, ed. Rodolfo O. de la Garza and Briant Lindsay Lowell. New York: Rowman and Littlefield.

Reichert, Joshua S. 1982. "The Migrant Syndrome: Seasonal U.S. Wage Labor and Rural Development in Central Mexico," *Human Organization* 40, no. 1 (Spring): 56–66.

United Nations General Assembly. 2006. "Globalization and Interdependence: International Migration and Development." Report of the Secretary General, sixtieth session, agenda item 54(c), May.

Traditional Mayan dance in which the head of a pig is carried through the town, performed during Tunkás's annual patron saint fiesta, February 2006.

9 Migration and Ethnicity

BLAIR LYMAN, MARÍA DE JESÚS CEN MONTUY, AND
EDITH TEJEDA SANDOVAL

Most scholarship on Mexican migration to the United States has focused on mestizo immigrants.[1] The growing interest in indigenous migration reflects the incorporation of new areas in southeastern Mexico into the U.S.-bound migration stream. The wave of Yucatecan migrants to the United States in the past thirty years has added a new dimension—an indigenous Maya identity—to the Mexican migratory experience. Contrary to a widely held perception that the Maya culture is dead, some eight million people today speak Maya in parts of Mexico, Guatemala, Belize, Honduras, and Nicaragua. Sixty-two percent of the residents of Tunkás speak at least some Maya (INEGI 2000).

The present study seeks to expand the literature on indigenous Mexican migration by examining the interplay between Tunkaseño migrants' identities, their roots in identity formation and categorization in Yucatán, and the effects of ethnic difference on the experiences of Yucatecos in Southern California. Our findings suggest that the ambiguity about migration's impacts on Mayan customs that we encountered in our fieldwork reflects the recentness of Tunkaseño migration to the United States. In addition, the self-identity, Maya language use, and interethnic relations of Tunkaseño migrants in the United States are shaped by the lack of interethnic conflict in Tunkás.

---

[1] The principal exceptions are the work on mostly Mixtec and Zapotec migrants from Oaxaca (see, for example, Kearney 1995; Fox and Rivera-Salgado 2004; Stephen 2004, 2007) and scattered studies on other indigenous migrant communities like the Purépecha in Michoacán (Dinerman 1982).

YUCATECAN MAYA IDENTITY

The category of "Maya" is ambiguous, given that cultural traditions can be invented, reconstructed, and appropriated. The Maya are a diverse and heterogeneous group, notwithstanding what Quetzil Castañeda calls an "assumption of an essential unity of ethnic, cultural, and social identity between all Maya as construed by 'Western imagination'" (Castañeda 2004: 37). Fundamentally, none of Mexico's indigenous cultures should be considered as an internally homogenous system. There is no standard form of being Nahua, Maya, or Chinanteco. Each of these denominations is created by socially heterogeneous clusters grouped around linguistic and cultural commonalities (Bartolomé 1997: 50).

Many contemporary anthropologists have argued that Maya culture is invented, imposed by outsiders and reproduced for tourists' pleasure to generate national and personal income in places like Chichen Itza, Yucatán's most famous archaeological site (Hervik 1999: 59). A *maya huinic* (Mayan man) does not think of himself as a builder of pyramids. Instead, he thinks of himself as a peasant or worker, neither of which signifies the loss of being Maya. Mayan identity need not refer to a specific historical moment. Rather, it is the current state of a tradition that could develop an idealized image of itself and of its past. In various studies, inhabitants of the Yucatán Peninsula are called "Yucatecan Maya." Gutiérrez Estévez argues that Yucatecos do not call themselves Maya, but use the terms mestizo, *macehual*, or *mayero*. The last term is generally used for those who know and use Maya as their native language (Gutiérrez Estévez 1992: 422). In this sense, the Maya language is a means of identification among Maya speakers and a symbol of identity (Rendón 1992: 32). In sum, "Maya" represents a vast category that includes all inhabitants of the Yucatán Peninsula who speak Maya.

The Ethnic Context of Yucatán

Perhaps one of the most influential and well-known historical events related to the Yucatán Maya is the Caste War of 1847–1901. Though some scholars have viewed the Caste War as an ethnic conflict in which the Yucatecan Maya fought solely to defend their culture against the Spanish-speaking descendants of the conquerors, there is much debate about the reasoning and formation of the resistance (Gabbert 2004a: 91).

One argument posits that the Caste War was a racial conflict in which indigenous Maya struggled for autonomy and independence from the state of Yucatán, resulting in one of the longest indigenous resistance movements in the Americas (Juárez 2002: 38). Other scholars postulate that the Caste War enabled the "emergence of an ethnic consciousness among the rebels whereas before there was no such identification by those we call Maya today." According to this view, neither side of the conflict was "composed in an ethnically exclusive fashion" but was, in fact, heterogeneous (Hostettler 2004: 189).

Whether the Caste War reflects the creation of a Maya identity in the face of opposition or simply the defense of a preexisting Maya identity, it remains significant in the social policies that the Mexican government developed to avoid future ethnic conflict. The government developed various indigenous education projects in the early 1900s as a way to assimilate, civilize, reform, and control populations that otherwise might join rebellions such as the Caste War and the Mexican Revolution (Eiss 2004: 122). The indigenous education project was connected to a much broader cause of assimilating indigenous populations into a reconstructed Mexican *patria*: to erase ethnic differences and replace them with a "spirit of national sameness" (Eiss 2004: 120). Although these education projects met great resistance, this resistance was not in defense of Maya culture, but instead reflected political, economic, and nonethnic cultural negotiations (Fallaw 2004: 152).

The various government programs and policies to Hispanicize the indigenous Yucatecan Maya contributed to the dramatically increasing number of Spanish speakers and decreasing percentage of Maya speakers in Yucatán during the twentieth century. Though several recent developments, such as the establishment of radio transmissions in Maya, have supported a growing presence of Maya in the public sphere, the future of the Maya language ultimately will depend on its attractiveness to young people (Gabbert 2004b: 109).

IMPACTS OF MIGRATION ON TUNKASEÑO CULTURE, ETHNICITY, AND IDENTITY

Our research in Tunkás demonstrates the complexity of ethnic definition and self-identification, resulting in ambivalent attitudes toward migration and its impacts on the town. When asked how they identified themselves, only 15 percent of Tunkaseños with U.S. migration experience, 12 percent of internal migrants, and 13 percent of nonmigrants chose Maya as their first group association, behind Yucatecan and Mexican (see table 9.1). Yet the Tunkaseños we interviewed frequently claimed that *"todos somos mayas"* (We are all Mayans).

Table 9.1 Primary Self-Identification by U.S. Migrants, Internal Migrants, and Nonmigrants

Identifier	U.S. Migrants	Internal Migrants	Nonmigrants
Maya	15%	12%	13%
Yucatecan	54%	47%	52%
Mexican	19%	20%	18%
Latin American	3%	2%	2%
Religious affiliation	9%	19%	15%

N = 558; p = 0.408.

This phenomenon of labeling oneself Yucatecan in one context and Maya in another could reflect the "situational identity" proposed by Jonathan Okamura, in which the social situation shapes the way a person self-identifies. An individual may choose to identify with one of a number of social (not necessarily ethnic) identities depending on the social setting and the perceived advantage or disadvantage. "Rather than place a dominant emphasis on ethnicity in his behavior, the actor may consider it in his interest to obscure rather than to assert his ethnic identity in a given situation so that the relationship proceeds in terms of other social statutes he holds" (Okamura 1981: 455).

While Tunkaseños seemed equally proud of being Maya, Yucatecan, and Mexican, to categorize oneself as Maya in Yucatán may not have as much political and social significance as asserting an indigenous identity elsewhere. As Castañeda explains, "Unlike Guatemala and Chiapas, ethnicity is not polarized in Yucatán. As impossible as it seems ... 'Maya ethnicity' is not polarized against another ethnicity—such as Ladinos or Mestizos" (2004: 52). This could be a consequence of a less confrontational relationship between indigenous and nonindigenous people in Yucatán today, as opposed to the antagonism that still exists between these two groups in Guatemala and Chiapas.

It should also be noted that the relatively higher numbers who self-identified as Yucatecan or Mexican rather than Maya were responding to a specific survey question: "To which group do you think you most belong?" Respondents were given five options: Latin American, Mexican, Yucatecan, Mayan, and Religious, in that order. Their answers— mainly "Yucatecan" and "Mexican"—contrast with their self-identification as Maya in our life-history interviews, when respondents were encouraged to speak more expansively. Thus the survey question itself may have influenced the choices of self-identification.

The contemporary literature suggests that varied experiences with internal and international migration also lead to varied ethnic self-identifications. For example, Alicia Re Cruz's work on migration effects in the Yucatecan pueblo of Chan Kom found that migration within Yucatán yields a change in ethnic self-identification and categorization by those who stayed behind:

> As seen from Chan Kom, Cancún is a dangerous entity that de-ethnifies Maya people. The urban Maya are thought to be members of another kind of society where they fall prey to the dangers of money, stress, and physical violence. Indeed, for los Antiguos, Cancún is a threat to the traditional order. However, for the migrants, Cancún represents an inexorable transition to a new form of socio-cultural order that allows them to be more "modernized," more "civilized" than their peasant counterparts (Re Cruz 2003: 500).

Re Cruz addresses two distinct issues here. The first is the threat of societal change that the elders see resulting from migration. The second is migration's connection to larger cities and a more "modern" person, hinting that nonmigrants are less "civilized" than their counterparts. In our survey in Tunkás, 46 percent of respondents stated that migration has neither hurt nor benefited Tunkaseño culture. And of those who felt there was an effect, elders were slightly more inclined to believe that Tunkás has benefited culturally from migration (see table 9.2).

Ambiguity about migration's effects on Tunkás is also evident when we compare the attitudes of Tunkaseños with U.S. migration experi-

ence, those who have only migrated within Yucatán, and those who
have never migrated. Table 9.3 shows that almost half of all U.S. migrants and nonmigrants felt that migration has had an impact on customs in Tunkás, while the other half felt there was no effect. Internal
migrants were also split, though they were more likely than the other
two groups to say that migration has affected local customs. In table 9.4
we see that about half of those who believed that migration did have an
effect on customs in Tunkás saw this effect as positive, while half said
that the impact was negative.

Table 9.2 Migration's Effect on Culture, by Age of Respondent

Migration's Effect	Age of Respondent	
	Under 30	Over 30
Beneficial	49%	57%
Harmful	51%	43%

$N = 241; p = 0.250.$

Table 9.3 Effect of Migration Experience on Change in Customs

Migration's Effect	U.S. Migrants	Internal Migrants	Nonmigrants
"Migration has *no* effect on customs"	53%	43%	54%
"Migration has an effect on customs"	47%	57%	46%

$N = 513; p = 0.303.$

Table 9.4 Evaluation of Migration Effects, by Respondent's Migration Experience

Evaluation	U.S. Migrants	Internal-only Migrants	Nonmigrants
Positive	49%	53%	56%
Negative	51%	47%	44%

$N = 244; p = 0.693.$

The somewhat surprising congruence of opinion across groups on
how migration is influencing the culture of Tunkás could reflect the fact
that migrants themselves are sharply ambivalent about the effects of
their own migrations, particularly when they observe changes in their
children. As Leslie Reese noted, "the host country exemplifies both

material good and moral decay" (2001: 456). These positive and negative influences contribute to the selective adoption of U.S. customs and values. Among Tunkaseño migrants, the same fraction (23 percent) said that migration was hurting/benefiting the customs of Tunkás.

The perceived beneficial and deleterious consequences of migration were quite varied among our interviewees. An enrichment of traditions was the most frequently cited benefit of migration (16 percent of responses). Among those who felt that migration had hurt Tunkaseño culture, no single problem stood out as the source of concern, but common responses included increased alcoholism (mentioned by ten of fifty-nine respondents); changes in language use and dress (each noted by eight respondents); and increased drug use and less cohesion in the community (each mentioned by seven respondents). This range of responses reflects the ambiguity within the community—not only in terms of *whether* migration has benefited or harmed culture and customs in Tunkás, but also *how* they have been affected.

Maya Language Use in Tunkás

One quite visible change in Tunkás in recent years is the steady decline in the use of the Maya language and in its acquisition by the younger generation. Re Cruz's observation of the association of "Maya" with "uncivilized" suggests one possible explanation for the low numbers of Tunkaseños who self-identify as Maya. The perceived link between the Maya language and economic backwardness is reflected in the low percentage of younger Tunkaseños able to speak Maya. While 90 percent of Tunkaseños between the age of 45 and 60 speak Maya, only 37 percent of those between the ages of 15 and 29 do so, and the fraction is even lower for Tunkaseños younger than 15 years of age. The fact that young children are not learning Maya has been documented throughout Maya territory. One scholar noted that "all of the languages in this family [Maya] show signs of language loss, principally because of the fact that children in at least some of the communities in which each language is spoken are no longer learning the language" (England 2003: 1). Many factors account for language loss in Yucatán, but at the forefront are the government's Mexicanization project and internal and international migration. Tunkaseños have been compelled to speak Spanish in the new economic markets to which they have migrated.

According to several of our informants, poorer Tunkaseños do not teach the Maya language to their children because they see it as connoting a lack of education. When asked whether some Tunkaseños wanted their children to speak only Spanish, Efrén, a nonmigrant in his forties, responded, "Yes, the majority. They don't want them to continue speaking Maya because they say that a person who speaks Maya doesn't study. They are *masiwales*, people who don't know anything." Many believe that the ability to speak Maya will not be a usable skill for their children, who will eventually migrate. Efrén explains, "Mostly from the outskirts, the *ranchitos*, they're the ones that don't want to speak Maya. They say that when they leave the town, they are going to go to the city, and there they won't speak Maya. That is why they don't want their children to learn Maya."

Still, the Maya language can be a source of pride and a reaffirmation of the migrants' Tunkaseño identity. Many express their identity by drawing a distinction between those who never left Tunkás and those who have migrated. When Tunkaseño migrants return home, they become the "other." The act of crossing the border makes them different, yet they do not lose their status as "Tunkaseños." Upon their return, the migrants look to reactivate their identity as part of a collective, but with certain elements that distinguish them as migrants. In other words, they redefine their identity to legitimize their membership in their native community. As one of our informants explained:

> I was born and raised in Tunkás, and my children were born here, but I had to go to the United States. There was no money and I left, but I couldn't stand being so far away for so long, so I returned. I was there for a few years and returned. I like Tunkás, I like my house. Then two of my children left and they live over there now; others live here. But they don't forget where they are from; we are from Tunkás. Yes, that is something to be proud of, but others disagree. Those who go over there, they forget where they were born. I don't forget. I speak Maya here in Tunkás and everywhere. I'm not ashamed of it.

> There are *paisanos* [other Yucatecos] that I met over there,
> and they recognized that I was from Tunkás. I like it that
> way, that they know where I come from.

Thus, speaking Maya is a strategic way for migrants to reincorporate into the Maya-speaking Tunkaseño community. The contrast regarding the use of the Maya language in Tunkás is between those who fear that Maya will mark their children as backward and uneducated and those who see in the Maya language a tool for reintegrating to or reaffirming their Tunkaseño identity.

Cultural Changes in Tunkás due to Migration

Language is part of a larger cultural constellation that is affected by migration. The influence of out-migration is also visible, for example, in the behavior of children in and out of school. A teacher in the town's primary school noted that many students, from both migrant and non-migrant families, are open-minded and socially liberal. She noted that students frequent a cave on the outskirts of Tunkás, where they kiss and engage in other "liberal" behaviors that she attributes to influences exerted by people from outside Tunkás. She also saw marked behavioral differences between students whose parents live in the United States and those whose parents are in Tunkás.

> The child whose father is absent wants to call attention to
> himself. For example, I have a student who is extremely
> rude. So I asked him, "What? Does nobody love you?"
> And he responded, "No." He didn't know the meaning of
> love. His parents were in the United States, and he was
> living with his sister.

In stating that this student "didn't know the meaning of love," the teacher hints at emotional instability in addition to discipline problems among students whose parents are out of the country. Although children of migrants have more resources, such as school supplies, they also show more emotional instability, typically manifested in aggression toward other children.

The annual fiesta provides perhaps the clearest example of Tunka-seños' ambivalence about the effects of migration in the town. This fiesta is a time when Tunkaseño identity is reinforced and migrants are heralded with processions of fraternal organizations like the Gremio de Braceros, celebrating migrants returning from *el norte*. At the same time that they celebrate their unity and "sameness" with other Tunkaseños, migrants are emphasizing their differences through their Americanized dress, music, and speech. One Tunkaseño expressed distaste for the changes: "Some return as *cholos*[2] and tell those who have never been to California to dress like them. Many people copy them even though they've never been to California."

These perceptions are important because the fiesta is a place where people assert their identity as Tunkaseños and where local, regional, and national pride come together. As Paul Eiss (2002: 297) noted, for "wealthier pueblo residents, the *gremios* hold out the prospect of social advancement through the legitimacy and status afforded by 'traditional' Yucatecan cultural practices and through multifarious acts of conspicuous consumption associated with the fiestas." In Tunkás, such wealth comes from remittances that migrants send home or bring with them when they return at fiesta time. With 38 percent of migrants in the United States sending money home for public celebrations, these traditional fiestas have become more extravagant, and alcohol consumption during the fiestas has increased.

Our schoolteacher informant observed that many students who return to school after spending time with returning migrant family members exhibit more behavioral problems, such as cursing and rudeness. An elderly Tunkaseño complained that many returning migrants fill their refrigerators only with beer—no food—for the duration of the fiesta. A local doctor believes that the increase in alcoholism in Tunkás is directly related to migration (see chapter 11 in this volume), claiming that returning migrants, who have more money to spend, drink more than those who never left.

---

[2] *Cholo* translates roughly as "gang member" or "homeboy" (Smith 1992).

TUNKASEÑO IDENTITY AND ETHNICITY IN THE UNITED STATES

Although Yucatán was the site of the Caste War, there is relatively little interethnic conflict in the state today. The lack of antagonism between Mayas and non-Mayas has eased the integration of many Tunkaseño migrants into the broader Mexican migrant community. We argue that the perceived relationship between indigenous and nonindigenous migrants and the self-categorization of Tunkaseño migrants are direct consequences of perceptions of identity and discrimination that Tunkaseños bring from home.

Tunkaseño Migrant Identity

The literature on ethnic identity and immigrant integration clusters around two seemingly opposed viewpoints. On one side are studies that focus on Mexican immigrants' successful assimilation into the broader U.S. society (Waters and Jiménez 2005; Alba and Nee 1997). On the other side are scholars who point to the role that transnationalism plays in retaining cultural and ethnic distinctiveness among immigrant groups in their new environments (Popkin 1999; Roberts, Frank, and Lozano-Ascencio 1999). Transnational communities are described as social spaces that migrants can appropriate and transform into a new kind of home that extends across national boundaries. Indigenous immigrants from Oaxaca and Guatemala have established transnational communities that have created cohesion, strengthened ethnic identity, and eased migrants' homesickness. Within the Kanjobal immigrant community in Los Angeles, the pan-Mayan movement in Guatemala[3] has spurred a "trend towards re-enacting ancestral customs in the context of contemporary cultural events" (Popkin 1999: 280). The pan-Mayan movement's promotion of indigenous culture gives pride, strength, and support to communities of indigenous Guatemalan immigrants, who collaborate with the movement's leaders in their home country.

---

[3] The pan-Mayan movement is focused on promoting indigenous scholarship, the mobilization of ethnic markers, the implementation of agricultural extension programs, and the promotion of national cultural rights legislation in the National Assembly (Popkin 1999: 279).

The Tunkaseño community in Southern California has also organized transnationally, as demonstrated by its participation in the 3 x 1 Program (see chapter 8, this volume) and the creation of the Gremio de Braceros. In contrast to the Mayas of Guatemala or Mixtecs from Oaxaca, Tunkaseños' organizations are not specifically for migrant political mobilization, nor were they created to reproduce or reaffirm cultural distinctiveness and pride. Mixtec and Zapotec migrants have created strong social and political organizations in both their home and host communities, drawing on social capital acquired from their experience with the *cargo* and self-governing systems of Oaxaca. In contrast, because of the newness of migration from Yucatán to the United States and the absence of Yucatecan Maya–centered social and political organizations in Southern California, the Tunkaseño migrant community has fewer avenues for expressing and celebrating Yucatecan Maya traditions. When asked whether Tunkaseños in Southern California made an effort to reproduce Mayan cultural practices, Luis, an immigrant who has lived in Anaheim for seventeen years, responded:

> Very little. If I had met you earlier, I would've taken you to a place called Pico Rivera. Yucatecans from Oxnard, Yucatecans from San Bernardino go there to do a type of cultural event, and they dance the Yucatecan Jarana. They do this every year.... There was a lot of Yucatecan food, *panuchos, empanadas, cochinita,* and *lechón al horno....* It's very hard, like the Aztecs. There aren't any Aztecs around today. Now they're mixed in. And the Maya, I think the same thing will happen to us. For example, if I speak Maya only a little and my children don't learn, it will be lost.

After Luis mentioned the one Yucatecan Maya cultural event he knew about, he immediately discussed the decline he sees in indigenous cultures, as if the former affects the latter. His assessment may be overly pessimistic, considering that many Tunkaseño immigrants continue to reproduce some of the cultural practices and behaviors that are characterized as Yucatecan, such as preparing Yucatecan foods, using hammocks, and incorporating Maya words in everyday conversation.

For Tunkaseños, the U.S. migration experience does not seem to affect their ethnic self-identification. Tunkaseños who have migrated to the United States still identify strongly with a local (Maya or Yucateco) identity (see table 9.5).

Table 9.5 Migrants' and Nonmigrants' Self-Identification

Self-Identification	Non–U.S. Migrant	U.S. Migrant
Maya or Yucateco	76%	76%
Mexican, Latin American	24%	24%

N = 487; p = 0.95.

Although Tunkaseños' self-identification may not depend on having migrated to the United States, there is a relationship between identity and settlement in that country. The longer a migrant has lived or felt established in the United States, the more likely he or she may be to identify more closely with a broader identity such as Mexican or Latin American, perhaps because this is the way they are labeled in the more ethnically diverse receiving society. Tunkaseño migrants who reported living primarily in the United States overwhelmingly identified as Mexican or Latin American as opposed to Maya or Yucateco, in contrast to Tunkaseño migrants who had been to the United States but who considered themselves still based primarily in Mexico (see table 9.6). Tunkaseño immigrants are following the pattern that emerged among Italian migrants in the early twentieth century, who, after migrating to the United States, identified themselves as Italian as opposed to giving a local village or regional identity (Cinel 1982).

Table 9.6 Self-Identification of Tunkaseño Migrants to the United States, by Place of Primary Residence

Place of Primary Residence	Self-Identification	
	Maya or Yucateco	Mexican or Latin American
Tunkás	64%	29%
United States	36%	71%

N = 195; p = 0.000.

Maya Language Use by U.S.-Based Migrants

The fact that 62 percent of Tunkaseño migrants speak Maya does not equate with their actual use of the Maya language while living in the United States. Some Tunkaseños complained that many migrants who returned home after working a few years in the United States no longer wanted to speak Maya. Efrén explained:

> Sometimes we speak in Maya, and they don't want to speak it. We poke fun at them. "You've only been over there one year, two years, and you forgot the words."... They don't forget, they just don't want to speak Maya.

This accords with the view of Luis, the Tunkaseño who has lived in Anaheim for seventeen years, when asked whether there are any Yucatecos who speak Maya in the United States:

> No, there aren't. Sometimes a few words. But it's not like we stop to speak (Maya) and say, "hey, this and that," no.... Some of us say words in Maya. But no, we don't stop and speak Maya with people.

Given that over half of the Tunkaseños surveyed speak Maya and three-fourths understand it, it seems somewhat strange that they do not commonly speak it in the United States. The low usage of Maya in the United States may be due to the fact that those who speak it are less likely to remain there than are those who speak only Spanish (see table 9.7).

Table 9.7 Ability to Speak Maya among Tunkaseño Migrants to the United States, by Place of Primary Residence

Place of Primary Residence	Can Speak Maya	Cannot Speak Maya
Tunkás	44%	25%
United States	56%	75%

$N = 394; p = 0.000.$

The fact that Maya speakers more often return to Tunkás than do Spanish speakers suggests that Maya speakers may feel a stronger attachment to their hometown. In fact, those who speak Maya are also less likely to want to legalize their status in the United States, perhaps because they do not intend to remain there (see table 9.8).

Table 9.8 Ability to Speak Maya among Tunkaseño Migrants to the United States, by Desire to Legalize Immigration Status

Desire to Legalize	Can Speak Maya	Cannot Speak Maya
No	56%	33%
Yes or already in process	44%	67%

N = 179; p = 0.005.

The decision to speak Maya in the United States can reflect both the migrant's affinity to Tunkás and, perhaps, a disconnect with the host society. Some of the Tunkaseños whom we interviewed mentioned that they spoke Maya not only when in Tunkás but also when they lived in the United States. Many, including a migrant in California, commented that they spoke Maya with their *paisanos* in the workplace:

> I speak Maya everywhere. I am from the town, and Maya is spoken in town. When I lived in Anaheim, I spoke it. They already knew over there that I was from Tunkás. At work, I spoke it since there were *paisanos*. We spoke Maya so they couldn't understand what we said. That's good, but people recognize that it is Maya. It feels so nice to speak it because you feel close to your land, your hometown, and even your home. But there are also people who are embarrassed to speak Maya. They arrive in the United States and forget where they are from. Now they only want to speak English, but I say that is wrong. For me, that is what is bad about those who leave and don't even know who they are. And they get worse because they are not even American, but they also don't want to feel Yucatecan. Those are the ones that are really messed up.

Unlike the case of the Q'anjob'al Maya from Guatemala, among whom "parents expressed a will to preserve their own language" (Fink 2003: 155), many Tunkaseños, both in Tunkás and in the United States, seemed to give little importance to teaching their children to speak

Maya. Luis, the Tunkaseño quoted above, was not taught Maya by his parents and therefore could not teach it to his children. Recent studies in Yucatán have confirmed the decline in the transmission of the Maya language from one generation to the next (Pfeiler and Zamisova 2006).

Beyond the desire to distance oneself from the negative images associated with speaking Maya, there is an economic incentive for emphasizing Spanish over Maya. In the United States, socioeconomic mobility trumps cultural reproduction, as Luis underscored when asked whether he would like his children to learn to speak a language other than Spanish and English: "I would like them to study another language, not just English and Spanish. That they study Italian or French too." Luis views Italian and French as valuable languages to learn, whereas Maya may not have the same prestige or usefulness. Tunkaseño migrants' low use of the Maya language may have eased their integration into the broader Mexican migrant community in Southern California by decreasing the differences between these two groups, as discussed in the following section.

INTERETHNIC CONFLICT AND PERCEPTIONS OF DISCRIMINATION

Recent studies of ethnic identity understand identity formation as something created through a process rather than being based strictly on the essence of cultural differences.

> Focusing on internal factors, some theories attribute the emergence and persistence of group identity to cultural commonalities. Structuralists, on the other hand, focus on the role of external factors in creating, shaping, and sustaining group identity. They attribute ethnic solidarity to a number of different factors, including economic conditions, common oppression, discrimination and racism (Bonacich 1972 and Blauner 1972, cited in Ochoa 2004: 86).

According to a structural analysis, it would seem likely that migrants' shared experience in the United States—marginalization as undocumented and racially stigmatized workers—would unite indigenous and nonindigenous Mexican immigrants alike. It might even erase some of the differentiation between these two groups that derives from the homeland.

On the other hand, studies have suggested that the racism that exists within Mexico persists in the United States, with indigenous workers placed in the most arduous and poorly paid positions, often under the supervision of the more established mestizos. And they are often called derogatory names by nonindigenous Mexican migrants (Calderón Chelius 1994; Popkin 1999). In contrast to many other indigenous migrant groups from Mexico, Tunkaseños seem to have few problems with nonindigenous Mexican migrants and have even forged friendships with non-Latinos. Tunkaseños and other Yucatecos have established baseball teams with nonindigenous Mexicans from Jalisco and Michoacán, and they often marry nonindigenous Mexican migrants, Chicanos, and other Latinos.

Although no antagonism is apparent between Tunkaseños and non-Mayan immigrants or Latinos, there are distinctions rooted in Mexico that some Tunkaseños retain while in the United States. Manuel, an older Tunkaseño migrant who has lived in the United States for many years, described the difference between Yucatecans and other Mexicans in the following terms:

> I'm not trying to speak well of my people or negatively about others, but the Yucatecans are peaceful people. Those from more northern areas of Mexico are very aggressive. In fact, you can see this in Mexico.... They carry guns on the street, they are very arrogant, and they don't care about putting a bullet in somebody. But the people from Yucatán are not fighters; they are peaceable people. The most they will do is throw a punch. It is rare to find a person from Yucatán that has the courage to kill someone. Here, you don't hear of such things, but over there [in northern Mexico] it happens every day.

The cultural and behavioral differences Tunkaseños claim to observe between Yucatecos and people from northern Mexico were not perceived to cause conflict between these groups, but they did create socially meaningful distinctions. Manuel explains how cultural differences can be a factor in choosing a marriage partner. When asked why he chose to marry a Tunkaseña instead of a woman from Jalisco, he responded:

> I've always had a good eye. Women from any country are very beautiful, but I've always noticed the culture. There are problems because of culture, their way of living, the cultural ways they were taught. If we go to El Salvador, there is a lot of war and the women there know how to carry guns. Not in my town. If we go to Guadalajara, their traditions are very nice, but we are not used to them. It is not that I am racist; it is just that I know that it is better to marry someone from one's own culture.

Here Manuel confirms that cultural differences exist, but he is careful to note that he has no problem with non-Yucatecans. One reason why Tunkaseño migrants associate easily with nonindigenous Mexicans may be the lack of perceived discrimination in Mexico. Both Tunkaseño migrants and nonmigrants feel strongly that skin color does not affect the way a person is treated in Yucatán (table 9.9), though they do feel that it is more likely to have that effect in Mexico more generally (table 9.10). The absence of perceived racial discrimination could also be due to the ethnic homogeneity of Tunkás and Yucatán, the high levels of bilingualism (according to INEGI, only 9 percent of Maya speakers in Yucatán are monolingual, and only 3 percent are monolingual in Tunkás), and acculturation to the dominant Mexican culture.

Because most Tunkaseños coming to the United States have not experienced ethnic discrimination and generally do not feel discriminated against in the United States (only 17 percent answered that they had been racially discriminated against in the United States), they feel little need to form an exclusive community and do not hesitate to socialize with non-Yucatecos and non-Mayas. Interethnic conflict has been associated with influencing identity: "the greater the level of discrimination, the more migrants will maintain a strong minority and counter-identity as a form of resistance and active opposition" (Tsuda 2003: 197). Tunkaseños' few experiences of racially based discrimination in Yucatán, in Mexico, or in the United States allow them to associate easily with people who are not Maya or Yucateco.

Table 9.9 Migrant and Nonmigrant Perceptions of Racial Discrimination in Yucatán

	Question: Does skin color affect a person's treatment in Yucatán?	
	Yes	No
Non–U.S. migrants	5%	95%
U.S. migrants	4%	96%

$N = 568; p = 0.619.$

Table 9.10 Migrant and Nonmigrant Perceptions of Racial Discrimination in Mexico

	Question: Does skin color affect a person's treatment in Mexico?	
	Yes	No
Non–U.S. migrants	18%	82%
U.S. migrants	23%	77%

$N = 555; p = 0.205.$

Many Tunkaseños also had favorable perceptions of and good relationships with Anglos in the United States. Manuel, who was quoted earlier, recalled his observations of Anglos' relations with Mexicans and Mexican immigrants and compared them to the relations between Chicanos and Mexican immigrants. "The Anglos I see are friendlier; they relate more with the people of the town. This is what most draws my attention—that the Anglos really like to relate to Latinos, while the Chicanos and Latinos, who are of Latino background, they want to discriminate against us, they want to push us aside." There is more perceived discrimination from Latinos or Chicanos who are U.S. citizens or have legal status than from Anglos. This is not to imply that there is no discrimination from Anglos, but Tunkaseños are acutely sensitive to discrimination from other Latinos, with whom they feel there should be some natural affinity. Manuel adds, "Sometimes it frustrates me to see an Anglo discriminate against a Latino, but it is very stupid for a Latino to discriminate against another Latino." Manuel's comment alludes to the fact that Tunkaseño migrants generally do not differentiate themselves from other "Latinos" and could therefore easily claim a Mexican or Latino identity.

In summary, due to the social and cultural grounding that Tunkaseño migrants bring from Tunkás, they assimilate easily into the broader Mexican migrant community and, as a consequence, may not feel the need to create a distinctly Mayan Tunkaseño community in the United States. Further, Maya speakers are less inclined to remain in the United States. These two outcomes demonstrate the importance and impact that cultural differences, sense of community, and identity have on migrant settlement behavior in the United States.

CONCLUSION

There is no consensus in Tunkás on whether or how migration has affected the local culture and customs. Some Tunkaseños see changes in migrants' use of spoken Maya, their dress, and their behaviors—changes that they attribute to foreign influences—but there have been no overt protests against these changes. The lamented decline in the use of the Maya language cannot be attributed solely to migration, of course, given that government education policies, social pressure, and the economic payoff of speaking Spanish also exert influence in this area. In general, children do not embrace the Maya language because it is not commonly spoken, except by elder Tunkaseños, and many parents are not committed to teaching it.

In the United States, migrants' experiences, ethnic expressions, and sense of identity differ tremendously between ethnic groups and relate directly to interethnic relations in their communities of origin. Because Tunkaseño migrants come from a region whose population is largely indigenous and where peaceful relations prevail between indigenous and nonindigenous residents, they are less inclined to express their ethnicity through speaking Maya in the United States. Further, the perception that racial discrimination and ethnic conflict are uncommon—in Yucatán, in Mexico generally, and in the United States—has fostered a Tunkaseño immigrant community that easily associates with non-Mayas and non-Yucatecans in the United States. Settled migrants express a connection and affiliation with the broader Mexican and La-tino community by choosing to label themselves as Mexican or Latin American rather than as Yucatecan or Mayan. On the other hand, other Tunkaseño migrants, most of whom speak Maya, demonstrate strong ties to their home community, preferring not to settle or legalize their status, thus reducing the prospect for a strong Maya cultural presence within the Tunkaseño community in Southern California.

Assuming that these trends in Tunkás and Southern California con-tinue, we foresee a settled Tunkaseño community that will continue to integrate into the broader Mexican migrant community. In Tunkás, we project that the effects of migration on Tunkaseño culture will be mini-mized because those migrants who return to live in Tunkás are the ones who are most inclined to speak Maya and may be connected more closely to Tunkaseño culture in general. Because these returning mi-grants appear less foreign than their U.S.-based counterparts, residents of Tunkás are likely to continue to tolerate well the cultural effects of migration.

References

Alba, Richard, and Victor Nee. 1997. "Rethinking Assimilation Theory for a New Era of Immigration," *International Migration Review* 31, no. 4: 826–74.

Bartolomé, Miguel Alberto. 1997. *Gente de costumbre y gente de razón: las identidades étnicas en México*. Mexico: Siglo Veintiuno.

Calderón Chelius, Leticia. 1994. "Migración indígena a Estados Unidos y la frontera norte," *El Cotidiano*.

Castañeda, Quetzil E. 2004. "We Are *Not* Indigenous!" *Journal of Latin Amer-ican Anthropology* 9, no. 1: 36–63.

Cinel, Dino. 1982. *From Italy to San Francisco: The Immigrant Experience*. Stan-ford, CA: Stanford University Press.

Dinerman, Ina. 1982. *Migrants and Stay-at-Homes: A Comparative Study of Rural Migration from Michoacán, Mexico*. La Jolla, CA: Center for U.S.-Mexican Studies, University of California, San Diego.

Eiss, Paul K. 2002. "Hunting for the Virgin: Meat, Money, and Memory in Tetiz, Yucatán," *Cultural Anthropology* 17, no. 3: 291–330.

———. 2004. "Deconstructing Indians, Reconstructing *Patria*," *Journal of Latin American Anthropology* 9, no. 1: 119–50.

England, Nora C. 2003. "Mayan Language Revival and Revitalization Politics: Linguists and Linguistic Ideologies," *American Anthropologist* 105, no. 4: 733–43.

Fallaw, Ben. 2004. "Rethinking Mayan Resistance: Changing Relations between Federal Teachers and Mayan Communities in Eastern Yucatan, 1929–1935," *Journal of Latin American Anthropology* 9, no. 1: 151–78.

Fink, Leon. 2003. *The Maya of Morgantown: Work and Community in the Nuevo New South.* Chapel Hill, NC: University of North Carolina Press.

Fox, Jonathan, and Gaspar Rivera-Salgado, eds. 2004. *Indigenous Mexican Migrants in the United States.* La Jolla, CA: Center for U.S.-Mexican Studies and Center for Comparative Immigration Studies, University of California, San Diego.

Gabbert, Wolfgang. 2004a. "Of Friends and Foes: The Caste War and Ethnicity in Yucatan," *Journal of Latin American Anthropology* 9, no. 1: 90–118.

———. 2004b. *Becoming Maya: Ethnicity and Social Inequality in Yucatán since 1500.* Tucson, AZ: University of Arizona Press.

Gutiérrez Estévez, Manuel. 1992. "Mayas y mayeros: los antepasados como otros." In *De palabra y obra en el nuevo mundo.* Vol. 1, *Imágenes interétnicas,* ed. M. León Portilla, Manuel Gutiérrez Estévez, G. H. Gossen, and J. J. Klor de Alba. Madrid: Siglo Veintiuno de España.

Hervik, Peter. 1999. *Mayan People Within and Beyond Boundaries: Social Categories and Lived Identity in Yucatán.* Amsterdam: Harwood Academic.

Hostettler, Ueli. 2004. "Rethinking Maya Identity in Yucatan, 1500–1940," *Journal of Latin American Anthropology* 9, no. 1: 187–98.

INEGI (Instituto Nacional de Estadística, Geografía e Informática). 2000. *XII Censo General de Población y Vivienda.* http://www.inegi.gob.mx.

Juárez, Ana M. 2002. "Ongoing Struggles: Mayas and Immigrants in Tourist Era Tulum," *Journal of Latin American Anthropology* 7, no. 1: 34–67.

Kearney, Michael. 1995. "The Local and the Global: The Anthropology of Globalization and Transnationalism," *Annual Review of Anthropology* 24: 547–65.

Ochoa, Gilda. 2004. *Becoming Neighbors in a Mexican Community: Power, Conflict, and Solidarity.* Austin, TX: University of Texas Press.

Okamura, Jonathan Y. 1981. "Situational Ethnicity," *Ethnic and Racial Studies* 4, no. 4: 452–65.

Pfeiler, Barbara, and Lenka Zamisova. 2006. "Bilingual Education: Strategy for Language Maintenance or Shift of Yucatec Maya?" In *Mexican In-*

digenous Languages at the Dawn of the Twenty-First Century, ed. Margarita Hidalgo. Berlin: Mouton de Gruyter.

Popkin, Eric. 1999. "Guatemalan Mayan Migration to Los Angeles: Constructing Transnational Linkages in the Context of the Settlement Process," *Ethnic and Racial Studies* 22, no. 2: 267–89.

Re Cruz, Alicia. 2003. "Milpa as an Ideological Weapon: Tourism and Maya Migration to Cancún," *Ethnohistory*.

Reese, Leslie. 2001. "Morality and Identity in Mexican Immigrant Parents' Visions of the Future," *Journal of Ethnic and Migration Studies* 27, no. 3: 455–72.

Rendón, Juan. 1992. "Notas sobre identidad, lengua y cultura." In *I Seminario sobre Identidad*, ed. Leticia Mendes y Mercado. Mexico City: Universidad Nacional Autónoma de México/Instituto de Investigaciones Antropológicas.

Roberts, Bryan, Reanne Frank, and Fernando Lozano-Ascencio. 1999. "Transnational Migrant Communities and Mexican Migration to the U.S," *Ethnic and Racial Studies* 22, no. 2: 238–66.

Smith, Robert. 1992. *Mexican Immigrant Women in New York City's Informal Economy*. New York: Columbia University–New York University Consortium.

Stephen, Lynn. 2004. "Mixtec Farmworkers in Oregon: Linking Labor and Ethnicity through Farmworker Unions and Hometown Associations." In *Indigenous Mexican Migrants in the United States*, ed. Jonathan Fox and Gaspar Rivera-Salgado. La Jolla, CA: Center for U.S.-Mexican Studies and Center for Comparative Immigration Studies, University of California, San Diego.

———. 2007. *Transborder Lives: Indigenous Oaxacans in Mexico, California, and Oregon*. Durham, NC: Duke University Press.

Tsuda, Takeyuki. 2003. *Strangers in the Ethnic Homeland: Japanese Brazilian Return Migration in Transnational Perspective*. New York: Columbia University Press.

Waters, Mary C., and Tomás Jiménez. 2005. "Assessing Immigrant Assimilation: New Empirical and Theoretical Challenges," *Annual Review of Sociology* 31: 105–25.

The Templo Evangélico Sinaí, one of three Pentecostal churches in Tunkás.

10 Migration and Religion

PAOLA GUZMÁN, ZOILA JIMÉNEZ-PACHECO, AND OSCAR RAMOS

Fireworks, brass and wind musical instruments, and the beat of a marching drum can be heard blocks away. A *gremio* is parading today in Tunkás.[1] Many more will parade throughout the week, as migrants return from the United States during the fiesta of San Tomás, Tunkás's patron saint. During the fiesta, migrants will visit with family and friends, stock their homes with items purchased in the United States, and enjoy Tunkás's familiar pace of life. Next week, the migrants will return to the United States and begin to save for next year's fiesta. As this *gremio* winds its way through town toward the central plaza and the Catholic church, it passes only blocks away from La Sinaí, a Pentecostal church whose pastor is preparing to celebrate the second anniversary of his tenure and the fiftieth anniversary of the church. La Sinaí sports new glass doors and recently renovated walls, and it is awaiting new wooden pews. Some of these expenses have been covered by church members in the United States.

For the past two decades, southern Mexico has experienced an intensification of two social trends: heavier migration to the United States and the growth of non-Catholic religious communities. In this chapter we explore the intersection of these trends in the migrant-sending community of Tunkás. Three questions are of particular interest: How do the Catholic and Protestant communities in Tunkás compare in terms of active participation in the migratory phenomenon? To what extent does Evangelicalism play a role in the decision to migrate? And how important is migration to the growth and stability of Tunkás's

---

[1] A *gremio* is an association organized along work or gender lines (such as the Gremio de Braceros or the women's *gremio*). A *gremio* meets periodically to honor the town's patron saint.

Evangelical communities, as measured by levels of conversion and religiosity?[2]

MIGRATION AND RELIGION IN YUCATÁN

Protestantism's appeal in southern Mexico lies in its relative accessibility to indigenous communities. While the Catholic Church invested authority in its clergy, which until 1965 still held Mass in Latin, nascent Protestant sects conducted their services in the Maya language and incorporated elements of indigenous religious practices into their own observances.[3] By frequently visiting people in the community, encouraging converted families who overcame alcoholism or domestic abuse to give testimony, and emphasizing the study of scripture, early Protestant pastors gave their congregations a more participatory role in their spiritual lives (Santana Rivas 1987: 126).

The hybridized continuity of indigenous religious practices in Protestant communities also helped attract converts. For example, *chaa chac*, a Mayan ritual celebrated in a cornfield at harvest time, cannot be carried out in its original form due to Protestantism's ban on idolatry. But this ceremony inspired the Protestant one that takes place in the church at harvest, when members pray for Jehovah's blessing for a good harvest (Vallado Fajardo 1989: 118).

While some Mexican towns have been home to Protestant communities since the 1800s (Bastian 1993: 38), Protestant congregations did not begin to multiply until the 1960s. Since then, increased migration has introduced Protestantism and other religious beliefs into many rural Yucatecan communities. In a study of Chan Kom, a rural Mayan pueblo in Yucatán that has recently become a source for Cancún-bound migrants, two new social categories distinguish those who adhere to Chan Kom's traditional agricultural economy and are members of the Catholic Church, now known as *los antiguos*, from those who migrate, convert to Protestantism, adopt urban clothing styles and values, and

---

[2] In southeastern Mexico, "Protestant" and "Evangelical" are generally used interchangeably, a usage we follow in this chapter.

[3] Ironically, Catholic critics of Tunkás's Evangelical communities say that Evangelicalism discourages Mayan pride, while the Catholic Church encourages it through the appropriation of Mayan practices in its rites.

are known as *los de Cancún*. Alicia Re Cruz (1998: 89–91) tells of a woman from Chan Kom who was ostracized after her husband migrated. The wife eventually migrated too and converted to Mormonism. In Chan Kom, Catholics blame such conversions to Protestantism on migration and consider it incompatible with their traditionally Catholic, peasant society.

RELIGION AND MIGRATION IN TUNKÁS

Unlike the linkages Re Cruz found between migration and the rise of Evangelicalism in Chan Kom, migration from Tunkás seems to have no statistical relationship to conversion to Evangelicalism. The Evangelical population of Tunkás numbers over 900—nearly a quarter of all residents—but only 28 percent of Evangelicals with migration experience (internal or international) and 26 percent of Evangelicals without migration experience are converts. This means that most Evangelicals, regardless of migratory experience, were born into Evangelical families. Tunkás's long history of religious diversity keeps Protestantism from being associated too closely with the rise in migration. Like most Catholics we interviewed in Tunkás, the local priest does not think that migration is the cause of the rise of Evangelicalism:

> Yes, it's true; many belong to a Protestant congregation because they are thankful to God that … they have stopped drinking. And, yes, there are many that dedicate themselves to reading the Bible and learning it by memory. And I ask myself, why isn't there any of that in this church? But I don't think it has anything to do with migration. Protestantism has been around for a long time.

The Presbyterian church in Tunkás, founded in 1927 by missionaries from Mérida, experienced a period of persecution from the Catholic church, which forced its earliest members to hold their meetings in secret in caves outside the town. Over time, the congregation grew and a local benefactor donated a house where services could be held. The congregation eventually built a church just two blocks from the Catholic church and the central plaza.

La Sinaí is the second-oldest Protestant church and the oldest of Tunkás's three Pentecostal churches. Dating from 1956, it was founded by an incipient congregation that found itself without a pastor and adopted a Pentecostal leader from Mérida. The church is sited between the Catholic church and the entrance to Tunkás, in the relatively wealthy town center. La Sinaí found stability during one pastor's thirty-three year tenure (1971–2004), which allowed the church to establish a Pentecostal presence in Tunkás, but this period also saw the splintering of the congregation into three separate groups. The original pastor's replacement was a nineteen-year-old who had only recently finished his seminary training.

The second Pentecostal church, founded in 1984, is located far from La Sinaí, on the outskirts of Tunkás, in an area of recently constructed, less prosperous houses. This congregation has had a single pastor, the only woman religious leader in Tunkás, who has been with the church since 1986. Tunkás's third Pentecostal church, Aposento Alto, was established in 1991, reportedly to accommodate people who had left the town's other two Pentecostal churches for various reasons. The church building is still under construction, awaiting further donations from congregants.

There are few socioeconomic differences between Catholics and Evangelicals in Tunkás in terms of education, median monthly income, and landownership (see table 10.1 for a summary of select characteristics of Catholics and Evangelicals in Tunkás). The Evangelicals' tendency to consume less alcohol is a major distinction they draw between themselves and Catholics. Because of the heavy alcohol consumption that accompanies the town's annual fiesta, Evangelical leaders say that they discourage their congregations from attending, although in general Evangelicals refrain from participating in nonreligious events. Despite theological differences, there is little evidence of the hostility between Protestants and Catholics that has marked relations in some Mexican and Central American communities. Even the local priest said that part of Evangelicalism's attraction is a tangible improvement in members' behavior, and he seemed to admire the Evangelicals' devotion to Bible study.

Table 10.1 Summary Profiles of Religious Groups in Tunkás

	Catholics	Evangelicals
Percentage of population	77%	23%
Median monthly income	US$280	$200
Landownership	61%	66%
Ever used alcohol	86%	74%
Median years of education	6	6
Migrated to U.S. at least once	35%	34%
Had family in U.S. prior to migrating	81%	80%
Share of U.S. migrants who send money home	86%	89%
Median monthly remittance by U.S. migrants	US$200	$200
Sent money home for a novena or *gremio*	50%	11%
Spent five years or more in U.S.	68%	51%
Spent seven years or more in U.S.	58%	32%
Desire to stay in U.S.	36% want legal permanent residence; 19% have it	30% want legal permanent residence; 9% have it
Plan to migrate to U.S. this year	25%	25%
Religious conversion from Catholicism		28%
Post-migration church attendance		
Less frequent	42%	43%
More frequent	24%	35%
Same	34%	22%
Mean weekly church attendance		
U.S. migrants	0.38 times	1.5 times
Nonmigrants	0.56 times	1.46 times
"Where do you place yourself and your family in relation to other families, on a scale of 1 to 10, in terms of living conditions (10 being the highest)?"	5.5	5.42

ADMINISTRATIVE/RHETORICAL RESPONSES TO MIGRATION

The Catholic Church

Waves of U.S.-bound migration from Mexico in the early twentieth century prompted the Catholic Church to develop a policy to discourage emigration or at least minimize its effects. The Church was alarmed by the number of migrants who were converting to Protestantism while they were in the United States (Craig 1983: 180–81). The Church's administrative response to migration included coordinated trips by priests from sending communities to receiving communities in the United States in order to reinforce migrants' ties to their hometowns. Parish offices in both countries shared information on migrants' behavior to ensure that migrants did not return to Mexico greatly altered by U.S. culture.

The Catholic Church's view of migration as a threat to the Mexican nation eventually gave way to the perception of migration as a human right. The Church began to encourage the migration of entire families rather than see their disintegration. In the traditional migrant-sending communities of Los Altos de Jalisco, David Fitzgerald found a variety of Church initiatives designed to assist local residents as they emigrated to the United States. Migrants receive a devotional book of migration-related prayers and Church teachings to assist them in their border crossings. Local priests receive a migration policy book from their diocese, which includes a template for migrant Masses and a database containing information about emigrants from their parish in the United States (Fitzgerald 2005: 11).

Church policies like those initiated in Los Altos de Jalisco arose in response to migration's impacts on sending communities, which were largely concentrated in west-central Mexico. In southern Mexico, where residents began to migrate internationally only in recent decades, the Church's response has been less developed. Catholic leaders in Yucatán have much in common with the Catholic Church in Mexico generally in their formal stance on emigration, but they have yet to adopt the administrative practices of traditional migrant-sending states like Jalisco. "We would prefer they stay," said the archbishop of Yucatán, "but the fact is that they go." While defending people's decision to migrate as a human right, the Catholic Church is wary of migration's disintegrative effect on families. "Mary and Joseph were migrants, but they went together," said Padre Alejandro, the priest who serves Tunkás (Tunkás is part of a much larger area that is served by a single priest). He recommends that when there is a necessity to migrate, families leave together in order to maintain a united family, a stance that echoes the Church's position in more established migration source states like Jalisco as well as the views of the archbishop of Yucatán.

The failure of the Catholic church in Tunkás to develop a sophisticated response to migration is largely due to Padre Alejandro's closer ties to the Catholic community in neighboring Cenotillo, where he resides, and his relatively loose ties to Tunkás. Padre Alejandro does not conduct an organized blessing of departing Tunkaseño migrants, although he does this in Cenotillo, where he believes the migratory phenomenon is more intense. The Catholic church in Tunkás has not compiled a registry of migrants, something that Catholic churches in Los Altos de Jalisco have found instrumental in maintaining strong institutional and cultural ties with migrants abroad. Tunkás has no local patron saint of migrants, nor has Padre Alejandro visited Tunkaseños in the United States, though he has visited migrants from Cenotillo who are in San Bernardino, California. When asked why he has not visited migrants from Tunkás, he responded: "Because there aren't any ... maybe a few, but not that many." The archbishop of Yucatán supports this view, pointing out that migration from Yucatán is significantly lower than that from Mexico's traditional sending regions.

Given that Padre Alejandro lives in Cenotillo, making him the only nonresident religious leader in Tunkás, he has not established the close relations with his congregation that his Protestant counterparts enjoy, and he is less likely to respond quickly to his Tunkaseño flock's needs, including the needs created by migration.

La Sinaí Pentecostal Church

In contrast to the preceding case, the pastor of La Sinaí is attempting to strengthen ties with migrant communities in the United States. Among his initiatives is a plan to send a family prominent in the Sinaí community to a receiving community for Tunkaseño migrants in the United States, to strengthen hometown ties with migrants who are unable to return or simply have not done so. Such a missionary visit could benefit the congregation in Tunkás; La Sinaí's church renovation was paid for by a migrant family who sent remittances for that purpose.

La Sinaí's pastor was also planning to incorporate migration into his sermons in 2006, an election year in which politics and migration were more intertwined than usual. A candidate for the Tunkás municipal presidency was a returned migrant who sought the pastor's support. As the pastor entered the political debate, he also hoped his congregation would explore migration within the context of Bible study.

The Filadelfia Pentecostal Church

Pastor Loida of the Filadelfia church, like the other Pentecostal ministers in Tunkás, says that there is little discussion of migration in her church or in her sermons. However, she is sympathetic to migrants, whom she believes go north solely out of necessity. Like the other ministers, she prays that one day there will be sufficient jobs in Tunkás so that townspeople will not have to leave. "It hurts us as ministers ... to see them compelled to go, not only to far-off places but even to Mérida or Cancún. But there are no jobs here." Pastor Loida says that only a few young men from her congregation have migrated. She holds ceremonies for those leaving and gives them advice and moral support to quiet their fears. The tightly knit Filadelfia community prays frequently for the migrants. Pastor Loida also believes that the young men will return to Tunkás to be reunited with their families once they have saved enough money. She says they only migrate to support their families and to be able to come back to a well-built house.

Of the three Pentecostal congregations, Filadelfia seems to have the most contact with members in the United States. The church has received large donations from U.S.-based migrants for various improvements, including a new roof and floor. Filadelfia also receives smaller donations such as Philadelphia Phillies baseball caps for the children of church members. Further, Pastor Loida maintains contact with church members who have migrated and with their pastors in the United States in order to monitor the migrants' behavior. Each returning migrant must bring her a letter from the pastor of the church attended in the United States to prove that he or she has been a dutiful Christian;

without it, the returnee will not be allowed to attend church in Tunkás. So strong are the ties that Pastor Loida maintains with migrants that a couple who migrated to the United States and then returned to Tunkás invited their U.S. pastor to come to their home community in Mexico to marry them.

Pastor Loida has arranged activities for members of her congregation to help them improve economically as well as spiritually. With support from the federal government, she acquired sewing machines and supplies with which the older women congregants can make hammocks for sale. Pastor Loida bases such efforts on her belief that a family's improvement begins with the woman's improvement. In the future she hopes to add a migrant support group to the list of activities she directs for her congregation.

Aposento Alto Pentecostal Church

Unlike the other Pentecostal churches in Tunkás, Aposento Alto does not maintain any contact with international or national churches. Aposento Alto's pastor loses contact with his congregants once they migrate, but because so few have left, he does not believe the church is affected by migration. He provides a religious service for migrants before they leave and meets with them to give them any needed support. Although this pastor is aware of the weak job market in Tunkás and the widely held perception that going to the United States is the only way out of poverty, he feels that migration is not necessary because God will help the faithful, wherever they are. He says that people can prosper in Tunkás if they have faith. But if they do not have faith, they will have to migrate. "If it's possible to not go, then that is better, because God can bless us even in our own land." This pastor does not have plans to create a support group for migrants or to develop any other project aimed specifically at their needs.

Divino Salvador Presbyterian Church

David Chan, leader of the smallest and oldest Protestant community in Tunkás, sees no need to enact administrative policies in response to migration's impacts on his congregation. Because few members of Divino Salvador have migratory experience, Chan explains that his main encounter with the phenomenon is via television: "We see everything that happens in the United States on television.... There are few migrants in the Evangelical churches, few people that go to the United States." Chan is only an observer of migration; his sole mention of a migration-related church policy involved an informal farewell session that takes place in the church, typically for first-time migrants to the United States:

> "I want you to pray for me," they say.... "I am going to the United States. I don't know when I will return. I don't know if I will return dead or alive, but pray to God. I will also pray for you while I am there." And they sing hymns, biblical songs. And then they sing a farewell song. A farewell, not from this world, but to another country. And then we say good-bye.

There is no organized effort to keep in contact with migrants once they leave Tunkás, though contact often continues through family and friends.

Since it benefits from the international network of Presbyterian churches, Divino Salvador has little need for migrant remittances. Leader Chan has received electronic keyboards and sound system equipment from a Presbyterian church in Korea, which recently sent a missionary group to provide free medical care in Tunkás and also to present him with a motor scooter. Chan is in contact with a Presbyterian doctor in Atlanta, whom he calls on his home telephone, also a gift from abroad. Given that migrant remittances do not represent a significant income prospect for this church, Chan's contacts with migrant members are generally limited to personal ties.

The lay leadership of the four Protestant churches in Tunkás is more actively involved in the everyday lives of the townspeople than are the Catholic clergy. These ministers all seem to agree that the weak job market in Tunkás is the main cause of out-migration. Although there are migration-related programs for Tunkaseños in the planning stages, there are as yet no formal migrant registries. The development of more ambitious migration policies in these churches likely depends on whether the U.S.-bound movement continues to grow in the future.

HOW RELIGION SHAPES MIGRANTS' BEHAVIOR

Catholics and Evangelicals in Tunkás have similar migratory profiles. They are equally likely to migrate (see table 10.1). Thirty-five percent of Catholics and 34 percent of Evangelicals have migrated only to the United States (no internal migration experience) at least once. Ten percent of each group have migrated only within Mexico. The same proportion of Catholics and Evangelicals reported that they were thinking about going to the United States to work in 2006.

There is little difference between Catholic and Evangelical migrants from Tunkás in terms of remittance behavior: over 85 percent in both groups report having sent money to relatives in Tunkás during their most recent sojourn in the United States, and the two groups tend to remit the same median amount monthly (table 10.1). Further, Catholic and Evangelical families spend these remittances similarly, with the large majority directing them to household costs or home improvements (see table 10.2). However, Evangelical families are somewhat more likely to use money earned in the United States to repay debts, while Catholic families are more likely to set it aside in savings or for their children's education. This difference is likely due to Catholics' higher average income; fewer Evangelicals are able to fund a trip to the United States with personal savings, and they are slightly more likely, therefore, to borrow the money in Tunkás. Fifty percent of Catholics, versus 11 percent of Evangelicals, report having sent money home for a novena[4] or *gremio*. The largely Catholic character of novenas and *gremios* (though some are secular) explains the lower Evangelical remittances in this category.

Catholics are significantly more likely than Evangelicals to plan to stay in the United States ($p = 0.052$). Thirty-six percent of Catholics say they want to obtain permanent U.S. resident visas, and another 19 percent have already done so or are in the process of doing so. Among

---

[4] A novena is a period of prayer lasting nine consecutive days, generally related to a particular entreaty.

Evangelicals, 30 percent want to obtain permanent U.S. legal residency, though only 9 percent have legalized or are moving through the legalization process (table 10.1). The higher proportion of Catholics who wish to stay in the United States could reflect differences in the time already spent there. Sixty-eight percent of Catholic migrants had lived five or more years in the United States, compared to 51 percent of migrant Evangelicals. This difference could influence their desire to stay in the United States as well as their ability to do so, in light of the increasing difficulty that undocumented migrants encounter when trying to obtain legal permanent residency. It is likely that there will be relatively more Catholic migration from Tunkás in the future, because Catholics are more likely to have legal permanent resident ("green card") status and will be able to sponsor close relatives' entry.

Table 10.2 Uses of Remittance Income, by Religious Affiliation

Use of Remittances	Catholics	Evangelicals
Household costs	76%	69%
Home improvements	12%	14%
Medicine	6%	8%
Land or animal purchase	3%	2%
Children's education	2%	0%
Debt repayment	0%	8%
Buy/expand a business	0%	0%
Savings	1%	0%
Other	0%	0%
Total	100%	100%

N = 342; p = 0.875.

Migration's effects on church attendance are mixed. Both Catholics and Evangelicals report nearly the same proportion of people who claim to attend church less frequently after migrating, but more Evangelicals than Catholics report attending church more often after migration (though the difference is not statistically significant) (see table 10.1).

The archbishop of Yucatán attributes the Catholics' decreased religiosity following migration to their inability to attend church in the

United States for fear of apprehension by the Border Patrol and because of physical distances between churches and the places where migrants live. These obstacles to church attendance should hold true for Evangelicals as well, but they do not. Evangelical groups in Tunkás tend to be more cohesive, and they are led by pastors who assign members more active community roles and also visit returning migrants to strengthen ties that may have weakened during their stay in the United States. The Catholic church in Tunkás does not make any such efforts, primarily because Padre Alejandro's residency in Cenotillo makes him both spatially and socially distant from his Tunkás congregation. Absent any efforts on his part to welcome migrants, these former congregants are less likely to resume church attendance.

The emergence of Tunkás's Evangelical communities is not related to international migration because they substantially predate the beginnings of U.S.-bound migration from Tunkás. However, some critics contend that Evangelicalism has harmed Mayan religious traditions such as the *gremios*, which are sponsored by the Catholic church. Tunkaseño Professor Rafael, who studies Mayan folklore, explains:

> Anything that has to do with the Mayan way of life is something bad according to the Evangelicals. For example, dancing and the wearing of jewelry, this is important for a Yucatecan woman. The Evangelicals see the use of all that as a symbol for sin. They don't let the children participate in the *gremios* because they see them as paganism. The Catholic church has preserved them because everything about the fiestas is for a Catholic saint.

Comparisons between Catholics and Evangelicals in Tunkás reveal relatively similar behaviors. Religious identity is not an indicator of higher status or associated with material advantages. Nor is religious identity associated with the perception of one's own higher status. When asked to compare themselves and their families to other families in Tunkás in terms of living conditions (on a scale of 1 to 10, with 1 representing the lowest and 10 the highest value), Catholics' responses paralleled those of Evangelicals (see table 10.1).

CONCLUSION

Religious differences in Tunkás do not significantly influence migratory behavior. There is little perception that the spread of Evangelicalism is the result of internal or international migration. Furthermore, religious institutions in Tunkás have only recently begun to develop as active participants in the migratory phenomenon. Tunkás's churches have yet to develop a sophisticated approach to managing the effects of migration, something that has occurred in Los Altos de Jalisco. In the case of the Catholic church, the development of such a response has been stymied because the priest resides in another town and also feels that there is little migration from Tunkás. Two of the Evangelical churches—the Presbyterian Divino Salvador and the Pentecostal Aposento Alto—do not have a sufficient number of migrants in their congregations to merit developing a program for them; migration simply does not figure into the pastors' goals for their churches. The Pentecostal Filadelfia and La Sinaí, however, are beginning to recognize the need to address migration-related issues among their congregations on both sides of the border. La Sinaí has already benefited economically from migrant remittances, and the pastor says he intends to maintain strong ties with his migrant members. Since Tunkás represents a relatively new migrant-sending community, church responses to migration are still evolving.

Unlike the nearly complete dominance of the Catholic Church in the historic heartland of Mexican out-migration in places like Los Altos de Jalisco and the conflictual heterogeneity of Protestants and Catholics in a Yucatecan community like Chan Kom, Tunkás represents a different case. Generations-old Evangelical religious communities are accepted, albeit grudgingly at times, as part of Tunkás. Therefore, the rise of Evangelical communities is not attributed to migratory activity. Whether religious identity will become a more significant factor in people's migration behavior may depend on how religious leaders respond to the needs and opportunities that international migration presents.

References

Bastian, Jean-Pierre. 1993. "The Metamorphosis of Latin American Protestant Groups: A Sociohistorical Perspective," *Latin American Research Review* 28, no. 2: 33–51.

Craig, Ann L. 1983. *The First Agraristas: An Oral History of a Mexican Agrarian Reform Movement.* Berkeley, CA: University of California Press.

Fitzgerald, David. 2005. "Emigration's Challenge to the 'Nation-Church': Mexican Catholic Emigration Policies, 1920–2004." UCLA Global Fellows Seminar Paper No. 5. http://repositories.cdlib.org/globalfellows/2005/5.

Re Cruz, Alicia. 1998. "Migrant Women Crossing Borders: The Role of Gender and Religion in Internal and External Mexican Migration," *Journal of Borderland Studies* 13, no. 2 (Fall): 83–98.

Santana Rivas, Landy Elizabeth. 1987. "Refuncionalización del protestantismo en el campo yucateco: el caso de Akil, Yucatán." Research Report. Mérida, Yucatán: Unidad de Ciencias Sociales, Centro de Investigaciones Regionales "Dr. Hideyo Noguchi," Universidad Autónoma de Yucatán.

Vallado Fajardo, Iván. 1989. "Cambios en la religiosidad popular en Zudzal, Yucatán." In *Religión y sociedad en el sureste de México,* vol. 4. México, DF: Centro de Investigaciones y Estudios Superiores en Antropología Social Sureste.

Bath time at a Tunkás home.

11 Migration and Health

SONIA PRELAT AND ALEJANDRA MACIEL

The study of migrant health has focused mainly on migrant populations in the United States, without investigating their nonmigrant counterparts in sending areas. This approach is useful in identifying health
problems of Mexican migrants in the United States, but it fails to isolate
whether factors associated with migration are the causes of these illnesses. Comparing the health status of migrants with that of nonmigrants from the same hometown provides the control group that has
been missing in many previous studies. This chapter discusses health
issues specific to Tunkaseño migrants, using nonmigrants as a control
group. In our assessment of depression and alcohol abuse among
Tunkaseños, we take a different approach, comparing Tunkaseño migrants to previously studied populations of Mexican migrants to understand how their behavior differs.

Our work views migrant health as a reflection of the culture and
structural conditions from which the migrants come and the milieu in
which they are presently immersed. Social, cultural, and environmental
conditions are addressed as we examine both the depression and anxiety that underlie the physical conditions of migrants and the traditional
medicine that they often employ to address such health concerns.

A DEMOGRAPHIC SNAPSHOT

The population pyramid for Tunkás has a broad base, with the highest
proportion of individuals (22 percent) between 10 and 19 years of age.
The distribution reveals a narrowing of the male population beginning
in the 25–29 age category and continuing through the 40–44 age category, after which the male population reaches the levels of the female
population (see figure 11.1). Given that males are more likely to migrate
and that the average age of U.S.-bound migrants is 37, it seems likely

that the contraction in the male population from 25 to 44 years of age is due to emigration.

Figure 11.1 Population Distribution in Tunkás, 2003, by Gender and Age

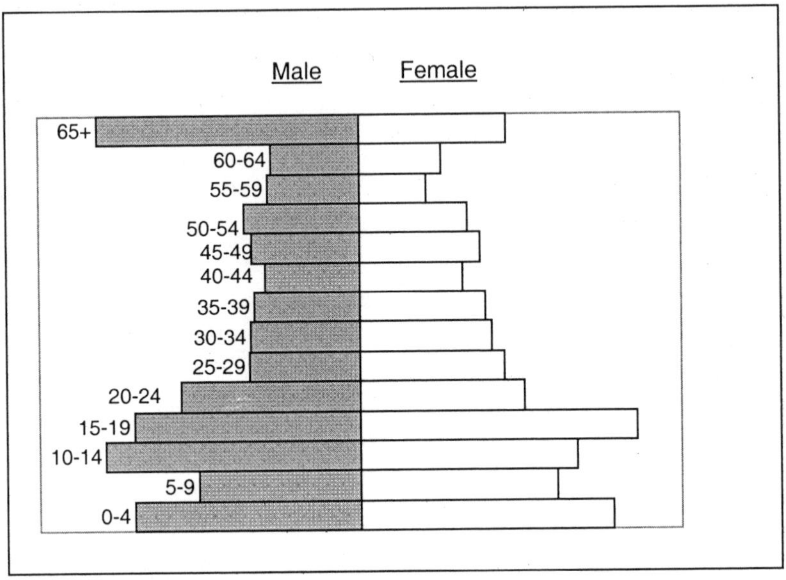

The effect of migration on the population distribution of Tunkás was first observed in a 2004 community study, in which Alfonso Martín Gómez Soler, resident medical student at the town's health clinic, noted that the departure of many young men in search of economic opportunities in the United States had removed a "high percentage of males of productive age from Tunkás" (Gómez Soler 2004: 13). The population distribution across age groups suggests that if limited job opportunities and low wages persist in Tunkás, a large proportion of those reaching working age may enter the workforce in the United States rather than in their hometown.

Our survey shows a slight difference between U.S.-bound migrants and nonmigrating Tunkaseños in terms of family planning. Seventy-five percent of migrating Tunkaseños, compared to 67 percent of nonmigrants, did not plan to have any more children, suggesting that migrants may be receptive to family-planning programs in Mexico and/or the United States, and that fertility behavior changes may occur as early as the first generation. These findings underscore the potential value of family-planning programs targeting first-generation migrants.

NUTRITION AND SERVICES

The Tunkaseño diet consists primarily of three staples: beans, corn tortillas, and chiles. Tunkaseños also eat other foods—generally tomatoes, lettuce, cabbage, and squash—two to three times a week. Households with more economic resources have a wider variety of protein, including beef and venison, in their diets, while lower-income families eat pigs and chickens they raise in their backyards.

Approximately 80 percent of the townspeople raise pigs in their yards for household consumption. Given the rudimentary and crowded housing conditions in Tunkás, the households' outdoor kitchens are usually in close proximity to dogs, cats, pigs, and chickens. The women generally cook on wood-fired stoves raised about a half-meter above the ground, exposing the food to dirt and animals. This arrangement greatly increases the risk of gastrointestinal illnesses and parasite infections, two major health problems in Tunkás.

The town's poor economy has restricted the development of infrastructure and urban services. The government has implemented an effective water distribution program, and potable water reaches 88 percent of the population, a fraction comparable to the neighboring municipalities of Cenotillo and Izamal. However, the municipal government has not established a community-wide sewerage system, leaving 80 percent of the population without adequate sanitary resources. This absence of basic infrastructure contributes to the high prevalence of gastrointestinal, urinary tract, and parasite infections in Tunkás. As outdoor fecal excretions dry, they become pulverized and airborne, increasing the risk of respiratory infections from inhalation of these particles. The town's doctors cite these types of infections as the primary reason for Tunkaseños' visits to their offices. The health-care resources available in Tunkás include a government-sponsored health clinic, three private doctors, two *parteras* (midwives), and one *huesero* (a "bone doctor" who incorporates herbs and spiritual rituals into his healing practices).

TUNKÁS AND THE LATINO HEALTH PARADOX

One might expect that moving from Mexico to the United States would improve migrants' health, given that the United States is a much richer country with technologically advanced medicine. Yet a large body of research consistently affirms that Latino immigrants are healthier than U.S.-born Latinos and that migrants' health outcomes decline with the length of time they spend in the United States. This finding has been called the "Latino health paradox" (Sorlie et al. 1993; Abraido-Lanza et al. 1999; Palloni and Arias 2004; Hummer et al. 2000; Weigers and Sherraden 2001).

One possible explanation for this apparent paradox is that migrants are a self-selected group of healthy people. The old, sick, and infirm are clearly less likely to migrate, especially given the harsh conditions of an undocumented border crossing. But some researchers argue that the rising numbers of health problems documented among migrants in the United States simply reflect the settled migrants' improved access to resources required to diagnose preexisting medical conditions, such as cancer, diabetes, cardiovascular disease, and HIV/AIDS (Burgos et al. 2005). These observers argue that settled migrants' higher incidence of self-reported disease cannot be unequivocally interpreted as a cause-and-effect relationship between migration and disease. It is difficult to determine whether migrants who are long-term residents of the United States are actually unhealthier or are simply more aware of their medical situation than are newcomers.

Still other authors argue that Mexican migrants are less willing than other migrant populations to change certain behaviors and that the Latino health paradox reflects their lack of faith in the effectiveness of American health-care practices. Thus they underreport disease relative to the second generation (see, for example, Reichman 2006). These researchers postulate that first-generation immigrants are highly resistant to change and that shifts in attitudes, behaviors, and beliefs can only occur in the second generation. Such resistance to acculturation has been attributed to these migrants' traditional rural backgrounds, strong family ties, geographic proximity to their place of origin, and the prevalence of "institutionalized discriminatory practices" that discourage their integration (Reichman 2006: 1–3). Nevertheless, Reichman insists, such measures of acculturation are superficial and fail to employ "behavioral measures of acculturation" that "satisfactorily predict attitudes" (p. 12). Using her own measures, Reichman conducted a study of Mexican migrant women in Santa Fe, New Mexico, and found that many modified their health care–seeking behaviors and attitudes about disease prevention within five to ten years of migration.

Our survey in Tunkás sheds new light on the Latino health paradox by comparing migrants to nonmigrants. Across the entire range of self-reported diseases we surveyed, Tunkaseño migrants are sicker than their nonmigrating counterparts. Rates of diabetes, hypertension, and high cholesterol are significantly higher for Tunkaseños with migration experience (see figure 11.2). This shows that migrants are not a self-selected group of healthy people; on the contrary, their health outcomes are worse than those of nonmigrants.

One possible explanation for the disparity between migrants and nonmigrants, as discussed above, may be that migrants are more likely to seek health care and, hence, to have diseases diagnosed. However, we found that the percentage of individuals seeking medical advice is roughly the same among nonmigrants (74 percent) and individuals with U.S. migration experience (77 percent). The share of Tunkaseños who seek no treatment whatsoever is lower for migrants (5 percent) than nonmigrants (8 percent). The remaining migrants and nonmigrants either self-medicate or use traditional medicine. Migrants appear to seek medical care at approximately the same rate in the United States (36 percent) and Mexico (41 percent), which leads us to conclude that Tunkaseño migrants are not simply more likely to report diseases that are equally prevalent among nonmigrants, but rather, that their health is indeed deteriorating as a consequence of migration.[1]

---

[1] However, these data do not allow us to discount the possibility that migrants who visit clinics in the United States are more likely to have a condition diagnosed than are nonmigrants who visit clinics in Mexico, given the more advanced medical infrastructure and training available in the United States.

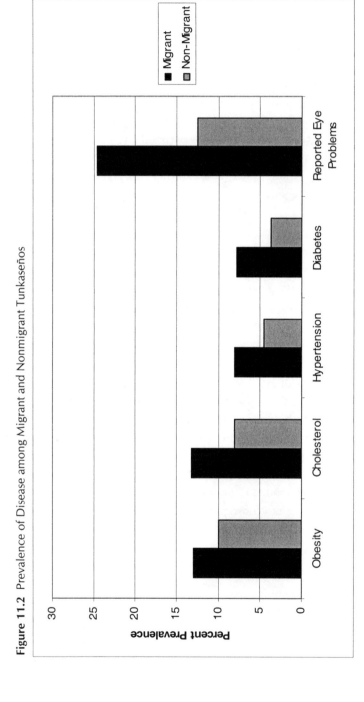

Figure 11.2 Prevalence of Disease among Migrant and Nonmigrant Tunkaseños

P values: obesity, 0.8968; cholesterol, 0.2254; hypertension, 0.0545; diabetes, 0.0363; eye problems, 0.0309.

N = 258 (nonmigrants), N = 313 (migrants).

USE OF TRADITIONAL MEDICINE

According to the World Health Organization, over 80 percent of the world's population uses some form of traditional medicine, and the majority of traditional medicine therapists come from indigenous societies (WHO 1993). Folk illnesses and traditional therapies are often associated with low economic status and marginalization from public services. Given this scenario, many researchers conclude that the use of traditional therapy is prompted by a lack of access to conventional medical help and that belief in folk illnesses, such as *mal de ojo* (the consequence of a piercing glance) and *mal aire* (bad air), will decline as urbanization advances. For example, Chávez (1984) documents that young Mexican migrants in San Diego, California, sought out traditional therapy in rural areas only when doctors were not available. Once in the United States, these respondents said, they would not visit folk practitioners.

This model is challenged, however, by Nigenda, Cifuentes, and Hill, who studied the increasing use of traditional medicine in Mexico City. According to Nigenda and colleagues, the availability of conventional medical help does not deter individuals from using traditional medicine as well. That is, the fact that conventional medicine is available does not imply a total shift from traditional to conventional methods. Instead, these authors conclude, "traditional medicine is extensively practiced in Mexico in parallel with the conventional medical system" (Nigenda, Cifuentes, and Hill 2004: 419).

Other researchers point out that the cost of modern health care leads many individuals to seek traditional therapy. Unable to afford visits to the community health clinic or to a private physician, they opt for a cheaper remedy: traditional medicine. Dr. Ignacio Gómez García, attending doctor at the town's clinic, pointed out that patients in Tunkás commonly go to both the clinic and the *herbatero* (herbalist) for treatment of the same ailment. Dr. Gómez offered as an example the case of a pregnant woman who receives prenatal care at the clinic and also visits a *sobadora* to help position the baby for delivery. He notes, further, that cost is not the deciding factor, given that the clinic does not refuse service to patients who cannot pay.

Our research shows that the prevalence of folk illnesses such as *mal de ojo* and *mal aire* does not differ between migrants and nonmigrants. Despite urbanization and possible acculturation, Tunkaseño migrants believe in the symptoms of *mal de ojo* (weakness and loss of appetite) and the harmful effects of *mal aire* to the same degree as nonmigrating Tunkaseños. Thus, in the Tunkaseños' case, belief in the power of folk illnesses has not decreased with exposure to U.S. practices and culture.

Even more surprisingly, U.S.-bound migrants are *more* likely to visit a *curandero, herbatero, sobador*, or *huesero* (29 percent) than their nonmigrating counterparts (22 percent), contradicting assertions that marginalization, lower economic status, and lower education levels are the principal predictors of traditional medicine use. On average, U.S.-bound migrants from Tunkás are more educated, more exposed to modern health-care practices, and of higher economic status than those who do not migrate; yet they are more likely to visit a traditional medicine practitioner.

The reasons for this "traditional medicine paradox" are not known, but our results suggest that researchers must look beyond socioeconomic status and acculturation. As mentioned previously, Mexican migrants are often described as resistant to change, an observation that might lead one to conclude that the use of traditional medicine serves as a "mechanism of resistance." However, 36 percent of our migrant interviewees had visited doctors in the United States within the previous two years. This clearly indicates that migrants are not rejecting modern health-care practices but rather are using them in conjunction with traditional medicine.

We propose that migrants' use of traditional medicine is a coping mechanism that enables them to integrate their cultural identity with their new reality. Traditional therapy, then, symbolizes much more than just a physical cure; it represents a spiritual connection to Tunkaseño land and culture. The fact that migrants hold onto these traditions more tightly than those who do not migrate may indicate that they associate traditional medicine with their homeland. The migrants' more frequent use of traditional therapy is most likely a result of several factors. Although our research is not conclusive in identifying which factors are most influential, it does provide strong evidence that migration to the United States does not depress use of traditional medicine.

MIGRATION AND ALCOHOLISM

Increases in alcohol consumption represent a public health concern in many Mexican migrant communities in the United States. Most studies of Mexican migrant alcohol use focus on male migrant farmworkers. These studies hold relevance for the Tunkaseño case because the majority (65 percent) of our survey interviewees in Tunkás are males; and even though most of our migrants were not employed as farmworkers, they have similar social networks and cultural backgrounds. Therefore, we expect that several of the predictors of migrant alcohol consumption identified in previous studies will apply in Tunkás as well.

In explaining the factors that regulate alcohol consumption in rural Mexico, Castro and Gutierres are quick to acknowledge the powerful role played by family traditionalism and the institutions that reinforce it. This value system emerged in an agrarian environment where family survival depends upon the members' willingness to make personal sacrifices for the collective well-being. As a result, family traditionalism consistently advocates empowering the group at the cost of the individual, and thereby minimizes the possibility of personal rebellion in the form of misconduct (Castro and Gutierres 1997: 510). Religion also plays a crucial role in reinforcing the values of family traditionalism. By urging the faithful to deny their personal desires and devote themselves wholeheartedly to God and Church, religion once also sought to empower the group at the cost of the individual. The Church also represented a fundamental unit of social organization, for it expected the whole community to participate in religious events. These frequent events not only fostered a powerful sense of community responsibility among the congregation; they also made it difficult for those engaging in deviant behaviors, such as excessive alcohol consumption, to escape the censorship of both their families and members of their church (Castro and Gutierres 1997: 510).

Researchers have confirmed that once an individual migrates, the family continues to play a key role in regulating personal conduct, including alcohol consumption. Two studies in particular, both conducted in migrant labor camps in upstate New York, identified social isolation as the most powerful factor affecting whether an individual would become a heavy or binge drinker (Watson et al. 1985; Chi and McClain 1992, cited in Watson et al. 1985: 446). Watson and colleagues concluded that "the importance of spouse, children, and other relatives cannot be overestimated as a moderating influence on drinking among male migrants" (p. 446). Indeed, high levels of alcohol abuse among male migrants can be partly attributed to the fact that most of them are placed in a social situation that promotes such behavior, and the social pressures that previously served to moderate their alcohol consumption are far away.

Upon arrival in a U.S. receiving community, male migrants often find themselves in an all-male environment with limited forms of entertainment. Heavy drinking is an opportunity to engage in a "sharing of identities and experiences that serve to re-enforce the importance of masculinity" and comes to be the principal activity of the majority of these groups (Watson et al. 1985: 450). Castro and Gutierres attribute such attitudes toward alcohol abuse principally to the fact that "norms condone it." Hailing from rural areas where jobs are monotonous and demand substantial physical exertion, many male migrants believe they have the right to use alcohol as a release (Castro and Gutierres 1997: 503). The disconnect that often arises between migrants and their U.S. host community makes the problem worse, according to Watson et al. (p. 448), because many migrants do not feel restricted by the kind of social contract that served to moderate alcohol consumption at home.

A migrant's alcohol abuse can also be affected by the amount of time spent in the United States. As migrants become increasingly acculturated in the United States, rates of alcohol abuse rise. The connection between increased acculturation and increased alcohol consumption becomes clear when one recognizes the enormity of the shift that adjustment to life in the United States requires. Defined by Castro and Gutierres as the transformation in "values, attitudes, behaviors, language, and lifestyle" involved in accepting the norms and traditions associated with a new cultural environment (p. 15), acculturation exerts a significant strain by forcing an individual to confront issues of class mobility, identity transformations, and warring value systems. In a study conducted in 1987 among Mexican Americans in urban Los Angeles, lifetime prevalence rates for alcohol abuse rose in direct proportion to levels of acculturation. This finding confirms that alcohol is frequently used to cope with the pressures of acculturation (Burnam et al. 1987, cited in Castro and Gutierres 1997: 16).

Surprisingly, our data from Tunkás show that rates of alcohol consumption did not increase significantly with migration. When asked to self-report their behavior in the United States, 73 percent of migrating Tunkaseños said that their alcohol consumption did not increase. Of these, 38 percent reported no change in their drinking habits upon migrating, and 35 percent reported drinking less alcohol in the United States. Our study suggests that the relative absence of significantly increased alcohol consumption may be due in part to Tunkaseño migrants' strong social networks. Thus the extended kinship network continues to play a role in regulating individual behavior, limiting alcohol consumption in much the same way that it does in Mexico.

Regular sending of remittances is one of the most important ways in which a migrant expresses the depth of his commitment to his family's well-being. For many migrants, the desire to supplement a limited family income with regular remittances represents one of the principal motives for migration. Following local values, the migrant sends home money that he could otherwise use for his own entertainment and comfort. We found that 86 percent of Tunkaseño migrants remitted money to relatives in the town during their most recent trip to the United States.

For many migrants, what most powerfully affected their behavior was the intensity of their connection to their nuclear family. Jesús, an evangelical Christian and father of two, said that despite the depression he experienced in the United States, "I did not allow myself to abuse alcohol because I had to send money home to my wife." Jesús never failed in his responsibility; his loyalty to his family was far more powerful than the pull of his depression. "I said to myself, 'This is why you came. You cannot turn into a drunk here.'" Vicente, another migrant, emphasized that his personal troubles were always subordinate to his concern for his family. Of his bimonthly telephone calls home, he says: "If they tell me they are healthy, I am happy. But when they are sick, you worry. But that is the life of a father, no? You love them a lot, but when you are far away, you can only send them money and hope for the best."

Our interviews with other Tunkaseño migrants confirmed that most were linked to a family system whose needs dictated the course of their life in the United States. Seventy-two percent of the migrants we surveyed were married, and many unmarried migrants were working specifically to accumulate the capital needed to support a family. We also found that 68 percent of Tunkaseños stayed with family members upon arrival in the United States, and 79 percent had relied on a relative or friend to obtain their most recent U.S. job. Our data suggest that maintaining strong ties to the sending community and with family and friends in the receiving community has a powerful effect on controlling alcohol consumption among migrants. In the course of several unstructured interviews we conducted in Tunkás, informants described abusers of alcohol as weak men incapable of upholding their family responsibilities.

MENTAL HEALTH

Many migrants to the United States must overcome depression if they are to succeed in their new environment. As early as 1978, the President's Commission on Mental Health asserted that "many of the objective features associated with Mexican migration to the United States would predispose toward poor mental health" (Vega, Kolody, and Valle 1987: 512). Further, the Commission identified isolation from emotional support systems in Mexico and the strenuous nature of a migrant's life in the United States as the factors that made migrants highly vulnerable to psychopathology. Though some of the assumptions that Vega, Kolody, and Valle made do not apply in the Tunkaseño case, the psychological strain produced by the factors they identified undoubtedly plays a role in Tunkaseños' depression.

Thirty-nine percent of the Tunkaseño migrants we surveyed reported an increase in feelings of depression during their first sojourn in the United States. We rely on the Fabrega Migration Adaptation Model (Fabrega 1969) to assess rates of depression among Tunkaseños. This model argues that the migration-adaptation process encompasses four "natural domains," each of which can be viewed as "an integral component for conceptualization and measurement" (Vega, Kolody, and Valle 1987: 512). Operating on the assumption that these factors "impinge universally on the migration experience" (p. 513), we will examine how depression among Tunkaseños fits the Fabrega model. Ultimately, our study reveals that the model succeeds in identifying several key causes of Tunkaseño depression, but it fails to identify one of the most fundamental stressors associated with migration: the impact on family members whom the migrant leaves behind. We employ qualitative data gathered in Tunkás to argue that no assessment of the stressors associated with migration is complete without examining the physical and emotional status of those who remain in the home community.

The first two domains of the migratory experience involve severing one's physical and emotional ties to the home country. Though Vega, Kolody, and Valle argue that each domain encompasses "intrapsychic and interpersonal elements," the first domain—in which the migrant experiences a sudden "break with a familiar sociocultural system" and disruption of those "family and other supportive ties" that have hitherto sustained him—seems to involve these elements more profoundly than the rest (p. 514). Feelings of fear, loss, and anxiety endemic to this state are often exacerbated by the migrant's undocumented status, which restricts his ability to visit his family once he has exited the home country (p. 515). The second domain of Fabrega's model encompasses the challenges of migratory passage. The degree of hardship varies significantly among undocumented Mexicans entering the United States, with the journey proving relatively uneventful for some and fraught with hunger and exhaustion for others. For some, it is even fatal (p. 515).

The third and fourth domains examine the migrant's interactions within the host country and his or her perceptions of those interactions. Adaptation factors, such as procuring shelter and viable employment, represent a migrant's foremost concern in the third domain. Many Mexican migrants rely upon extended family networks to facilitate this transition. Despite migrants' ties to a larger support system, Vega, Kolody, and Valle observe that several factors inhibit the adaptation process in the Mexican case: "Mexican migrants are often segregated, destitute, minimally educated, and are often seeking employment under marginal circumstances ... that render them highly exploitable" and therefore vulnerable to the types of stressors that stimulate depression (p. 516).

In the fourth and final domain of the Fabrega model, the migrant must assess whether he has achieved the improved living standard that was the object of his migration. Operating on the assumption that unfulfilled expectations frequently precipitate negative mental health outcomes, Fabrega emphasizes that it is "neither the structure of opportunity nor the level of goal striving" in the social and work environment that most affects migrant depression, but rather how socially and materially successful the migrant perceives himself to be in those environments (Vega, Kolody, and Valle 1987: 516).

An analysis of Tunkaseños' struggles and successes in terms of this model demonstrates that although transnational social networks have a powerful stabilizing influence on the migrant, they cannot shield him or her from the multiple stresses associated with migration to the United States. Among the stressors exerting a strong impact on Tunkaseños are estrangement from family, difficult border crossings, and loneliness. Most Tunkaseños we interviewed described the consistent efforts they made to connect with their families and offset the stresses associated with the disruption of family ties. Ninety-four percent contacted their family in Tunkás at least once a month while they were in the United States. Jesús, who was quoted above, explained how his frequent calls home and the time he spent with members of his extended family in the United States alleviated his depression. He credited his wife's constant support for sustaining him throughout his U.S. sojourn: "My wife and I have been together for a long time.... We met in elementary school.... We've always kept in contact; we talk about everything. We are very close."

Despite their desire to maintain close ties with the home community, Tunkaseño migrants in the United States make infrequent visits to their hometown. Sixty-one percent of the migrants we interviewed reported spending more time in the United States than in Tunkás. Nineteen percent return once a year; 17 percent return less than once every four years; and 41 percent have not returned at all since leaving Tunkás. With 45 percent of migrants citing financial constraints (including the cost of a smuggler to help them reenter the United States after a home visit) and the risks associated with clandestine border crossings as the main reasons for their infrequent visits home, we can infer that undocumented status is a key deterrent to return migration.

An added stressor associated with the infrequency of trips home is the migrant's awareness of what his family endures during his absence. When asked about this, Don Clemente noted how difficult it was to be separated from his wife and children: "The children are growing up, and they need their father." And about his wife: "She had it very hard because one of the children got sick, and she had to find a solution." Ultimately the struggles of his family impelled him to return, but not before he himself had experienced significant mental and emotional hardship.

Our examination of the migrant's relationship to his nuclear family and the suffering that his absence often engenders reveals the crucial role these factors play in migrants' depression. Even though many migrants demonstrate a desire to remain connected to their hometown, the relative infrequency with which they actually return home appears to have a fundamental impact on their rates of depression.

Eighty-one percent of the Tunkaseño migrants surveyed cross the border without papers or with false or borrowed papers. Sebastián vividly described the arduous journey he undertook over the mountains in order to circumvent areas more heavily surveilled by the Border Patrol. Once on the U.S. side, a tire on the minivan his group was traveling in blew out. According to Sebastián, "Half of the people with us were picked up by the Border Patrol. The rest of us went with another *coyote*. Our *coyote* escaped." Sebastian spoke with sadness about two women who "almost didn't make it" across the border; they were in the group seized by "la Migra." When asked what enabled him to avoid apprehension, he alluded to his determination: "Right there I said, 'I am going to get out of this.'"

Jesús adopted a similar attitude when crossing the border. Though aware of the enormous risks involved, he knew that he could not let his fear paralyze him. When asked what he was thinking as he walked across the border, he responded: "Just about walking, about continuing. We focused on the main goal. There was no time for anything else."

Such testimony confirms that the border presents truly formidable challenges to Tunkaseño migrants and that their success depends largely on their determination. Whether the stresses of the crossing represent a potential source of depression appears largely dependent on the individual migrant's mental preparedness for the journey.

Another important stressor is linked to the cost of crossing the border, which often runs to several thousand dollars. Vicente alluded to the burden of knowing that he needed to repay everyone who had loaned him money for his most recent border crossing. He noted that when a migrant arrives in the United States, he is not free to work for himself. The debt weighs heavily: "They loan you money, and you have to repay what they gave you. Then there are the fees for crossing the border.... You have to pay all of the people; you owe the money. If you don't pay it back, you're a *mala paga* [deadbeat]." For Vicente, his sense of personal security rested upon his ability to repay those who had helped him. Until he discharged those debts, he feared becoming a "*mala paga*" and experienced all the anxiety and depression that such fears engender.

A majority of the Tunkaseños whom we observed in Anaheim and Inglewood, California, eased the adaptation process by living in ethnic enclaves dominated, if not by Tunkaseños, at least by other Yucatecans. In one apartment complex in Anaheim, groups of Tunkaseño men drink beer, fix each others' cars, and watch television together. Fifty-nine percent of the migrants surveyed reported having Tunkaseños as neighbors. More than any other factor, proximity to friends and relatives from Tunkás determined migrants' choice of destination within the United States: 93 percent chose their most recent destination because they had relatives or friends there.

Nevertheless, many immigrants coming from small towns like Tunkás struggle to find their way in U.S. cities. Don Clemente described the bewilderment he felt when arriving in the United States. Simple tasks like crossing the street were a struggle. The noise and the challenge of getting around almost overwhelmed him, but he relied on a group of friends from Tunkás. "They helped me, and I gradually became more accustomed." Don Clemente's case illustrates how reliance on a transnational social network enables migrants to fend off depression.

For Vicente, the most difficult aspect of adjustment to life in the United States was overcoming his fear of the Border Patrol. When asked if he would consider settling permanently in the United States, he responded: "With papers, yes.... How can I put it? La Migra persecutes you. I don't like it. It means you are not free." Vicente's fear of deportation was constant: "Sometimes they say the Migra is seizing undocumented workers. That makes me afraid."

Jesús is a good example of an immigrant who used available social infrastructure to facilitate his adaptation to the receiving community. For example, he enthusiastically described the difference his church in the United States made for his sense of connectedness and mental well-being. For a time his work consumed him, and his religious commitment began to wane. Then he started attending Evangelical church services, and he says that the change he experienced was significant. "I see the difference because it brings spiritual comfort ... because you go and pray, and when you leave you feel peaceful, happy, and not worried anymore." Ultimately, by attending church three times a week, Jesús was able to alleviate the anxiety and depression that had afflicted him in the course of his stay.

Finally, a migrant's mental health is affected by the subjective perception of whether he has achieved the social and financial success he initially sought through migration. Sebastián described his job in the United States with great pride, eagerly showing photographs of himself and his co-workers:

> I worked in the Hilton with the Americans. I also worked with blacks; in fact, I worked with everybody. I had a lot of responsibility. That's why the boss was so upset when I left. It was a lot of responsibility to walk away from. "Bring your family here," my boss told me. "I need you here," he said. One day I cooked for four thousand people. That's a lot of people.

Vicente also speaks with pride when describing his relationship to his job in the United States: "I was very willing to work. I like it when they tell me I've done a good job.... I like to keep busy, even if I work slowly, until the job is finished and done well." For both Vicente and Sebastián, work provided a stimulating challenge in addition to the financial compensation for their efforts. Such experiences can help alleviate symptoms of depression and improve a migrant's sense of self-worth.

But what of the family members who stay behind? Despite the intense commitment of men like Don Clemente and Vicente to support their families, our findings and previous research both confirm that the absence of the male head of household disrupts a family. Because the migrant's decision to migrate depends on the emotional and economic support of his family, migration's impacts are rarely restricted to the migrant alone. Our survey data reveal that nearly 40 percent of individuals who borrowed money to migrate borrowed from family members. Almost inevitably, migration requires economic sacrifice by the entire family and a restructuring of the family system to accommodate the migrant's absence. By not exploring such a crucial component of the migratory process, Fabrega fails to address all of the factors that "impinge universally on the migration experience" (Vega, Kolody, and Valle 1987: 513).

The literature shows that a parent's absence increases the stress on the remaining parent and the children. The remaining parent tries to compensate by shouldering more responsibilities, a decision that often compromises their emotional and physical well-being (Amato and Gilbreth 1999). Nobles (2006) points out that migration often involves a long period of parent-child separation, sometimes longer than what follows the dissolution of a union. Paradoxically, migration, which increases household income through remittances, often makes family members who stay behind more susceptible to depression, anxiety, and poor overall health.

Fifty-six-year-old Eligia, whose husband migrated to Anaheim when she was twenty-eight in order to "build this humble house," describes her distress during her husband's absence: "I felt so sad. All I did was cry, and I think I also carried lots of anxiety (*nervios*) inside.... I didn't know if he was going to return alive, and I was pregnant. What was I going to do?" Eligia attributes six miscarriages to the anxiety that her husband's absence caused. She feels guilty, believing that her crying angered God and eventually led to her last miscarriage: "I think God said that I was crying all the time and that's why my child was born dead." Despite her husband's periodic visits, Eligia says she missed out on a normal married life. Twenty-eight years later, she is still affected by her husband's absence as she considers the prospect of growing old alone. Eligia attributes her current physical illnesses to the depression that her husband's migration triggered.

Celmy, a 28-year-old housewife, noted a similar pattern of physical consequences in her 6-year-old son who, at age 3, got sick when her husband migrated:

> They told me it was emotional, because he wouldn't eat. He was sad and got sick a lot. I don't know how much medicine he took, but nothing worked. I took him to another doctor, and he said that there was nothing wrong with the child. All I could do was cry because I saw how thin my child was getting.... He almost died from the same emotional illness. He started vomiting; he turned pale, pale. He didn't have any color. So much medicine he was taking, and nothing made him better.

Marcos, Eligia's 17-year-old son, also described his childhood longing for his father:

> When I went to school, my friend's father would pick him up, and my mom couldn't pick me up. I walked home from school alone. Sometimes the bullies would make fun of me, saying I didn't have a dad. My mom said I did have a dad, that he would be back soon, but I had my doubts. The kid next door would ride a horse to the fields with his dad, and I would ask my mom when my dad would be back because I wanted to go out on a horse and do all the things that a boy does with his dad.

Marcos recalled the moment he realized that his father would never be able to give him what he needed: "It was a total change. I learned to move forward in life alone, not to count on anyone."

Research has shown that children in single-parent households tend to have less access to capital, which impairs their educational and health outcomes (McLanahan and Sandefur 2006). This explanation does not generally apply to children's outcomes in Tunkás, however, because most single-parent Tunkaseño households receive remittances, so migrants' children actually have more access to resources than their counterparts in two-parent households. The poor mental health and educational outcomes of the children of migrants are most likely attributable, then, to parental separation stress (Strohschein 2005). Lamb and Tamis-Lemonda (2004) suggest ways that the simple presence of the male parent in a household facilitates a child's development and provides emotional support. Marcos asserts that his father was never around to teach him how to work like a man, to explain the physical changes he was undergoing, or simply to play with him. A child's developmental pathways are significantly altered when a parent is gone.

Ultimately, several factors—including the stress associated with clandestine border crossings and estrangement from family members—stand out as powerful catalysts of migrant depression, while the absence of the migrant has a profound effect on the family left behind.

CONCLUSION

Despite its status as a recent sending community, Tunkás cannot escape the pervasive influence of American culture. Tunkaseños display many of the health issues that characterize more experienced migrants from other parts of Mexico. Consistent with the "Latino health paradox," it does appear that Tunkaseño migrants are getting sicker in the United States: they exhibit higher levels of diabetes, hypertension, high cholesterol, and self-reported eye problems than nonmigrating Tunkaseños. As in the case of mestizo migrants, the pressures of border crossing, family separation, and adjustment to life in the United States can induce stress and spur a decline in physical and emotional health. Both our quantitative and qualitative data show that migration's impacts extend well beyond the migrant, altering the structure of the family that stays behind.

On the other hand, Tunkaseño migrants benefit from strong ties to social networks based on kinship and common origin. By remitting money home regularly and relying heavily on social networks in the United States, Tunkaseños retain stronger family ties than many of their mestizo counterparts. The strength of these family ties explains why many Tunkaseños stay in the United States only for a short time, citing as their principal reason for returning home their desire to be with their families. Their use of traditional Yucatecan medicine may also represent a coping mechanism, enabling Tunkaseños to retain their cultural heritage despite acculturative pressures in the United States. Thus Tunkaseños rely on both social networks and traditional medicine in their efforts to cope with the many stressors of migration.

References

Abraido-Lanza, Ana F., Bruce P. Dohrenwend, Daisy S. Ng-Mak, and J. Blake Turner. 1999. "The Latino Mortality Paradox: A Test of the 'Salmon Bias' and Healthy Migrant Hypotheses," *American Journal of Public Health* 89, no. 10.

Amato, Paul, and Joan Gilbreth. 1999. "Nonresident Fathers and Children's Wellbeing: A Meta-analysis," *Journal of Marriage and the Family* 61, no. 3 (August): 557–73.

Burgos, A. E., et al. 2005. "Importance of Generational Status in Examining Access to and Utilization of Health Care Services by Mexican American Children," *Pediatrics* 115, no. 3: 322–30.

Castro, Felipe G., and Sara Gutierres. 1997. *Drug and Alcohol Use among Rural Mexican Americans.* Monograph No. 168. Washington, DC: National Institute on Drug Abuse Research.

Chávez, Leo. 1984. "Doctors, Curanderos, and Brujas: Health Care Delivery and Mexican Immigrants in San Diego," *Medical Anthropology Quarterly* 15, no. 2 (February): 31–37.

Fabrega, H. 1969. "Migration and Adaptation: The Nature of the Problem." In *Behavior in New Environments*, ed. E. Brody. Beverly Hills, CA: Sage.

Gómez Soler, Alfonso Martín 2004. "Estudio de comunidad: Centro de Salud Tunkás, Yucatán 2003–2004." Mexico: Centro Cultural Universitario Justo Sierra Escuela de Medicina.

Hummer, R. A., R. G. Rogers, S. H. Amir, D. Forbes, and W. P. Frisbie. 2000. "Adult Mortality Differentials among Hispanic Subgroups and Non-Hispanic Whites," *Social Science Quarterly* 81, no. 1: 459.

Lamb, Michael E., and Catherine S. Tamis-Lemonda. 2004. "The Role of the Father." In *The Role of the Father in Child Development*, ed. Michael E. Lamb. Hoboken, NJ: John Wiley & Sons.

McLanahan, Sara, and Gary Sandefur. 2006. *Growing Up with a Single Parent: What Hurts, What Helps*. Cambridge, MA: Harvard University Press.

Nigenda, Gustavo, Enrique Cifuentes, and Warren Hill. 2004. "Knowledge and Practice of Traditional Medicine in Mexico: A Survey of Healthcare Practitioners," *International Journal of Occupational and Environmental Health* 10: 416–20.

Nobles, Jenna. 2006. *The Contribution of Migration to Children's Family Contexts*. Los Angeles, CA: California Center for Population Research, University of California, Los Angeles.

Palloni A., and E. Arias. 2004. "Paradox Lost: Explaining the Hispanic Adult Mortality Advantage," *Demography* 41, no. 3: 385–415.

Reichman, Jill S. 2006. *Immigration, Acculturation, and Health: The Mexican Diaspora*. New York: LFB Scholarly Publishing.

Sorlie, Paul D., Eric Backlund, Norman J. Johnson, and Eugene Rogot. 1993. "Mortality by Hispanic Status in the United States," *Journal of the American Medical Association* 270, no. 20.

Strohschein, Lisa. 2005. "Parental Divorce and Child Mental Health Trajectories," *Journal of Marriage and Family* 67, no. 5: 1286–1300.

Vega, William A., Bohdan Kolody, and Juan Valle. 1987. "Migration and Mental Health: An Empirical Test of Depression Risk Factors among Immigrant Mexican Women," *International Migration Review* 21, no. 3.

Watson, J., G. Mattera, R. Morales, S. J. Kunitz, and R. Lynch. 1985. "Alcohol Use among Migrant Laborers in Western New York," *Journal of Studies on Alcohol* 5, no. 46 (September).

Weigers, M. E., and M. S. Sherraden. 2001. "A Critical Examination of Acculturation: The Impact of Health Behaviors, Social Support, and Economic Resources on Birth Weight among Women of Mexican Descent," *International Migration Review* 34: 804–39.

WHO (World Health Organization). 1993. "Implementation of the Global Strategy for Health for All by the Year 2000." Eighth Report on the World Health Situation. Geneva: WHO.

Demonstrators in Tunkás's central plaza call for comprehensive immigration reform in the United States, May 2006.

12 Migration and Political Participation

ILEANA BEATRIZ RUIZ ALONSO, MILTON JOVANNI SARRIA, AND ARTURO SEVERO VÁZQUEZ

> *Some of my friends in the United States are very interested in Tunkás politics. They come back for the fiestas and take advantage of their visit to talk politics. It's clear they would like to pitch in and help the town. They also understand the needs of a rural community and want to know who is serving as municipal president. But it's not the same to hear about it from someone from the town as to see it for yourself.*
> –Jaime, 55-year-old returned migrant living in Tunkás.

With immigration at the forefront of public debates in both the United States and Mexico, the potential participation of migrants in home-country politics has become a salient issue. Are persons with U.S. migration experience more engaged in the politics of the sending or the receiving country? Is it possible to be politically involved on both sides of the border? McCann, Cornelius, and Leal (2005) have summarized the theoretical debate over migrants' political incorporation as follows:

> It is quite possible to argue that political incorporation in one national context fosters fuller engagement in the other.... In the case of Mexican immigrants, continued involvement in public or communal affairs in Mexico may strengthen one's feelings of personal efficacy, one's sophistication about problems that affect both Mexico and the United States (e.g., environmental pollution, crime, troubled public schools), and one's desire to participate even more in collective action" (p. 9).

In this chapter we focus particularly on "political binationals": the segment of Tunkaseño migrants who have developed attachments to the U.S. political system while maintaining a foothold in home-country politics. We examine various forms that migrants' political involvement may take, including an expressed interest in U.S. and Mexican politics, voting in U.S. and Mexican elections, and seeking citizenship in the United States. We explore the effects of longer residence in the United States, having one's home base in Mexico versus the United States, and various sociodemographic attributes on these modes of political incorporation. Finally, we analyze the path toward U.S. citizenship upon which many Tunkaseño migrants seem to have embarked.

COGNITIVE POLITICAL INVOLVEMENT

Political events in the United States, such as immigration policymaking, have a direct impact on migrants, especially those who spend long periods in the United States or choose to reside there permanently. Accordingly, one would expect them to be more attentive to politics in their new host country than to the political system that they left behind. But when we asked Tunkaseños with U.S. migration experience if they were more interested in the politics of the United States, Mexico, or both, a majority responded that they were more interested in the politics of their native country. One-quarter of them reported a stronger interest in U.S. politics, and about one in five claimed an interest in the politics of both countries (figure 12.1).

Not surprisingly, where migrants spend most of their time strongly influences the locus of their political interest. We found that migrants who live primarily in Tunkás are more interested in the politics of Mexico, while migrants based primarily in the United States are more interested in the politics of that country (see table 12.1). These findings likely indicate that migrants who view the United States as their main place of residence have achieved a certain level of assimilation into U.S. society. Assimilation encourages a migrant to take more interest in the politics of the receiving country because it confers a sense of belonging to the social and political system. On the other hand, migrants still based in Tunkás tend to view U.S. migration as a temporary solution to their economic problems and assume that decisions made by public officials in their home country will affect them when they return from the United States.

Figure 12.1 Primary Locus of Political Interest among Tunkaseño Migrants

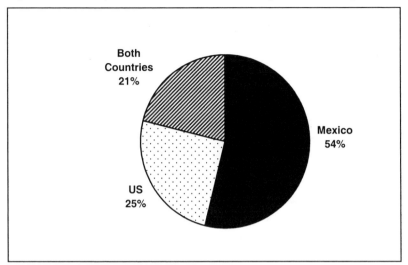

Table 12.1 Relationship between Locus of Political Interest and
Principal Place of Residence

Primary Locus of Political Interest	Migrant's Primary Place of Residence	
	Tunkás	United States
Mexico	68%	28%
United States	12%	48%
Both Mexico and the United States	20%	24%

N = 169; $p < .05$.

We also find that Tunkaseño migrants' locus of political interest is affected by their length of residence in the United States (see table 12.2). Migrants who had spent the least time in the United States (four years or less) had the highest proportion (67 percent) of those most interested in Mexican politics. As migrants remain longer in the United States, their political interest tends to shift toward the receiving country.

Table 12.2 Relationship between Locus of Political Interest and Length of U.S. Residence

Primary Locus of Political interest	Length of Residence in United States		
	4 Years or Less	More than 4 and Less than 11 Years	More than 11 Years
Mexico	67%	57%	32%
United States	15%	17%	47%
Both Mexico and United States	18%	26%	21%

N = 182; $p < .05$.

A third group of migrants interviewed in our survey displayed a political interest in both countries. Based on the theory that involvement in home-country and host-country politics is mutually reinforcing, we posit that as migrants spend more time in the United States, their interest in the politics of the two countries will rise. In fact, we find that binational political interest rises among our interviewees from 18 percent among those with four years or less of U.S. residence to 26 percent among those with between four and eleven years in the United States. But the relationship appears to be curvilinear: binational political involvement falls to 21 percent among migrants with more than eleven years of U.S. residence (table 12.2). This finding may be explained by the impracticality of participating significantly in the politics of both countries over the longer term (McCann, Cornelius, and Leal 2005: 7).

It is noteworthy that Tunkás migrants with the shortest stays in the United States have the greatest interest in the politics of Mexico, even though the politics of the United States can have a stronger impact on their daily lives. For example, the consequences of changes to U.S. immigration policy currently under consideration would fall more heavily on recent migrants than on migrants who have been in the country for some time. The general lack of interest in U.S. politics that we found to exist among Tunkaseño migrants recently arrived in the United States could be attributed to the fact that these migrants are marginalized from the U.S. political process, in part because they do not remain there long enough to become informed about the U.S. political system.

Although Mexican politics presents its own complexities and problems of accessibility, migrants tend to believe that they can more easily access and understand the way politics operate in their home country. Their idea of political life in Mexico comes from known elements that allow them to form opinions about their government. For example, migrants can rate an administration or a political figure as more or less corrupt than another (Calderón Chelius and Martínez Saldaña 2002: 89). Moreover, an understanding of U.S. politics—and social assimilation as well—is hindered by a lack of English language proficiency (Bueker 2006: 159).

Socioeconomic status is another important explanatory factor. Among Tunkaseños, we found that 60 percent of low-income migrants but only 48 percent of high-income migrants reported that they were primarily interested in the politics of Mexico. Thus, as Tunkás migrants ascend the income ladder, they tend to lose interest in the politics of the home country (see table 12.3). However, higher income also predisposes the migrant to be politically binational. We found that interest in the politics of both countries was much more prevalent (29 percent) among high-income migrants, compared with only 13 percent of low-income migrants. This finding is consistent with previous research showing that low socioeconomic status is a significant impediment to Mexican migrants' incorporation into one or both national systems (McCann, Cornelius, and Leal n.d.).

Table 12.3 Relationship between Locus of Political Interest and Income

Primary Locus of Political Interest	Income Level	
	Low	High
Mexico	60%	48%
United States	27%	23%
Both Mexico and United States	13%	29%

N = 183; $p < .05$.

A MULTIVARIATE MODEL OF BINATIONAL POLITICAL INCORPORATION

To assess the relative influence of various demographic and socioeconomic factors on migrants' political incorporation, we used multinomial

Table 12.4 Predictors of Primary Locus of Political Interest

Predictors	Mexico versus Both Mexico and United States			U.S. versus Both Mexico and United States		
	Coefficient (β)	Odds Ratio	Significance (p)	Coefficient (β)	Odds Ratio	Significance (p)
Voting in the 2006 election (yes)	.996	2.7	.335	**-4.34**	**.013**	**.016**
High income	-1.18	.307	.090	**-2.69**	**.068**	**.023**
U.S. location	**-2.44**	**.087**	**.022**	-1.29	3.63	.341

N = 108; p < .001.

logistic regression analysis to predict the probability that a respondent would be interested in both sending- and receiving-country politics. The predictor variables were the respondent's age, total years of residence in the United States, number of family members in the United States, documented status, education, gender, income (low income was the reference category/dummy variable), primary place of residence (Tunkás was the reference category), and intention to participate in the 2006 elections ("no" was the reference category). A test of the full model versus a model with intercept only was statistically significant, $X^2 = 89.58$ (N = 108), $p < .001$. The model had an overall success rate of 74.5 percent.

Table 12.4 shows the logistical regression coefficient, odds ratio, and significance of the predictors. Using a .05 criterion of statistical significance, income, migrant location, and participation in the 2006 Mexican elections had significant partial effects. The inverted odds ratio for migrant location indicates that a Tunkás migrant based in the United States is 11.4 times more likely to be interested in the politics of both countries than in the politics of Mexico. The inverted odds ratio for voting in the 2006 Mexican elections indicates that a migrant who was planning to vote in these elections was 77 times more likely to be interested in the politics of both countries than in the politics of the United States. Looking at the inverted odds ratio for income scale, we found that a high-income migrant was 14.7 times more likely to be interested in the politics of both countries rather than in the politics of the United States. In sum, our model indicates that a Tunkás migrant who is incorporated binationally would be more likely to have his primary residence in the United States, be contemplating voting in the 2006 Mexican elections, and fall in the high-income category.

Voting Participation among Migrants

Mexican expatriates have long sought to participate in Mexican elections from abroad, though this demand did not become widespread until the 1988 Mexican presidential campaign (Pineda 1999: 83). Such participation depends on the would-be voters' ability to have a political presence in both their country of origin and the country in which they reside (Calderón Chelius and Martínez Saldaña 2002: 138; Tomás

Rivera Policy Institute 2003). Comparing Tunkaseño migrants with those who had never migrated, we found major differences in rates of participation in the 2000 Mexican elections (see figure 12.2). About 77 percent of nonmigrants claimed that they had voted in the 2000 Mexican presidential election, compared with 51 percent of Tunkaseños with U.S. migration experience. The lower frequency of participation among migrants can be attributed in part to their inability to cast absentee ballots in that election.

Figure 12.2 Voting in Mexico's 2000 and 2006 Presidential Elections, by Migration Experience

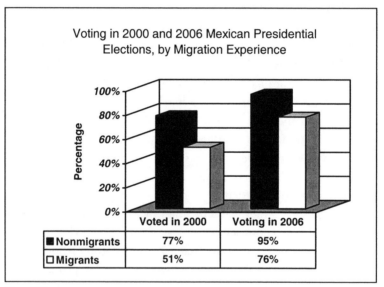

N = 718.

We found that 95 percent of nonmigrants in Tunkás were thinking about voting in the 2006 Mexican presidential election, and more than three-quarters (76 percent) of Tunkás migrants were planning to vote—a 25 percent increase over their self-reported participation rate in the 2000 election. This difference might be attributed to a change in Mexico's constitution—approved in 1996 but not implemented until 2005–2006—that allows expatriates to vote in presidential elections without having to return to Mexico. However, when we asked migrants where they would be voting in 2006, 91 percent said they would vote in Tunkás, while only 9 percent said they would be voting from the United States, making it unlikely that Mexican voting reforms are fundamentally driving greater interest in home-country voting participation among migrants. Given that our survey was conducted six months before the July 2006 presidential election, we have no way of knowing what proportion of our interviewees actually voted, but the total number of absentee ballots cast by U.S.-based migrants (about 33,000) suggests that no more than a handful of Tunkaseños—if any—chose to exercise that right in 2006.[1]

DETERMINANTS AND CONSEQUENCES OF NATURALIZATION IN THE UNITED STATES

> *I think that if immigrants were U.S. citizens, we'd take more interest in U.S. politics. After I naturalized as a U.S. citizen I voted in all the elections over there. But before I became a citizen I wasn't much interested in their politics. My duty as a U.S. citizen is to vote, no matter how good or bad the candidates might be.* —Manuel, 52-year-old returned migrant living in Tunkás

Citizenship is an integral part of the democratic process in the United States. Whether acquired at birth or through naturalization, it signifies inclusion and participation in the national community. Understanding why and how some Tunkaseño migrants have become U.S. citizens can shed light on their process of incorporation into U.S. society. In this section, we examine the determinants and consequences of Tunkaseño

---

[1] Our survey did not include items on party or candidate preference in 2000 or 2006. However, Tunkás has long been governed by the Institutional Revolutionary Party (PRI). All 26 municipal presidents since 1941 have been from that party. In the 2004 midterm elections, according to the Yucatán Electoral Institute, most voters in Tunkás (936) cast their votes for candidates of the PRI, followed by those of the National Action Party (PAN), with 784. Only three persons voted for the Labor Party, or PT; five for the Green Party, PVEM; and 11 for the Convergencia Party.

migrants' becoming naturalized U.S. citizens. Based on a review of the literature on naturalization, we identified several factors that may increase Tunkaseño migrants' interest in becoming U.S. citizens:

- immigration status (documented or undocumented),

- primary place of residence (whether Tunkás or the United States is considered "home"),

- English proficiency, and

- number of years spent in the United States.

When we asked Tunkaseño migrants whether they would be interested in becoming naturalized U.S. citizens, about 58 percent answered affirmatively; 26 percent had no desire to naturalize, and 15 percent responded that they already had U.S. citizenship (see figure 12.4).

Figure 12.4 Tunkaseño Migrants' Interest in Becoming a U.S. Citizen

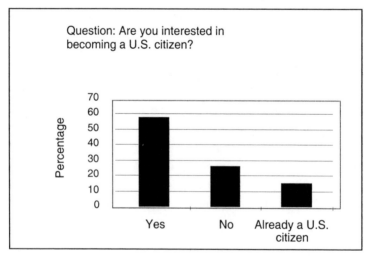

N = 118.

Not surprisingly, legal status in the United States powerfully affects naturalization aspirations (figure 12.5). Approximately 85 percent of documented migrants in our sample expressed interest in becoming a

U.S. citizen, compared with about 60 percent of currently undocumented migrants, who face a much longer and less certain road to U.S. citizenship.

Figure 12.5 Tunkaseño Migrants' Interest in U.S. Naturalization, by Immigration Status

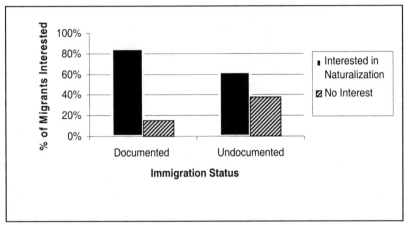

N = 111; p < .05.

A second determinant of Tunkaseño migrants' interest in U.S. citizenship is whether they consider their home to be Tunkás or the United States. Nearly 90 percent of migrants who considered the United States their home reported being interested in becoming a U.S. citizen, while only 41 percent of Tunkás-based migrants were interested in U.S. citizenship (figure 12.6).

Length of residence in the United States is one of the most consistently positive predictors of both naturalizing and voting among Mexican immigrants (Bueker 2006: 185). Among our interviewees, nearly 91 percent of migrants with more than eleven years of residence in the United States reported an interest in U.S. citizenship. The level of interest in citizenship decreases as total time in the United States declines (see figure 12.7). As length of U.S. residence increases, migrants also become more culturally assimilated, obtain better jobs, and become more economically secure—all attributes that encourage immigrants to seek U.S. citizenship (Bueker 2006).

Figure 12.6 Tunkaseño Migrants' Interest in U.S. Naturalization, by Location of Primary Residence

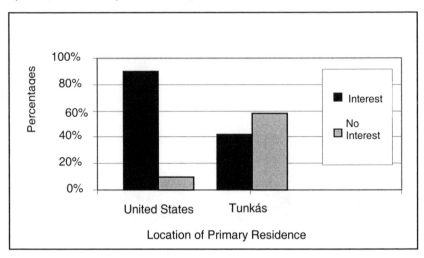

N = 110; *p* < .05.

Figure 12.7 Tunkaseño Interest in U.S. Citizenship by Time Spent in the U.S.

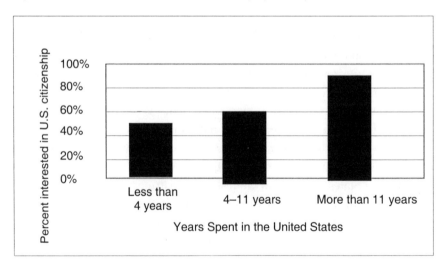

N = 109; *p* < .05.

Migrants' English language skills also affect their interest in naturalization. Nearly 92 percent of Tunkaseño migrants who could speak
English expressed interest in acquiring U.S. citizenship. Those who
have acquired some English skills have a strong advantage here, given
that the naturalization process requires a candidate to demonstrate
English proficiency. Proficiency in English also facilitates economic
integration, which then positions migrants to become politically incorporated, including as naturalized U.S. citizens. Finally, English-
speaking migrants are more likely to develop contacts and social relationships with native-born members of the U.S. population, which may
also encourage naturalization.

Logistic regression analysis was employed to predict the probability
that a Tunkás migrant would be interested in becoming a U.S. citizen.
The predictor variables were place of primary residence (Tunkás was
the reference variable), time in the United States, number of relatives in
the United States, ability to speak English (two dummy variables coding speak English), knowledge of Bush's immigration reform proposals
("no" was the reference variable/dummy), documented status, and
marital status (three dummy variables coding marital status). A test of
the full model versus a model with intercept only was statically significant (N = 94; $p < .001$). The model was able to correctly classify 91 percent of migrants who were interested in becoming U.S. citizens and 63
percent of those who were not, for an overall success rate of 83 percent.

Table 12.5 shows the logistic regression coefficient (B), significance,
and odds ratio for each of the predictors. Employing a $p = .05$ criterion
of statistical significance, migrant location, time in the United States,
and knowledge of Bush's immigration reform proposals all had significant partial effects. The odds ratio for migrant location indicates that
when holding all other variables constant, a Tunkás migrant who resides primarily in the United States is 7.1 times more likely than a migrant based in Tunkás to be interested in becoming a U.S. citizen, and
migrants who had spent more time in the United States were more
likely to be interested in naturalizing. In addition, migrants who knew
about the Bush immigration reform proposals were 5.3 times more
likely to be interested in becoming U.S. citizens than those who knew
nothing about them.

Table 12.5 Logistic Regression Predicting Interest in Becoming a U.S. Citizen

Predictors	Coefficient (β)	Significance (p)	Odds Ratio
U.S. is main residence	**1.965**	**.005**	**7.14**
Time in U.S. (years)	**.073**	**.017**	**1.1**
Number of relatives in U.S.	.006	.768	1.006
Speak English:			
Some	−.233	.748	.792
Proficient	.430	.724	1.54
Knowledge of President Bush's immigration reform proposal: Yes	**1.660**	**.025**	**5.3**
Documented status in the U.S.: Yes	.997	.174	2.71
Marital Status:			
Married	1.063	.405	2.9
Single	.949	.511	2.583

N = 94; $p < .05$.

CONCLUSION

We have found that as Tunkaseño migrants become assimilated into U.S. society, they become more interested in the politics of the host country. But one out of five migrants—and nearly one-quarter of those whose primary residence is in the United States—are political binationals, cognitively involved in both the sending and receiving country's politics. We also find that a large majority of Tunkaseño migrants—especially those who are proficient in English—are interested in becoming U.S. citizens. Unlike previous generations of Mexican migrants to the United States, today's *norteños* are staying longer and putting down roots, which may lead to significantly higher naturalization rates in the future. A legalization program benefiting currently undocumented migrants that includes a guaranteed path to U.S. citizenship would assure this outcome.

References

Bueker, Catherine Simpson. 2006. *From Immigration to Naturalized Citizen: Political Incorporation in the United States.* New York: LFB Scholarly Publishing.

Calderón Chelius, Leticia, and Jesús Martínez Saldaña. 2002. *La dimensión política de la migración mexicana.* México, D.F.: Instituto Mora.

McCann, James, Wayne A. Cornelius, and David Leal. 2005. "Binational Political Incorporation of Mexican Migrants: How Do 'Old Country' Connections Shape Engagement in U.S. Politics?" Unpublished paper, Purdue University, University of California–San Diego, and University of Texas at Austin.

McCann, James, Wayne A. Cornelius, and David Leal. n.d. "Absentee Voting in 2006 and the Potential for Transnational Civic Engagement among Mexican Expatriates." In *Mexico's Disputed Election: Issue Emergence and Democratic Consolidation in 2006,* ed. Jorge I. Domínguez and Chappell Lawson. Stanford, Calif.: Stanford University Press. Forthcoming.

Pineda, Raúl Ross. 1999. *Los mexicanos y el voto sin fronteras.* Culiacán, Sin., México, D.F., and Chicago: Universidad Autónoma de Sinaloa, Centro de Estudios del Movimiento Obrero y Socialista, and Salcedo Press.

Tomás Rivera Policy Institute. 2003. *Immigrant Politics at Home and Abroad.* Los Angeles: TRPI.

APPENDIX

Survey Questionnaire Administered to Persons with U.S. Migration Experience in Tunkás, Yucatán

EMPLEO Y RESIDENCIA DURANTE 2005

¿Es usted casado(a), soltero(a), viudo(a), divorciado/a, separado/a, unión libre?

¿Tiene Ud. o su familia terrenos en Tunkás, o cerca del pueblo?

¿Son terrenos ejidales?

¿Son propios? ¿Arrendados?

En total, ¿cuántos parientes tiene Ud. que viven actualmente en los EE.UU.?

[Si ha migrado dentro de México, así como a los EE.UU.] ¿De lo que aprendió en _____, qué es lo que más le sirvió en los EE.UU.?

[Si trabajaba en Estados Unidos durante parte del 2005] Cuando estuvo en Tunkás antes de salir, ¿a qué se dedicaba?

¿Dónde pasa más tiempo: aquí en Tunkás, o en EE.UU.?

[Si pasa más tiempo en EE.UU.] ¿Qué tan seguido viene a Tunkás normalmente?

Desde su primer viaje a EE.UU., ¿viene a Tunkás menos o más seguido ahora?

¿Por qué?

HISTORIA MIGRATORIA DEL ENTREVISTADO

(sobre el primer viaje a los Estados Unidos:)

¿En que trabajaba antes de migrar, esa primera vez?

Antes de que usted se fuera a los EE.UU. *por primera vez*, ¿ya tenía parientes viviendo en los EE.UU.?

¿Quién le dio alojamiento cuando llegó a EE.UU. la primera vez?

¿Estaban otros parientes en la misma casa con usted? (sin contar esposa e hijos)

¿Estaban otros paisanos en la misma casa con usted? (sin contar esposa e hijos)

Cuando usted necesitó dinero allá en Estados Unidos ¿a quién se lo pidió?

¿Cómo escogió el lugar donde vivía en los Estados Unidos?

Si entró sin papeles o con papeles chuecos, ¿qué tan difícil fue pasar al otro lado?

En ese primer viaje, ¿lo agarraron en la frontera? ¿Cuántas veces?

(sobre el último viaje a los Estados Unidos:)

En esta última temporada en los EE.UU., ¿se quedó más tiempo de lo que tenía planeado?

¿Por qué fue a los EE.UU., esta última vez?

En el mes en que se fue a los EE.UU. esta última vez, ¿tenía algún trabajo pagado, aquí en Yucatán?

¿Ud. se fue porque aquí en el pueblo no le iba bien, o porque en los EE.UU. había más oportunidades?

¿Cómo consiguió su último trabajo en los EE.UU.?

En su último intento de ir a EE.UU., ¿pasó con papeles, o tuvo que entrar sin papeles?

[Si entró sin papeles] ¿Tuvo que usar pollero, o entró sin pollero?

[Si usó pollero] ¿Cómo logró conseguir el pollero?

¿Cuánto le pagó al pollero?

¿El pollero cumplió con todo lo que prometió?

¿El pollero cometió algún tipo de maltrato o abuso?

En total, ¿cuánto dinero tuvo que juntar para hacer este viaje a los EE.UU., incluyendo el transporte?

¿Cómo logró juntar el dinero para hacer este viaje?

¿A qué parte llegó primero para cruzar la frontera?

¿Cuánto tiempo tardó desde que llegó a la frontera, hasta que llegó a su primer lugar de trabajo?

[Si caminó] ¿Cuánto tiempo caminó?

¿Su experiencia cuando cruzó la frontera la última vez, fue lo que había imaginado antes de salir de Tunkás?

¿Fue más fácil?

¿Más difícil?

Antes de irse a la frontera, ¿había escuchado o había visto algún anuncio sobre los peligros de cruzar la frontera? ¿Esto afectó su decisión de irse, de alguna manera?

Al intentar cruzar la frontera ¿le robaron o asaltaron?

¿La migra lo agarró en la frontera?

[Si fue agarrado] Entonces, ¿cuántas veces intentó cruzar la frontera?

Entonces, ¿pudo pasar o no, después de que lo agarraron, la última vez?

¿Por qué regresó usted a Tunkás esta última vez?

INTENCIONES DE EMIGRAR

¿Ha pensado en irse a los EE.UU. este año para trabajar?

[Si la respuesta es sí] ¿Por qué piensa irse?

¿Qué tipo de trabajo piensa tener en los EE.UU., la próxima vez que se vaya? ¿Por qué ese tipo de trabajo?

¿Este trabajo ya está arreglado con el mismo patrón, será arreglado por algún pariente o amigo que ya vive en los EE.UU., o usted tendrá que buscarlo?

¿Cuánto piensa que va a ganar en ese trabajo?

[En caso de que no ha pensado en ir a los EE.UU.] ¿Por qué no piensa irse a los EE.UU. este año?

¿Sabe algo, o ha escuchado, de las operaciones de la Migra para impedir la entrada de los indocumentados por San Diego, Arizona o Texas?

¿Actualmente, qué tan difícil es evadir la Migra al cruzar la frontera?

¿Conoce usted a alguien que se haya quedado en EE.UU. por temor a la vigilancia en la frontera?

Actualmente, ¿qué tan peligroso es cruzar la frontera, si uno no tiene papeles?

¿Conoce Ud. a alguien que se fue a los EE.UU. y que se haya muerto al cruzar la frontera?

¿Sabe algo, o ha oído hablar, de la propuesta del presidente Bush para trabajadores migrantes?

¿Qué es lo que propuso el presidente Bush?

Si se aprueba la propuesta de Bush, ¿es más probable que Ud. se vaya a los EE.UU. a trabajar, o no tendría ningún efecto sobre sus intenciones?

TRABAJO Y VIDA EN LOS ESTADOS UNIDOS

Actualmente, ¿qué tan difícil es conseguir trabajo en los EE.UU., para un yucateco o mexicano que no tiene papeles?

Durante su trabajo más reciente en los EE.UU., ¿el patrón le pidió algún documento de identificación?

[Si la respuesta es sí] ¿Qué tipo de documento?

Durante este viaje más reciente (o actual) a los EE.UU., ¿pudo (puede) mandar dinero a sus parientes de aquí de Tunkás o Yucatán?

¿Me podría decir como cuánto dinero lograba juntar para mandar, y cada cuándo?

¿Cómo mandaba el dinero?

¿Para qué se usó este dinero?

¿Ha mandado dinero para una novena o gremio?

De los aparatos electro-domésticos en la casa, ¿cuáles de ellos se compraron con dinero ganado en los EE.UU.?

¿Me podría decir cuánto dinero trajo consigo, cuando regresó a Tunkás?

Durante su última estancia en los EE.UU., ¿tenía (tiene) cuenta bancaria en los EE.UU.?

Durante esta estancia en los EE.UU., ¿Ud. tuvo que pagar impuestos por el dinero que ganó en los EE.UU.?

Durante esta temporada más reciente (o actual) en los EE.UU., ¿mandó a sus hijos a la escuela allá?

Cuando se encuentra en los EE.UU., ¿participa Ud. en algún club social o deportivo de yucatecos y/o tunkaseños? ¿Cuál?

¿A cuántas reuniones de este grupo asistió Ud. el último año que estuvo en EE.UU.?

Cuando está Ud. en los EE.UU., ¿cada cuándo se pone en contacto con sus familiares en Tunkás?

¿Cómo se mantiene en contacto con ellos, principalmente?

Durante su estancia más reciente en los EE.UU., ¿en qué tipo de casa vivió?

¿Con cuánta gente compartía ese lugar?

¿De dónde era la mayoría de sus vecinos (del barrio)?

¿Tenía vecinos de Tunkás?

¿Qué ha sido lo más difícil para usted, de vivir en los EE.UU.?

¿Lo han tratado mal en EE.UU., por ser inmigrante?

[Si la respuesta es sí] ¿De qué manera?

¿Recibió Ud. o algún miembro de su familia "food stamps", o sea, estampillas de comida?

¿Recibió usted o algún miembro de su familia "el welfare"?

OPINIONES SOBRE SU PUEBLO

En su opinión, ¿la migración de gente de aquí a los EE.UU. ha beneficiado o ha perjudicado la economía de Tunkás?

¿En qué ha beneficiado?

¿En qué ha perjudicado?

En su opinión, ¿la migración de gente de aquí a los EE.UU. ha beneficiado o ha perjudicado las costumbres y las formas de vivir de la gente en Tunkás?

¿En qué ha beneficiado?

¿En qué ha perjudicado?

En su opinión, ¿qué sería necesario para que menos gente se fuera de este pueblo, para trabajar o vivir?

En su opinión, ¿por qué no mejora la producción agrícola y ganadera en Tunkás?

Algunas personas dicen que una persona joven, nacida aquí en el pueblo, puede progresar en la vida sin salir del pueblo. Otras dicen que para superarse, una persona joven nacida aquí tiene que salir a otra parte. ¿Qué piensa Ud.?

Algunas personas nos dicen que es mejor que los niños crezcan en Yucatán. Otras nos dicen que es mejor que se críen en EE.UU. ¿Qué opina Ud.?

SITUACIÓN ECONÓMICA PERSONAL

En relación a hace 5 años, ¿Ud. y su familia viven mejor, igual, o peor? ¿Por qué?

En comparación con ahora, ¿cómo cree que van a vivir Ud. y su familia, dentro de 5 años – mejor, igual, o peor? ¿Por qué?

En el último año, ¿diría Ud. que la situación económica de Tunkás o Yucatán ha mejorado o ha empeorado?

¿Diría Ud. que dentro de un año la situación económica de Yucatán mejorará o empeorará?

Aquí tiene una escalera de 10 escalones. En el número "10" está una familia con las mejores condiciones de vida en este pueblo actualmente. En el número "1" está la familia con las peores condiciones de vida. ¿En cuál escalón se ubicaría Ud. y su familia, actualmente?

¿Usted o su familia participan en el programa "Oportunidades"?

¿Ha escuchado algo sobre el "Programa 3x1 para Migrantes" aquí en Tunkás?

¿Qué es lo que ha hecho este programa?

¿Qué cosas le gustaría que los migrantes apoyaran aquí?

¿Alguien de su familia participa en el Programa PROCAMPO?

¿En qué utilizan el apoyo de PROCAMPO?

PLANES PARA EL FUTURO

¿Está pensando en irse a vivir fuera de Tunkás, de manera permanente?

¿A dónde piensa ir?

¿Por qué quiere ir a ese lugar en vez de otro?

¿Cuál es la razón más importante por la cual Ud. no se ha ido de Tunkás?

[En caso de vivir actualmente en los EE.UU.] ¿Hay alguna razón por la cual volvería a vivir aquí en Tunkás, en Yucatán u otro lugar en México, de manera permanente?

[En caso de haber estado "sin papeles" durante su última temporada en EE.UU.] ¿Piensa arreglar sus papeles para quedarse en los EE.UU.?

[En caso de ser residente permanente legal durante su última temporada en EE.UU.] ¿Le gustaría hacerse ciudadano norteamericano?

POLÍTICA, IDENTIDAD, Y ETNICIDAD

¿Le interesa más lo que pasa en la política de México o en la política de los EE.UU.?

¿Tiene credencial de elector?

[Si no es ciudadano norteamericano] ¿Piensa votar en las elecciones para presidente de México, este año?

¿En dónde piensa votar en las elecciones para presidente este año – en Tunkás o en los EE.UU.?

¿Logró votar en las elecciones mexicanas, en el año 2000?

¿Ha ocupado Ud. algún cargo público o religioso en Tunkás?

¿Qué tipo de cargo?

¿A qué grupo piensa que pertenece más — comunidad latinoamericana, comunidad mexicana, comunidad yucateca, comunidad maya o comunidad religiosa?

¿Ud. considera que en México el color de la piel afecta o no afecta el trato que reciben las personas?

¿Alguna vez en Yucatán lo han discriminado por su color de piel?

¿Alguna vez en EE.UU. lo han discriminado por su color de piel?

EDUCACIÓN

¿Hasta qué año llegó Ud. en la escuela?

[Si ha sido migrante en EE.UU.] ¿Estudió en México o en los EE.UU.?

¿Sabe Ud. inglés? ¿Cuánto?

[Si ha sido migrante en EE.UU.] ¿Asistió a clases de inglés en los EE.UU.?

SALUD

¿Se ha enfermado en los últimos dos años?

[Si se ha enfermado] ¿Quién lo atendió?

[Si ha migrado a EE.UU.] ¿Ha recibido usted o algún miembro de su familia atención médica en un hospital o una clínica en los EE.UU.?

¿Cómo fue la atención que recibió?

¿Quién pagó la atención médica?

¿Ha sufrido algún accidente o enfermedad relacionado con su trabajo en los EE.UU.?

¿De qué clase?

Durante su estancia en EE.UU., ¿diría usted que pesa más, pesa menos, o pesa igual que antes de irse a los EE.UU.?

¿Cuánto más, o cuánto menos?

¿Fuma o ha fumado cigarros de tabaco?

Al estar en los EE.UU., ¿fuma más, menos, o igual que en Yucatán?

[Preguntar solo a migrantes actuales] ¿Ha tomado alcohol alguna vez?

Cuando se encuentra en Tunkás, ¿toma más, menos, o igual que en EE.UU.?

¿Ha tenido o tiene cáncer, diabetes, hipertensión, sobrepeso/obesidad, enfermedades del hígado, problemas del corazón, infarto, colesterol, asma, problemas de los ojos, enfermedades transmitidas sexualmente o SIDA?

¿Alguna vez le han hecho pruebas para detectar SIDA?

¿Cuál fue su resultado?

[Preguntar solo si el entrevistado ha sido migrante a EE.UU.] Durante su primera estancia en los EE.UU., ¿se sentía más, menos, o igual de deprimido, ansioso, o irritable que antes de salir de Yucatán?

¿En este último año, alguna vez se ha sentido deprimido, ansioso o irritable?

¿Ha sufrido de mal de ojo?

¿Ha sufrido de mal aire?

¿Ha ido con un curandero, yerbatero, sobador o huesero?

¿Piensa tener (más) hijos?

¿Cuántos (más)?

RELIGIÓN

¿Cada cuándo asiste a una iglesia?

¿A qué iglesia pertenece Ud.?

[Si es evangélico] ¿Ha cambiado de religión?

¿En dónde cambió – aquí en Tunkás, o en los EE.UU.?

¿Ud. asiste ahora a su iglesia menos seguido o más seguido que antes de irse a los EE.UU. la primera vez?

VIVIENDA

¿Cuántos espacios tiene esta casa?

¿Tiene fosa séptica o drenaje?

¿Tiene agua potable?

Durante los últimos 12 meses, ¿vivió en esta casa todo el tiempo?

CUADRO A. Información sobre habitantes del hogar e hijos del jefe que no viven en el hogar

# en hogar	Nombre	Sexo	Relación al jefe	Año en que nació	Lugar donde nació	¿Vive en el hogar?	Ocupación actual	Ingresos (dólares)	por (B)	Lengua Maya habla/entiende		Religión
1		M / F				Sí/No				Sí/No	Sí/No	
2		M / F				Sí/No				Sí/No	Sí/No	
3		M / F				Sí/No				Sí/No	Sí/No	
4		M / F				Sí/No				Sí/No	Sí/No	
5		M / F				Sí/No				Sí/No	Sí/No	
6		M / F				Sí/No				Sí/No	Sí/No	
7		M / F				Sí/No				Sí/No	Sí/No	
8		M / F				Sí/No				Sí/No	Sí/No	
9		M / F				Sí/No				Sí/No	Sí/No	
10		M / F				Sí/No				Sí/No	Sí/No	
11		M / F				Sí/No				Sí/No	Sí/No	
12		M / F				Sí/No				Sí/No	Sí/No	

B. Códigos de frecuencia del pago

1 = Hora
2 = Día
3 = Semana
4 = Quincena
5 = Mes

C. Códigos de religión

1 = Católica
2 = Evangélica
3 = Ninguna
4 = Otro

CUADRO B. Información sobre personas en Cuadro A con experiencia migratoria en EE.UU.

# en hogar	Nombre	# viajes a EE.UU.	Viaje	Lugar de destino (ciudad y estado)	Año en que llegó ahí	Tiempo que duró este viaje	Doc (A)	Ocupación en EE.UU.	Ingresos (dólares)	por (B)	Tiempo total vivido en EE.UU.
1			1er								
			último								
2			1er								
			último								
3			1er								
			último								
4			1er								
			último								
5			1er								
			último								
6			1er								
			último								
7			1er								
			último								
8			1er								
			último								
9			1er								
			último								
10			1er								
			último								
11			1er								
			último								
12			1er								
			último								

A. Códigos de documentación

1 = Residente legal
2 = Contratado- Bracero (1942-1964)
3 = Contratado - H2A
4 = Contratado - H2B
5 = Turista
6 = Ciudadano
7 = Tarjeta cruce local
8 = Visa de estudiante
9 = Indocumentado

B. Códigos de frecuencia del pago

1 = Hora
2 = Día
3 = Semana
4 = Quincena
5 = Mes

CUADRO C. Información sobre personas en Cuadro A con experiencia migratoria dentro de México

# en hogar	Nombre	# viajes en MX	Viaje	Lugar de destino (municipio y estado)	Año en que llegó ahí	Tiempo que duró este viaje	Ocupación en destino	Ingresos (dólares)	por (B)	Tiempo total vivido en otras partes de México
1			1er							
			último							
2			1er							
			último							
3			1er							
			último							
4			1er							
			último							
5			1er							
			último							
6			1er							
			último							
7			1er							
			último							
8			1er							
			último							
9			1er							
			último							
10			1er							
			último							
11			1er							
			último							
12			1er							
			último							

B. Códigos de frecuencia del pago

1 = Hora	2 = Día	3 = Semana	4 = Quincena	5 = Mes